BASICS

C++

Todd Knowlton

Computer Education Consultant

Lubbock, TX

**South-Western
Computer Education**
an imprint of Course Technology

Thomson Learning™

Australia • Canada • Mexico • Singapore • Spain • United Kingdom • United States

Managing Editor: Carol Volz
Senior Product Manager: Dave Lafferty
Production Manager: Angela McDonald
Art Coordinator: Mike Broussard
Consulting Editor: Custom Editorial Productions, Inc.
Marketing Manager: Susanne Walker
Production: Custom Editorial Productions, Inc.

ISBN: 0-538-69493-9, Spiral Cover Text
ISBN: 0-538-96815-X, Soft Cover Text
ISBN: 0-538-69494-7, Soft Cover Text/Data CD Package

1 2 3 4 5 6 BM 03 02 01 00

Printed in the United States of America

South-Western Computer Education, an imprint of Course Technology, is a division of Thomson Learning.

How to Use This Book

What makes a good programming text? Sound instruction and hands-on skill-building and reinforcement. That is what you will find in *C++ Basics*. Not only will you find a colorful, inviting layout, but also many features to enhance learning.

Objectives— Objectives are listed at the beginning of each lesson, along with a suggested time for completion of the lesson. This allows you to look ahead to what you will be learning and to pace your work.

SCANS—(Secretary's Commission on Achieving Necessary Skills)—The U.S. Department of Labor has identified the school-to-careers competencies. The eight workplace competencies and foundation skills are identified in exercises where they apply. More information on SCANS can be found on the *Electronic Instructor*.

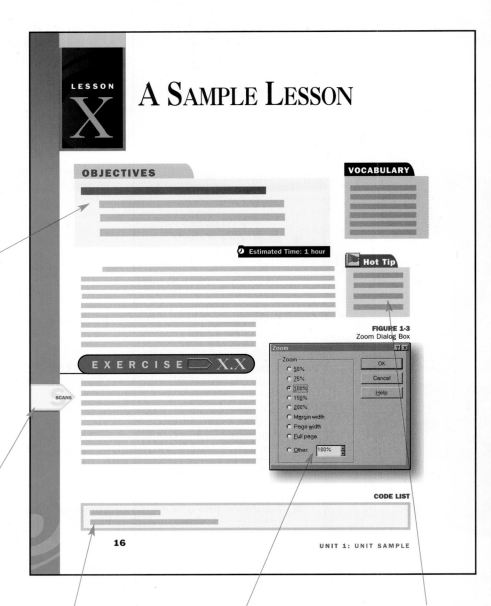

FIGURE 1-3
Zoom Dialog Box

Code Lists— Code lists display entire programs or components of a program to emphasize conceptual discussion.

Enhanced Screen Shots—Screen shots now come to life on each page with color and depth.

Marginal Boxes— These boxes provide additional information for Notes, Hot Tips, warnings (Important), fun facts (Did You Know?), and Concept Builders.

How to Use This Book

Summary—At the end of each lesson, you will find a summary to prepare you to complete the end-of-lesson activities.

Review Questions—Review material at the end of each lesson and each unit enables you to prepare for assessment of the content presented.

Lesson Projects—End-of-lesson hands-on application of what has been learned in the lesson allows you to actually apply the techniques covered.

Critical Thinking Activity—Each lesson gives you an opportunity to apply creative analysis to solve problems.

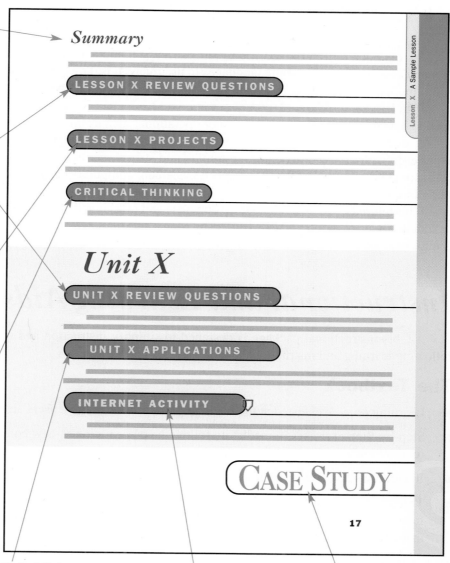

Summary

LESSON X REVIEW QUESTIONS

LESSON X PROJECTS

CRITICAL THINKING

Unit X

UNIT X REVIEW QUESTIONS

UNIT X APPLICATIONS

INTERNET ACTIVITY

CASE STUDY

Lesson X   A Sample Lesson

17

End-of-Unit Applications—End-of-unit hands-on application of concepts learned in the unit provides opportunity for a comprehensive review.

Internet Activity—Hands-on project that incorporates Internet resources for research and completion.

Case Studies—Case studies reinforce material covered in several units using C++ programs in real-world scenarios.

PREFACE

This book will introduce you to programming computers using a language called C++, just one of many computer programming languages in use today. It is, however, one of the most widely used programming languages. Many of the applications you use every day were written using C++.

The lessons in this book do not assume you have any previous programming experience. You do need to have knowledge of basic computer operations, such as how to use your operating system.

This book will build a foundation in the basics of C++ programming. You will even gain some experience with object-oriented programming and string, vector, and matrix classes. The lessons in this book are good preparation for an advanced placement computer science course or other more advanced study in C++.

This tutorial takes 30 to 40 hours to complete and is designed for use with most major C++ compilers, including DOS, Windows, and Macintosh. More information about C++ and up-to-date information about this book is available at **http://www.programcpp.com/basics**.

Instructional and Learning Aids

This instructional package is designed to simplify instruction and to enhance learning with the following learning and instructional aids:

The Textbook

- Learning objectives listed at the beginning of each lesson give users an overview of the lesson.

- Step-by-Step exercises immediately follow the presentation of new concepts for hands-on reinforcement.

- Illustrations and code samples explain complex concepts and serve as reference points.

- Three case studies allow students to learn from complete C++ programs and then extend the functionality of those programs. The case studies allow students to see practical programs that make use of the concepts learned in the lessons.

END OF LESSON

- Lesson summaries provide quick reviews reinforcing the main points in each lesson.

- True/false and written questions gauge students' understanding of lesson concepts and software operations.

- Projects offer minimal instruction so students must apply concepts previously introduced.

- Critical thinking activities stimulate the user to apply analytical and reasoning skills.

END OF UNIT

- Review questions provide a comprehensive overview of unit content and help in preparing for tests.

- Unit applications for reinforcement ask the student to apply all the skills and concepts presented in the unit.

- Internet activities require the student to obtain information from the Internet to complete the activity, reinforcing Internet skills.

END OF BOOK

- A rich set of appendices, including quick references for common compilers.

- The glossary is a collection of the key terms from each lesson.

- A comprehensive index supplies quick and easy accessibility to specific parts of the tutorial.

Other Components

- The Activities Workbook provides additional exercises and programming projects to reinforce each lesson.

- The Instructor's Manual provides teaching suggestions, solutions, and other resources.

- The Electronic Instructor package is a CD-ROM that includes data files; solutions for exercises, projects, and applications; lesson plans specific to each lesson; student lesson plans that help students work through each lesson; reproducible tests with answers; and other features such as scheduling suggestions, SCANS information for exercises in the book, guidelines for working with students at differing ability levels, and other useful information.

- Testing software allows the instructor to generate printed tests, online exams, and an instructor gradebook.

Acknowledgments

This book is the result of the work of many people over several years. It is built on the work of my previous C++ books. The feedback of the many students and teachers who have used my earlier books has been invaluable.

I thank Dave Lafferty and Carol Volz at South-Western for their support. I also thank Stephen and Melissa Collings, Marcelia Sawyers, Trey Stoffregen, Mark Leech and Matt Weaver for their work on the manuscript and testing; and Roseann Krane from Monte Vista High School in Danville, California, for her review of the text. Roseann is a dear friend and an awesome teacher.

I owe a special thanks to my editor, Cat Skintik. I have had the privilege of working with Cat on many projects and it is always a pleasure.

Most importantly, I thank my wife, Melissa, for putting up with my schedule, and my daughters, Kaley and Amy, for allowing me to be wrapped around their little fingers.

Todd Knowlton

TABLE OF CONTENTS

UNIT 1   YOUR FIRST C++ PROGRAM

UNIT 2   DATA AND OPERATIONS

STRINGS AND SCREEN INPUT AND OUTPUT

UNIT 3

DECISION MAKING AND LOOPS

UNIT 4

START-UP CHECKLIST

A course in C++ programming has requirements different from a software applications course. C++ is a language that is used on various types of computers and operating systems. The compiler software required to write C++ programs is available from a variety of software publishers, including Microsoft, Inprise, and Metrowerks. This Start-Up Checklist will help you ensure that you have the items necessary to successfully complete this text.

■ A compiler or development environment capable of compiling standard C++ source code is required. Use the most recent version available for your operating system. Check your compiler's system requirements before installing the compiler. Also verify that the compiler you are using supports template classes.

■ If you need help using your compiler, consult your compiler's documentation or refer to Appendix G in this book for general guidelines and addresses of resources on the Web.

■ You will need the data files that accompany this book. These files are primarily text files containing C++ source code for students to compile in the exercises and activities in the book.

■ Some activities require Internet access and a Web browser. However, all the material can be learned without Internet access.

■ Instructors should have access to the *Electronic Instructor* for complete lesson plans and solutions.

■ For up-to-date information, updates to the text and data files, and links to important resources, go to **http://www.programcpp.com/basics**.

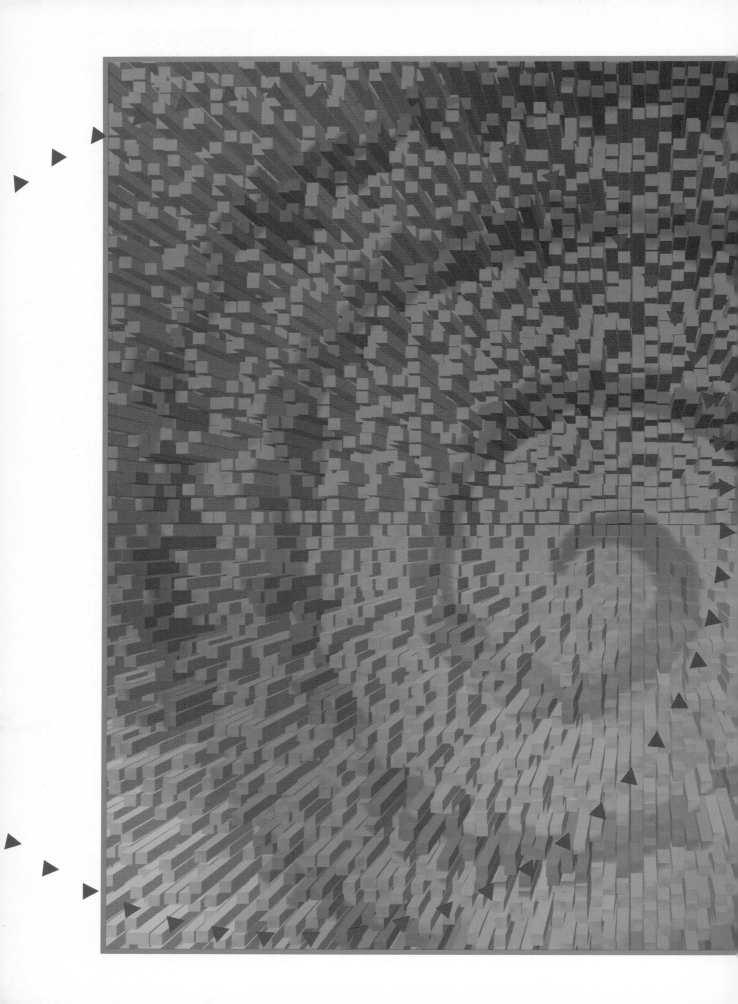

YOUR FIRST C++ PROGRAM

Estimated Time for Unit: 2 hours

1

INTRODUCING PROGRAMMING LANGUAGES

What Is a Computer Program?

Computers are complex machines. They are, however, just machines. Think of a computer as a machine that follows instructions. From the moment a computer is turned on, it begins executing instructions, and it does not stop until you turn it off. These instructions are put into a logical sequence to create *programs*.

When you perform a particular task with your computer, such as use a word processor, a computer program provides the instructions to the computer. Programs such as word processors and games are called *application programs*. Figure 1-1 shows an example of an application program. But even when you are not running a particular application program, the computer is still executing programs.

When a computer is first turned on, it follows instructions that are embedded in its hardware on chips called *read-only memory* or *ROM*. On some computers, these instructions are called the *BIOS* or *basic input/output system*. The programs in ROM do very basic operations and help the computer get its operating system started.

FIGURE 1-1
Microsoft PhotoDraw is an example of an application program.

FIGURE 1-1
Microsoft PhotoDraw is an example of an application program.

Operating Systems

The *operating system* is a set of programs that takes charge of fundamental system operations. Application programs rely on the operating system to handle the details. Let us look at some of the things an operating system does.

1. **The operating system manages the hardware resources.** The operating system allocates memory to programs and system operations. It also can allocate processor time in situations in which multiple programs are running.

2. **The operating system maintains the system of files.** The operating system organizes programs and files into directories.

3. **The operating system controls input and output operations.** Keyboard input, mouse movements, displaying to the screen, and printing all involve the operating system.

4. **The operating system loads programs and supervises their execution.** When you issue a command to start a program, the operating system loads the program into memory and allows it to begin executing. The operating system regularly interrupts the program so that other programs can run and housekeeping chores such as updating the system date and time can take place.

Some operating systems you may have seen or used are Microsoft Windows, the Mac OS, Unix, and MS-DOS.

Many operating systems use graphical user interfaces as a control center from which programs are loaded. A *graphical user interface* is a system that allows the computer user to interact with the computer through pictures. Graphical user interface is often abbreviated as GUI, pronounced "gooey."

An example of an operating system with a graphical user interface is Microsoft Windows, shown in Figure 1-2. Modern operating systems such as Microsoft Windows do more than allow you to see your files and launch programs. They allow multiple programs to be run at the same time and provide resources that programs can share. They allow computers to network with each other and the Internet. They also make it easier to learn new programs, because each program has the same look and feel.

FIGURE 1-2

Microsoft Windows is an operating system with a graphical user interface.

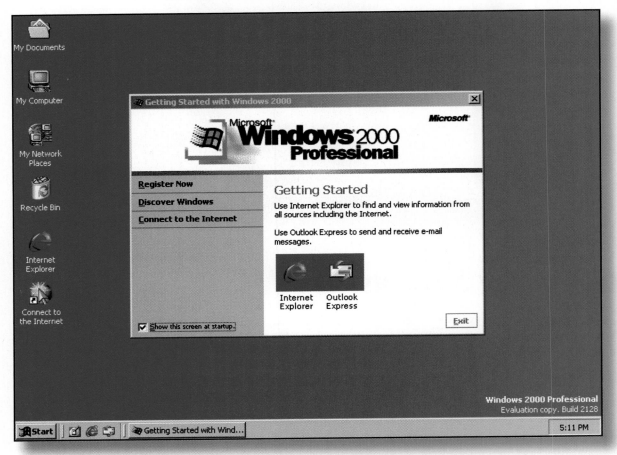

The Computer's Language

The device in the computer that actually processes the instructions being provided by ROM, the operating system, and application programs is the *microprocessor*. Figure 1-3 shows an example of a microprocessor. A microprocessor is designed to "understand" a set of commands called an *instruction set*. Although there are similar instructions among different microprocessors, each model has its own instruction set. Microprocessors can accept and carry out operations that are written in the format of their own unique instruction set only. This is one reason why software written for one kind of computer does not automatically work on another kind of computer.

FIGURE 1-3

The Intel Pentium III processor is an example of a popular microprocessor.

All instructions must be provided to the microprocessor in its native language, called ***machine language***. Machine language is actually a combination of circuits that can be either on or off. The number system commonly used to represent this world of ons and offs is called the *binary number system*. In the binary number system, ones and zeros are used to represent the on and off conditions.

Programming a computer in machine language means programming in the combinations of ones and zeros that the microprocessor understands. Writing a program in machine language is difficult because even a simple program requires hundreds or even thousands of microprocessor instructions. Another problem is that the numbers used to represent the instructions are difficult for people to understand. Figure 1-4 shows a short machine language program. Each line is one instruction to the microprocessor.

Concept Builder

You may have learned that computers use a system of on and off circuits to represent all data and instructions. To learn more about how computers represent data and instructions, and to learn more about the binary number system, read Appendix B.

FIGURE 1-4

Machine language is the language of the
microprocessor. This machine language
program adds 3 + 2 and stores the result.

```
01010101
10001011  11101100
01001100
01001100
01010110
01010111
10111111  00000011  00000000
10111110  00000010  00000000
10001011  11000111
00000011  11000110
10001001  01000110  11111110
01011111
01011110
10001011  11100101
01011110
11000011
```

Introduction to Programming Languages

Supplying computers with instructions would be extremely difficult if machine language were the only option available to programmers. Fortunately, special languages have been developed that are more easily understood. These special languages, called ***programming languages***, provide a way to program computers using instructions that can be understood by computers and people.

Like human languages, programming languages have their own vocabulary and rules of usage. Some programming languages are very technical, and others are made to be as similar to English as possible. The programming languages available today allow programming at many levels of complexity.

Assembly Language

The programming language most like machine language is ***assembly language***. Assembly language uses letters and numbers to represent machine language instructions (see Figure 1-5). However, assembly language is still difficult for novices to read.

Assembly language programming is accomplished using an assembler. An *assembler* is a program that reads the codes the programmer has written and assembles a machine language program based on those codes.

FIGURE 1-5

In assembly language, each microprocessor instruction is assigned a code that makes the program more meaningful to people. It is still difficult, however, for the untrained person to see what the program will do.

MACHINE LANGUAGE	ASSEMBLY LANGUAGE
01010101	PUSH BP
10001011 11101100	MOV BP, SP
01001100	DEC SP
01001100	DEC SP
01010110	PUSH SI
01010111	PUSH DI
10111111 00000011 00000000	MOV DI, 0003
10111110 00000010 00000000	MOV SI, 0002
10001011 11000111	MOV AX, DI
00000011 11000110	ADD AX, SI
10001001 01000110 11111110	MOV [BP-02], AX
01011111	POP DI
01011110	POP SI
10001011 11100101	MOV SP, BP
01011110	POP BP
11000011	RET

Low-Level versus High-Level Languages

Machine language and assembly language are called *low-level languages*. In a low-level language, it is necessary for the programmer to know the instruction set of the microprocessor in order to program the computer. Each instruction in a low-level language corresponds to one or only a few microprocessor instructions. In the program in Figure 1-5, each assembly-language instruction corresponds to one machine-language instruction.

Most programming is done in *high-level languages*. In a high-level language, instructions do not necessarily correspond one-to-one with the instruction set of the microprocessor. One command in a high-level language may represent many microprocessor instructions. Therefore, high-level languages reduce the number of instructions that must be written. A program that might take hours to write in a low-level language can be done in minutes in a high-level language. Programming in a high-level language also reduces the number of errors because the programmer does not have to write as many instructions, and the instructions are easier to read. Figure 1-6 shows a program written in four popular high-level languages. Like the machine language and assembly language programs you saw earlier, these high-level programs add the numbers 3 and 2 together.

Another advantage of programs written in a high-level language is that they are easier to move among computers with different microprocessors. For example, the microprocessors in Macintosh computers use an instruction set different from that for microprocessors in most computers running Microsoft Windows. An assembly language program written for a Windows computer will not work on a Macintosh. However, a simple program written in a high-level language can work on both computers with little or no modification.

FIGURE 1-6
The same program can be written in more than one high-level language.

BASIC

```
10 I = 3
20 J = 2
30 K = I + J
```

VISUAL BASIC

```
Private Sub cmdCalculate_Click()
  Dim intI, intJ, intK As Integer
  intI = 3
  intJ = 2
  intK = intI + intJ
End Sub
```

PASCAL

```
program AddIt;

var
  i, j, k : integer;

begin
  i := 3;
  j := 2;
  k := i + j;
end.
```

C++

```
int main()
  {
  int i, j, k;
  i = 3;
  j = 2;
  k = i + j;
  return 0;
  }
```

So why use a low-level language? It depends on what you need to do. The drawback of high-level languages is that they do not always provide a command for everything the programmer wants a program to do. Using assembly language, the programmer can write instructions that enable the computer to do anything the hardware will allow.

Another advantage is that a program written in a low-level language will generally require less memory and run more quickly than the same program written in a high-level language. This is because high-level languages must be translated into machine language before the microprocessor can execute the instructions. The translation is done by another program, and is usually less efficient than the work of a skilled assembly-language programmer. Table 1-1 summarizes the advantages of low- and high-level languages.

TABLE 1-1
Low- and high-level languages

Advantages of Low-Level Languages	Advantages of High-Level Languages
Better use of hardware's capabilities	Require less programming
Require less memory	Fewer programming errors
Run more quickly	Easier to move among computers with different microprocessors
More easily read	

Interpreters and Compilers

Programmers writing in a high-level language enter the program's instructions into a text editor. A *text editor* is similar to a word processor, except the files are saved in a basic text format without the font and formatting codes that word processors use. The files saved by text editors are called *text files*. A program in the form of a high-level language is called **source code**.

Programmers must have their high-level programs translated into the machine language that the microprocessor understands. The translation may be done by interpreters or compilers. The resulting machine language code is known as **object code**.

INTERPRETERS

An **interpreter** is a program that translates the source code of a high-level language into machine language. It translates a computer language in a way similar to the way a person might interpret between languages such as English and Spanish. Each instruction is interpreted from the programming language into machine language as the instructions are needed. Interpreters are normally used only with very high-level languages. For example, the versions of BASIC that were included with early computers were interpreted languages.

To run a program written in an interpreted language, you must first load the interpreter into the computer's memory. Then you load the program to be interpreted. The interpreter steps through the program one instruction at a time and translates the instruction into machine language, which is sent to the microprocessor. Every time the program is run, the interpreter must once again translate each instruction.

Because of the need to have the interpreter in memory before the program can be interpreted, interpreted languages are not widely used to write programs that are sold. The buyer of the program would have to have the correct interpreter in order to use the program.

COMPILERS

A **compiler** is another program that translates a high-level language into machine language. A compiler, however, makes the translation once, then saves the machine language so that the instructions do not have to be translated each time the program is run. Programming languages such as PASCAL and C++ use compilers rather than interpreters.

Figure 1-7 shows the steps involved in using a compiler. First, the source code is translated using the compiler to a file called an **object file**. An object file, however, is incomplete. A program called a **linker** is used to create an executable program. The linker combines the object file with other machine language necessary to create a program that can run without an interpreter. The linker produces an **executable file** that can be run as many times as desired without having to be translated again.

Although using a compiler involves more steps than using an interpreter, most C++ compilers automate the task and make it easy for the programmer to use. Most compilers allow you to compile and link in a single operation. In fact, most modern compilers are part of a complete programming environment that helps you create source code, compile, link, run, and *debug* your programs. An example of a complete software development environment is Microsoft Visual C++, shown in Figure 1-8.

FIGURE 1-7
Compiling a program involves a compiler and a linker.

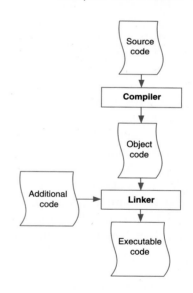

9

FIGURE 1-8
Microsoft Visual C++ is one example of a software
development environment that includes a compiler.

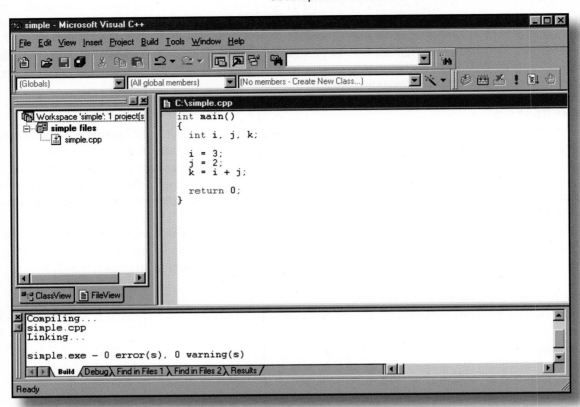

Programs you use regularly, such as word processors and games, are examples of programs written with a compiler. Compiled programs require less memory than interpreted programs because a compiled program does not require that an interpreter be loaded into memory. Compiled programs also run faster than interpreted programs because the translation has already been done. When a compiled program is run, the program is loaded into memory in the machine language the microprocessor needs.

Concept Builder

Debugging a program refers to correcting programming errors. These errors, known as bugs, can be caused by errors in keying source code, errors in the logic of the program, or other errors.

Choosing and Using a Language

How do you know what programming language to use? The choice of programming language is sometimes a complex decision. When choosing a language, you should consider the needs of the program you are creating. How important is speed? Will the program do anything that may require features that are not available in some of the higher-level languages? Who will maintain the program?

Experience is the best preparation for making this decision. That is why most professional programmers have worked with various languages to gain an understanding of the differences that exist among them.

You should not become so accustomed to working in one or two languages that you begin to believe no other languages are necessary. Think of programming languages as tools. Some languages are appropriate for a wide range of tasks—some are appropriate for specific tasks only. The smart programmer knows the available tools and how (and when) to use them.

After a language has been chosen, how do you use a programming language to actually make the computer do something you want it to do? The answer to that question is found in the remaining lessons of this book. Computers operate by following a set of steps, called an *algorithm*. A programming language allows you to provide the computer with algorithms that will produce the results you desire.

Hot Tip

To learn more about algorithms and the programming process, read Appendix C.

In the next lesson, you will begin to learn how to assemble the commands and necessary C++ language structures to build a functional computer program. You will also learn about the structure of a C++ program and compile and execute your first C++ program.

Summary

- Computers are complex machines that follow instructions called programs.

- Application programs are programs that perform tasks for the user.

- Input and output operations and loading of executable files are handled by the operating system. The operating system loads a program and turns over control of the system to the program. When the program ends, the operating system takes control again.

- At the heart of the work a computer does is a device called a microprocessor. The microprocessor responds to commands called machine language.

- High-level programming languages allow programmers to work in a language that people can more easily read. Machine language and assembly language are low-level languages because each instruction in the language corresponds to one or only a few microprocessor instructions. In high-level languages, instructions may represent many microprocessor instructions.

- An interpreter or compiler must translate high-level languages into machine language. An interpreter translates each program step into machine language as the program runs. A compiler translates the program before it is run and saves the machine language as an object file. A linker then creates an executable file from the object file.

- There are many factors to consider when choosing a programming language. Experience will teach you what language is appropriate for a specific task.

VOCABULARY REVIEW

Define the following terms:

algorithm
assembly language
compiler
executable file
graphical user interface (GUI)
high-level language
interpreter
linker

low-level language
machine language
object code
object file
operating system
programming language
source code

LESSON 1 REVIEW QUESTIONS

TRUE/FALSE

Circle the T if the statement is true. Circle the F if it is false.

T F 1. A word processor is an example of an application program.

T F 2. The programs in a typical computer's ROM provide programs such as spreadsheets and video games.

T F 3. The operating system controls input and output operations of a computer.

T F 4. An instruction set is a system for interacting with computer users through pictures.

T F 5. A compiler creates a source code file.

T F 6. The programming language most like machine language is C++.

T F 7. Programs written in low-level languages usually require less memory than those written in high-level languages.

T F 8. High-level languages are more difficult to read than low-level languages.

T F 9. An interpreter creates an object file that a linker makes into an executable file.

T F 10. Most modern compilers are programs that must be run separately from the linker.

WRITTEN QUESTIONS

Write your answers to the following questions.

11. What does the acronym ROM stand for?

12. List three operations managed by operating systems.

13. What is the device that processes the instructions in a computer?

14. What is the name of the number system commonly used to represent the state of being on or off?

15. Give an example of a low-level programming language.

16. List three examples of high-level programming languages.

17. List two advantages of a low-level language.

18. Describe the process involved when using a compiler to program a computer.

19. Describe one advantage that compiled programs have over interpreted programs.

20. Why is it important for professional programmers to have worked with various programming languages?

LESSON 1 PROJECT

Make a chart of at least 12 high-level languages. Include a brief description of each language that tells the primary use of the language or its historical significance. If you can find the date the language was created, include that on your chart. Some languages to consider are Ada, ALGOL, BASIC, C, C++, COBOL, FORTRAN, Java, LISP, Logo, Oberon, PASCAL, PL/I, Scheme, and Smalltalk.

Given that the following languages are listed in order from highest level to lowest level, answer the questions that follow.

BASIC, PASCAL, C++, assembly language

1. What language would be most appropriate for writing a quick, temporary program with the least effort and shortest code?
   a. BASIC
   b. C++

2. What language would be most appropriate for writing a program that must control the flow of data through a custom-built hardware device?
   a. PASCAL
   b. assembly language

ENTERING, COMPILING, AND RUNNING A C++ PROGRAM

OBJECTIVES

When you complete this lesson, you will be able to:

- Describe the process required to enter, compile, link, and run a C++ program.

- Explain the structure of a C++ program.

- Access the text editor and enter C++ source code.

- Compile, link, and run C++ programs.

- Modify source code.

- Create a standalone program.

- Load, compile, and run an existing source code file.

⏱ **Estimated Time: 1 hour**

VOCABULARY

braces
case sensitive
comments
compiler directive
function
header file
lowercase
main function
statement
uppercase

Using a C++ Compiler

You learned in the last lesson that C++ is a compiled language. You also learned that compiling a C++ program is just one step in the process of writing and running a C++ program. C++ source code has to be entered into a text editor, translated by a compiler, and made into an executable program by a linker.

Your task in this lesson will be to create an actual C++ program on your system. You will first examine the structure of a C++ program. Then you will enter a simple program into the text editor and compile, link, and run the executable file that is created.

Various brands of C++ compilers are available. It is important that you learn to use your particular compiler while you are in this lesson. At the appropriate point in this lesson, you will be directed to seek information specific to your compiler.

💡 Did You Know?

The C++ language evolved from a language called C. The language C got its name because it is a descendent of a language called B. Both languages were developed at Bell Laboratories. There was no A language. The language B probably got its name because it was based on a language named BCPL.

C++ Program Structure

C++ programs have the basic structure illustrated in Figure 2-1. They are:

1. **Comments.** *Comments* are remarks that are ignored by the compiler.

2. **Compiler directives.** *Compiler directives* are commands for the compiler that are needed to effectively compile and run your program.

3. **Main function.** The ***main function*** is where every C++ program begins.

4. **Braces.** *Braces* are special characters used to mark the beginning and ending of blocks of code.

5. **Statement.** A *statement* is a line of C++ code. Statements end with a semicolon.

FIGURE 2-1

A C++ program has several parts.

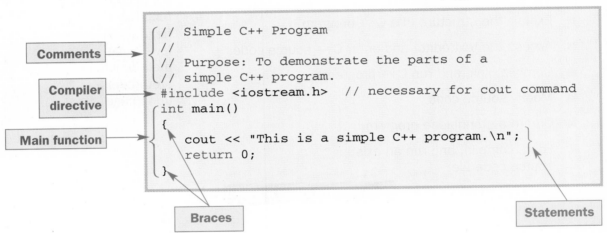

```
// Simple C++ Program
//
// Purpose: To demonstrate the parts of a
// simple C++ program.
#include <iostream.h>    // necessary for cout command
int main()
{
    cout << "This is a simple C++ program.\n";
    return 0;
}
```

Comments

Compiler directive

Main function

Braces

Statements

Let us examine each part of a C++ program in more detail.

Comments

When writing a program, you may think that you will always remember what you did and why. Most programmers, however, eventually forget. But more important, others may need to make changes in a program you wrote. They probably will be unaware of what you did when you wrote the program. That is why comments are important.

Use comments to:

- explain the purpose of a program.
- keep notes regarding changes to the source code.
- store the names of programmers for future reference.
- explain the parts of your program.

Code List 2-1 is an example of a program that is well documented with comments. The comments at the top of the program assign the program a name, identify its programmer as Jonathan Kleid, and indicate that the purpose of the program is to calculate miles per gallon and price per mile. Within the program, comments help the reader identify what the lines in the program do.

> **Concept Builder**
>
> As you will learn later in this course, a C++ program can have other functions in addition to the main function.

```cpp
// Travel Efficiency
// Programmer: Jonathan Kleid
//
// Purpose: Calculates miles per gallon and price per mile when
// given miles traveled, number of gallons used, and gas price.
#include <iostream.h> // necessary for cin and cout commands
int main()
{
  // Variable declarations
  float MilesTraveled;      // stores number of miles
  float GallonsUsed;        // stores number of total gallons used
  float PricePerGallon;     // stores price per gallon
  float PricePerMile;       // stores price per mile
  float MilesPerGallon;     // stores number of miles per gallon
  // Ask user for input values.
  cout << "How many miles did you travel? ";
  cin  >> MilesTraveled;
  cout << "How many gallons of gas did you use? ";
  cin  >> GallonsUsed;
  cout << "How much did one gallon of gas cost? $";
  cin  >> PricePerGallon;
  // Divide the number of miles by the number of gallons to get MPG.
  MilesPerGallon = MilesTraveled / GallonsUsed;
  // Divide price per gallon by miles per gallon
  // to get price per mile.
  PricePerMile = PricePerGallon / MilesPerGallon;
  // Output miles per gallon and price per mile.
  cout << "You got " << MilesPerGallon << " miles per gallon,\n";
  cout << "and each mile cost $" << PricePerMile << "\n";

  return 0;
}
```

Comments, which are ignored by the compiler, begin with a double slash (//) and may appear anywhere in the program. The comment can take up an entire line or can appear to the right of program statements, as shown in Code List 2-2. Everything to the right of the // is ignored. Therefore, do not include any statements to the right of a comment. Be sure to use the forward-leaning slash (/) rather than the backslash (\) or the compiler will try to translate your comments and an error message will result.

```cpp
float MilesTraveled;      // stores number of miles
float GallonsUsed;        // stores number of total gallons used
float PricePerGallon;     // stores price per gallon
float PricePerMile;       // stores price per mile
float MilesPerGallon;     // stores number of miles per gallon
```

Compiler Directives

Directives are instructions to the compiler rather than part of the C++ language. The most common compiler directive is the #include directive, which instructs the compiler to treat the text file that is enclosed in brackets as if it were keyed into the source code. See Figure 2-2.

FIGURE 2-2

The #include compiler directive inserts other code into your program as if it were actually keyed into your program.

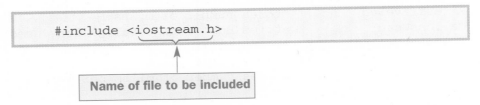

```
#include <iostream.h>
```

Name of file to be included

So why do you need other code included in your source code? The code you are including makes additional commands available to you. For example, the #include <iostream.h> directive that you have seen in programs in this lesson makes a set of input and output commands available. These commands make it easy to get input from the user and print it to the screen.

The main Function

Every C++ program has a main function (see Figure 2-1). A *function* is a block of code that carries out a specific task. Although simple programs can be written entirely within the main function, C++ programs are typically divided into multiple functions, which are accessed through the main function. No matter how many functions you have, the main function runs first.

Suppose, for example, that your program needs to calculate the area of a circle. A function could be written to calculate the area of a circle. That function could be used (or "called") wherever the calculation is needed in the program. You will see examples of this sort in a later lesson when you learn to use and create functions.

You may have noticed that the word *int* appears before the word *main* in Figure 2-1. The main function returns an integer value (a whole number) to the operating system when the program ends. Functions written in C++ often return a value of some kind to the function that called it. The main function is "called" by the computer's operating system. The int keyword allows the main function to return an integer to the operating system. When you learn to work with multiple functions, this will make more sense. For now, it is best to get in the habit of putting the int before the word main when you write your main function.

The parentheses that follow the word main are required. They tell the compiler that main is a function. All functions have parentheses, although many of them have information inside the parentheses. You will learn more about using functions in a later lesson.

The program ends with a return 0; statement. The return statement is what actually returns the value to the operating system or calling function. In this case, it returns a value of 0 to the operating system.

Braces

Braces are used to mark the beginning and end of blocks of code. Every opening brace must have a closing brace. Notice in Code List 2-3 that the `main` function is enclosed in a set of braces. Providing comments after each closing brace helps to associate it with the appropriate opening brace. Also, aligning the indention of opening and closing braces is a good idea.

CODE LIST 2-3

```
// comments.cpp
// This program prints the common uses for comments
// to the screen.
// Program written by Greg Buxkemper
#include <iostream.h>  // necessary for output statements
int main()
{
    cout << "Use comments to:\n";
    cout << " - explain the purpose of a program.\n";
    cout << " - keep notes regarding changes to the program.\n";
    cout << " - store the names of programmers.\n";
    cout << " - explain the parts of a program.\n";
    return 0;
} // end of main function
```

Statements

Functions contain statements that consist of instructions or commands, which make the program work. Each statement in C++ ends with a semicolon.

Semicolons

You must have a semicolon after every statement. The semicolon terminates the statement. In other words, it tells the compiler that the statement is complete. Notice, however, that directives such as `#include` and function declarations such as `int  main()` are exempt from being punctuated by semicolons.

C++ and Blank Space

C++ allows for great flexibility in the spacing and layout of the code. Use this feature to make it easier to read the code by indenting and grouping statements as shown in the sample program in Code List 2-1.

Uppercase or Lowercase

In the computer, *A* and *a* are different characters. The capital letters are referred to as ***uppercase***, and small letters are called ***lowercase***.

C++ is known as ***case sensitive*** because it interprets uppercase and lowercase letters differently. For example, to a C++ compiler, the word *cow* is different from the word *Cow*. Be careful to use the same combination of lettering (either uppercase or lowercase) when you enter source code. Whatever capitalization was used when the command was originally named is what must be used. In most cases, you will use lowercase letters in C++ programs. If you key a command in uppercase that is supposed to be lowercase, you will get an error.

From Source Code to a Finished Product

Hot Tip

You can also check
http://www.programcpp.com/
basics on the Internet or refer
to the documentation that came
with your compiler.

The exact process required to enter source code and compile, link, and run will vary depending on the compiler you are using. There are several compilers available for you to use. Additional information about compilers is provided in Appendix G.

Entering Source Code

The first step is to enter your C++ source code into a text file. Most C++ compilers have an integrated programming environment that contains a text editor you can use. An integrated programming environment allows you to enter your source code, compile, link, and run the program while your text editor is on the screen.

S TEP-BY-STEP 2.1

1. Start your text editor with a new, blank file.

2. Enter the C++ source code exactly as it is shown below.

```cpp
// myprog.cpp
// My first C++ program
#include <iostream.h>
int main()
{
  cout << "My first C++ program.\n";
  return 0;
}
```

Concept Builder

The "\n" causes the compiler to move the cursor to the beginning of the next line after printing the output to the screen.

3. Save the file as **myprog.cpp** and leave the program on your screen for the next Step-by-Step exercise.

Compiling, Linking, and Running the Program

Most compilers allow you to compile, link, and run with a single command from the integrated environment.

S TEP-BY-STEP 2.2

1. Compile, link, and run the program you entered in Step-by-Step 2.1. If your compiler allows all of these operations to be performed with a single command, use that command. If your program fails to compile or link, check to see whether you entered the code exactly as shown in Step-by-Step 2.1 and try again.

2. If your program runs successfully, you should see the text *My first C++ program* on the screen, similar to the output shown in Figure 2-3. Otherwise, ask your instructor for help.

3. Leave the source file open for the next exercise.

Concept Builder

The "Press any key to continue..." message that appears in Figure 2-3 is automatically generated by the Microsoft Visual C++ compiler. If your output window appears and then immediately disappears, check your compiler's documentation for specific information about your compiler. Or, check http://www.programcpp.com/basics on the Internet.

FIGURE 2-3

The output of the program should appear on your screen or in a window on your screen.

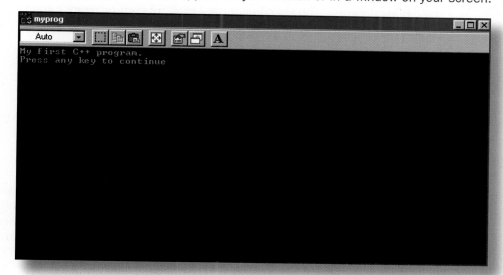

Making Changes and Compiling Again

You can add, change, or delete lines from a program's source code and compile it again. The next time the program is run, the changes will be in effect.

STEP-BY-STEP ▷ 2.3

1. Add the statement below to the main function, substituting your name in place of Allison Brackeen.

```
cout << "By Allison Brackeen\n";
```

Your program should now appear like the one below, except your name should be on the new line.

```
// myprog.cpp
// My first C++ program
#include <iostream.h>
int main()
{
    cout << "My first C++ program.\n";
    cout << "By Allison Brackeen\n";
    return 0;
}
```

(continued on next page)

2. Compile, link, and run the program again to see the change.

3. Save the source code file and leave it open for the next exercise.

Creating a Standalone Program

Compiling, linking, and running the program probably created a standalone program on the disk. The executable file is typically located in the same directory as the source code. A standalone program becomes important if you want to pass the program you have created on to another user. By passing on the standalone program, you make it possible for the recipient of your program to run the program even if he or she does not have to have a C++ compiler. By distributing a standalone program, you also do not have to share your program's source code.

Concept Builder

When you purchase a computer program in a store, you are purchasing a standalone program.

STEP-BY-STEP ⇨ 2.4

1. If a standalone program was generated as a result of completing Step-by-Step 2.3, quit the integrated programming environment and run the standalone program from the operating system. Otherwise, complete steps 2 through 4 below.

2. Select the option that allows you to compile and link to disk so that a standalone executable file is created.

3. Quit the integrated programming environment.

4. Run the executable program from the operating system.

Hot Tip

When you run the standalone program, the program is likely to disappear from your screen as soon as the output is printed to the screen. In a later lesson, you will learn how to write code that will cause the program to pause until you are ready for the program to end.

Loading and Compiling an Existing Source File

Often you will load an existing source code file and compile it. Most integrated programming environments have an Open command that can be used to open source files.

STEP-BY-STEP ⇨ 2.5

1. Start your integrated programming environment.

2. Open the source file **travel.cpp**. Your instructor will either provide you with a work disk or give

you instructions for accessing the file from the hard disk or network.

3. Compile, link, and run the program.

4. When the program prompts you for data, enter values that seem realistic to you and see what output the program gives.

5. Run the program several times with different values.

6. Close the source file and quit.

Congratulations

Congratulations. You now know the basics of creating and running C++ programs. From here you will simply add to your knowledge to enable you to write more useful programs. If you feel you need more experience with compiling and running C++ programs, repeat this lesson or ask your instructor for additional help. Future exercises require that you know how to compile, link, and run.

Summary

■ A C++ program has several parts.

■ Comments are remarks that are ignored by the compiler. They allow you to include notes and other information in the program's source code.

■ Directives are commands for the compiler, rather than part of the C++ language.

■ All C++ programs have a `main` function. The `main` function is where the program begins running.

■ Braces mark the beginning and end of blocks of code.

■ Statements are the lines of code the computer executes. Each statement ends with a semicolon.

■ C++ allows you to indent and insert space in any way that you want. You should take advantage of this flexibility to format source code in a way that makes programs more readable.

■ C++ is case sensitive, which means that using the wrong capitalization will result in errors.

■ Most C++ compilers have an integrated programming environment that contains a text editor for entering source code. The programming environment allows you to enter source code, compile, link, and run while your text editor is on the screen.

VOCABULARY REVIEW

Define the following terms:

braces	header file
case sensitive	lowercase
comments	main function
compiler directive	statement
function	uppercase

TRUE/FALSE

Circle the T if the statement is true. Circle the F if it is false.

T   F   1. Comments begin with \\.

T   F   2. Comments may appear on the same line with program statements.

T   F   3. Compiler directives are not part of the C++ language.

T   F   4. The .hfl extension indicates that the file is a header file.

T   F   5. The parentheses after the word main indicate to the compiler that it is a function.

T   F   6. The int keyword that appears before the word main indicates that the function is an internal function.

T   F   7. Every opening brace must have a closing brace.

T   F   8. It is a good idea to align the opening and closing braces in source code to improve readability.

T   F   9. Every C++ statement ends with a colon.

T   F   10. Capital letters are called uppercase letters.

WRITTEN QUESTIONS

Write your answers to the following questions.

11. List four uses for comments.

12. What compiler directive inserts source code from another file into your program?

13. What is a function?

14. What purpose do braces serve?

15. What does the term "case sensitive" mean?

16. What company developed the compiler you are using?

17. What is the name of the compiler you are using and its version number?

18. What command or commands are used to run a program with your compiler?

19. What command opens a source code file from a disk?

20. What command saves a source code file?

LESSON 2 PROJECTS

PROJECT 2A

Enter the program shown below but substitute your name and the appropriate information for your compiler. Compile, link, and run. Save the source code as **compinfo.cpp**.

```
// compinfo.cpp
// By Jeremy Wilson
#include <iostream.h>
int main()
{
  cout << "This program was compiled using\n";
  cout << "Colossal C++ version 2.5.\n";
  return 0;
}
```

PROJECT 2B

Enter the program shown in Code List 2-3, compile it, link, and run. After you have run the program, close the source file.

PROJECT 2C

Open the source file **braces.cpp**. Look at the program and observe how the pairs of braces match up. Compile, link, and run the program. After you have run the program, close the source file and quit.

CRITICAL THINKING

Write a program that prints the message of your choice to the screen. Make the message at least four lines long. Save the source code file as **my_msg.cpp**.

Your First C++ Program

MATCHING

Write the letter of the description from Column 2 that best matches the term or phrase in Column 1.

Column 1	Column 2

_____ 1. algorithm

A. The set of commands a microprocessor is made to understand

_____ 2. assembler

B. A program that links object files created by a compiler into an executable program

_____ 3. compiler

C. A program that reads assembly language and converts it into machine language

_____ 4. executable file

D. A program in the form of a high-level language

_____ 5. instruction set

E. A program that translates a high-level language into machine language but does not save the machine language

_____ 6. interpreter

F. The device in the computer that processes the instructions

_____ 7. linker

G. A set of sequential instructions followed to solve a problem

_____ 8. microprocessor

H. The machine language code produced by a compiler

_____ 9. object code

I. A program that translates a high-level language into machine language, then saves the machine language

_____ 10. source code

J. The output of a linker

WRITTEN QUESTIONS

Write your answers to the following questions.

1. What is an application program?

2. What is the purpose of the binary number system?

3. What kinds of programs are usually found in a computer's ROM?

4. Why does a program written in a low-level language typically require less memory?

5. Is PASCAL a high- or low-level language?

6. What term refers to correcting programming errors?

7. What character or characters tell the compiler that the text to follow is a comment?

8. What character is used to end a C++ statement?

9. What is the file extension typically used to signify a header file?

10. When a C++ program is executed, what function is run first?

APPLICATIONS

APPLICATION 1-1

In the spaces below, write the name of the parts of the C++ program shown below.

```
// Simple C++ Program          ←——— A

#include <iostream.h>          ←——— B

int main()          ←——— C
{
  cout << "Hello World!\n";   } E
  return 0;
}          ←——— D
```

A._____

B._____

C._____

D._____

E._____

APPLICATION 1-2

Write a program that lists to the screen the name and description of three high-level programming languages. Use three of the languages that you researched in the Lesson 1 Project.

INTERNET ACTIVITY

In this Internet activity, you will use the Internet to learn more about your microprocessor and your compiler.

1. Open your Web browser.

2. Go to the Web address below.

   http://www.programcpp.com/basics

3. On the home page, click the link called **Internet Activities from the book**.

4. On the Internet Activities page, click the **Unit 1 Internet Activity** link.

5. Click the **Microprocessors** link. Links to the Web pages of major microprocessor companies appear. Determine whether the manufacturer of your microprocessor appears in the list.

6. If the manufacturer of your microprocessor appears in the list, visit the site by clicking the appropriate link. Otherwise, search the Internet for the manufacturer of your microprocessor.

7. While on the Web site of the microprocessor manufacturer, list the latest microprocessors released by the company or print Web pages that list the microprocessors they have available.

8. Return to the Unit 1 Internet Activities page.

9. Click the **Compilers** link. Links to the Web pages of major compiler developers appear. Determine if your compiler appears on the list.

10. If the developer of your C++ compiler appears on the list, visit its site by clicking the appropriate link. Otherwise, search the Internet for the developer of your compiler.

11. While on the Web site of the compiler developer, list the latest compilers released by the company or print Web pages that list the compilers they have available.

12. Close your Web browser when finished.

DATA AND OPERATIONS

Estimated Time for Unit: 5 hours

VARIABLES AND CONSTANTS

OBJECTIVES

When you complete this lesson, you will be able to:

■ Explain the terms data structure, variable, and constant.

■ Explain the different integer variable types used in C++.

■ Declare, name, and initialize variables.

■ Use character variables.

■ Explain the different floating-point types and use variables of those types.

■ Describe Boolean variables.

■ Use constants.

⏱ **Estimated Time: 2 hours**

VOCABULARY

ASCII
Boolean variable
characters
constant
data type
declaring
exponential notation
floating-point number
identifier
initialize
integer
keyword
string
variable

Understanding Variables and Constants

Computer programs process data to provide information. The job of the programmer is to properly organize data for storage and use. Computers store data in many complex arrangements called *data structures*.

Any organized way of storing data in a computer is a data structure. The simplest type of data storage takes place in data structures known as *primitive data structures,* or simply *primitives*. These primitive data structures come in two varieties: variables and constants.

A *variable* holds data that can change while the program is running. A *constant* is used to store data that remains the same throughout the program's execution.

C++ has more than a dozen types of variables to store numbers and characters. Some variables are for storing *integers* (whole numbers); other variables are for *floating-point numbers* (real numbers).

You may recall from math courses that an integer is a positive or negative whole number, such as –2, 4, or 5133. Real numbers can be whole numbers or decimals and can be either positive or negative, such as 1.99, –2.5, 3.14159, or 4.

When programming in C++, you must select a type of variable, called a *data type*, that best fits the nature of the data itself. In this lesson, you will first learn about the data types used to store variables and how to use them in your programs. Then you will learn how to use data types for characters and floating-point numbers. Finally, you will learn how to work with constants in your programs.

Integer Data Types

When you are working with either positive or negative whole numbers, you should use integer data types for your variables. Several integer data types are available in C++ (integer data types can vary by compiler). Selecting which integer data type to use is the next step.

Table 3-1 lists some of the most common integer data types. The table also shows the range of values each type typically holds and the number of bytes of memory required to store a variable of that type. However, these ranges and number of bytes occupied may vary among compilers, especially in regard to the int type.

Concept Builder

In general, new C++ compilers use 4 bytes for the int type. Older compilers or compilers for older operating systems are more likely to use only 2 bytes for the int type.

TABLE 3-1
Common integer data types

Data Type	Minimum Range of Values	Minimum Number of Bytes Occupied
char	−128 to 127	1
unsigned char	0 to 255	1
short	−32,768 to 32,767	2
unsigned short	0 to 65,535	2
int	−2,147,483,648 to 2,147,483,647	4
unsigned int	0 to 4,294,967,295	4
long	−2,147,483,648 to 2,147,483,647	4
unsigned long	0 to 4,294,967,295	4

S TEP-BY-STEP ▷ 3.1

1. Locate the reference manual or online documentation for your compiler.

2. Search for the sizes of the integer data types used in your compiler. Figure 3-1 shows the information found in the Microsoft online documentation.

3. Record the information specific to your compiler or print the information from your online documentation.

FIGURE 3-1

Your compiler should include information about the size of the integer data types.

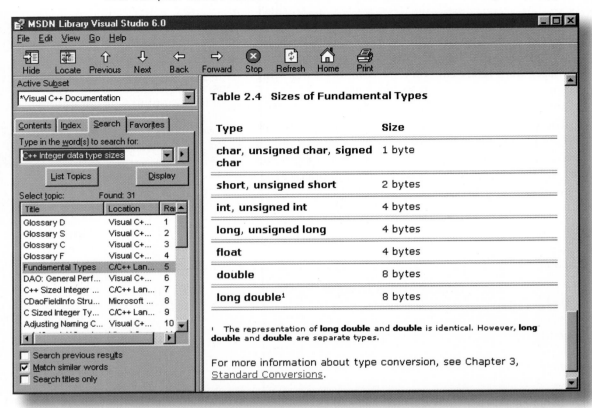

Take a moment to notice the range of values that each type can hold (Table 3-1). For example, any value from −32,768 to 32,767 can be stored in a variable if the short data type is chosen. If you need to store a value outside of that range, you must choose a different data type such as int or long.

An unsigned variable can store only positive numbers. For example, if you were to store the weights of trucks in variables, an unsigned data type might be a good choice. A truck can't weigh less than zero. If you are sure that the integers you are storing cannot be less than zero and will not exceed 65,535, then an unsigned short may be a good choice.

Why would you want to use the short type when the long type has a bigger range? The answer is that you *can* use the int or long types when a short would do, but there is more to consider. Notice the third column of Table 3-1. The variables with the larger ranges require more of the computer's memory. Saving memory used to be much more important than it is today. Computers now have vast amounts of memory. However, conserving space may become more important when lots of data is involved.

In addition, it often takes the computer longer to access the data types that require more memory. Also, it is more common than ever for data to be transferred over networks such as the Internet. The smaller the space occupied by data, the faster the data can be delivered. Having all of these data types gives the programmer the ability to use only what is necessary for each variable, decrease memory usage, and increase speed.

Declaring and Naming Variables

Indicating to the compiler what type of variable you want and what you want to call it is called *declaring* the variable.

Declaring Variables

You must declare a variable before you can use it. The C++ statement declaring a variable must include the data type followed by the name you wish to call the variable and a semicolon. An integer variable named i is declared in Code List 3-1.

CODE LIST 3-1

```
#include <iostream.h>  // necessary for cout command

int main()
{
  int i;    // declare i as an integer

  i = 2;    // initialize i to 2
  cout << i  << '\n';
  return 0;
}
```

Initializing Variables

The compiler assigns a location in memory to a variable when it is declared. However, a value already exists in the space reserved for your variable. A random value could have been stored when the computer was turned on, or the location could retain data from a program that ran earlier. Regardless, the memory location now belongs to your program and you must specify the initial value to be stored in the location. This process is known as initializing.

To *initialize* a variable, you simply assign it a value. In C++, the equal sign (=) is used to assign a value to a variable. In Code List 3-1, the variable i is initialized to the value of 2.

STEP-BY-STEP ▷ 3.2

1. Enter the program shown in Code List 3-1 into a blank editor screen.

2. Save the source code file as **ideclare.cpp**.

3. Compile and run the program. The program should print the number 2 on your screen. If no errors are encountered, leave the program on your screen. If errors are found, check the source code for keyboarding errors and compile again.

4. Change the initialization statement to initialize the value of i to –40 and run again. The number –40 is shown on your screen. Save the source code again and close the program. You may have to close a project or workspace to completely close the current program.

Table 3-2 shows that declaring variables for other data types is just as easy as the example in Code List 3-1. You can also see in Table 3-2 that variable names can be more interesting than just i.

TABLE 3-2
Variables for other data types

Data Type	Example C++ Declaration Statement
short	short temperature;
unsigned short	unsigned short k;
int	int DaysInMonth;
unsigned int	unsigned int Age_in_dog_years;
long	long PopulationChange;
unsigned long	unsigned long j;

Did You Know?

C++ will allow you to declare a variable anywhere in the program as long as the variable is declared before you use it. However, you should get into the habit of declaring all variables at the top of the function. Declaring variables at the top of the function makes for better-organized code, makes the variables easy to locate, and helps you plan for the variables you will need.

Naming Variables

The names of variables in C++ are typically referred to as *identifiers*. When naming variables, use descriptive names and consider how they might help the programmer recall the variable's purpose. For example, a variable that holds a bank balance could be called balance, or the circumference of a circle could be stored in a variable named circumference. The following are rules for creating identifiers.

Note

Recall from the previous lesson that C++ is case sensitive. The capitalization you use when the variable is declared must be used each time the variable is accessed. For example, total is not the same identifier as Total.

■ Identifiers must start with a letter or an underscore (_). You should, however, avoid using identifiers that begin with underscores because the language's internal identifiers often begin with underscores. By avoiding the use of underscores as the first character, you will ensure that your identifier remains out of conflict with C++'s internal identifiers.

■ As long as the first character is a letter, you can use letters, numerals, or underscores in the rest of the identifier.

■ Use a name that makes the purpose of the variable clear, but avoid making it unnecessarily long. Most C++ compilers will recognize only the first 31 or 32 characters.

■ There can be no spaces in identifiers. A good way to create a multiword identifier is to use an underscore between the words; for example, last_name.

■ The following words, called *keywords*, must NOT be used as identifiers because they are part of the C++ language. Your compiler may have additional keywords not listed here.

```
asm            catch          continue
auto           char           default
break          class          delete
case           const          do
```

double	new	switch
else	operator	template
enum	private	this
extern	protected	throw
float	public	try
for	register	typedef
friend	return	union
goto	short	unsigned
if	signed	virtual
inline	sizeof	void
int	static	volatile
long	struct	while

Table 3-3 gives some examples of illegal identifiers.

TABLE 3-3
Illegal identifiers

Improper C++ Variable Names	Why Illegal
Miles per gallon	Spaces are not allowed.
register	register is a keyword.
4Sale	Identifiers cannot begin with numerals.

STEP-BY-STEP ▷ 3.3

1. Open the source code file named **ideclare.cpp** that you saved in Step-by-Step 3.2.

2. Save the source code as **intdecl.cpp**.

3. Change the name of the variable i to MyInteger. Be sure to change the name in every line of code where it appears.

4. Compile and run the program. The output of the program should be unaffected by the change in the variable name.

5. Close the current program.

Declaring Multiple Variables in a Statement

You can declare more than one variable in a single statement as long as all the variables are of the same type. For example, if your program requires three variables of type int, all three variables could be declared by placing commas between the variables like this:

```
int x, y, z;
```

Characters and the Char Data Type

TABLE 3-4
ASCII codes

As you probably know, all data in a computer is represented by numbers, including letters and symbols. Letters and symbols, called *characters*, are assigned a number that the computer uses to represent them. Most computers assign numbers to characters according to the *American Standard Code for Information Interchange (ASCII)*. Table 3-4 shows some of the ASCII (pronounced "ask-e") codes. For a complete ASCII table, see Appendix A.

The basic ASCII code is based on 7 bits, which gives 128 characters. About 95 of these are upper and lowercase letters, numbers, and symbols. Some of the characters are used as codes for controlling communication hardware and other devices. Others are invisible characters such as Tab and Return. Most computers extend the ASCII code to 8 bits (a whole byte) to represent 256 characters. The additional 128 characters are used for graphical characters and characters used with foreign languages.

When a computer stores a character, software keeps track of whether the number stored is to be treated as an integer or interpreted as a character. To make it easy, C++ includes a char data type especially for storing characters. The char data type, however, is just an integer. If you use the char data type, the integer you store will be interpreted as a character when you print the character to the screen.

For example, the program shown in Code List 3-2 declares a variable of type char, initializes it, and outputs the character to the screen.

Character	Equivalent Decimal Value
$	36
*	42
A	65
B	66
C	67
D	68
a	97
b	98
c	99
d	100

 Did You Know?

Fonts used on modern operating systems such as Microsoft Windows and the Macintosh OS also use the ASCII codes. Have you ever changed a font and noticed that some special characters changed to unrecognizable characters or squares? That happens when the font you selected does not have a character for that particular ASCII value or uses an ASCII value for a different character. All the standard characters—letters, numerals, and basic punctuation—are consistent among fonts.

CODE LIST 3-2

```
#include <iostream.h>  // necessary for cout command

int main()
{
  char MyChar;    // declare MyChar as a char

  MyChar = 'A';   // initialize MyChar to 'A'
  cout << MyChar  << '\n';
  return 0;
}
```

STEP-BY-STEP ▷ 3.4

1. Enter the program shown in Code List 3-2 into a blank editor screen.

2. Save the source code file as **chardecl.cpp**.

3. Compile and run the program. The program should print the letter *A* on your screen. If no errors are encountered, leave the program on

your screen. If errors are found, check the source code for keyboarding errors and compile again.

4. Change the initialization statement to initialize the value of `MyChar` to *B* and run again. The letter *B* is shown on your screen. Save the source code again and close the program.

Each variable of the char data type can hold only one character. In order to store words or sentences, you must string characters together. A group of characters put together to make a word or phrase is called a ***string***. You will learn more about characters and strings in a later lesson.

Floating-Point Data Types

Integer variables are inappropriate for certain types of data. For example, tasks as common as working with money call for using floating-point numbers. Just as there is more than one integer data type, there is more than one data type for floating-point variables.

Table 3-5 lists the three floating-point data types and their range of values. The ranges of floating-point data types are more complicated than the range of integers. Selecting an appropriate floating-point type is based on both the range of values and the required decimal precision.

TABLE 3-5
Floating-point data types

Data Type	Approximate Range of Values	Digits of Precision	Number of Bytes Occupied
float	3.4×10^{-38} to 3.4×10^{38}	7	4
double	1.7×10^{-308} to 1.7×10^{308}	15	8
long double	3.4×10^{-4932} to 1.1×10^{4932}	19	10

When you are choosing a floating-point data type, first look to see how many digits of precision are necessary to store the value you need to store. For example, to store π as 3.1415926535897 requires 14 digits of precision. Therefore you should use the double type. You should also verify that your value will fit within the range of values the type supports. But unless you are dealing with very large or very small numbers, the range is not usually as important an issue as the precision.

 Note

The information in Table 3-5 may vary among compilers. Check your compiler's manual for exact data type ranges and bytes occupied for both integers and floating-point numbers.

Let us look at some examples of values and what data types would be appropriate for the values:

- Dollar amounts in the range $-99,999.99 to $99,999.99 can be handled with a variable of type float. A variable of type double can store dollar amounts in the range $-9,999,999,999,999.99 to $9,999,999,999,999.99.

- The number 5.98×10^{24} kg, which happens to be the mass of Earth, can be stored in a variable of type float because the number is within the range of values and requires only three digits of precision.

Assigning a floating-point value to a variable works the way you probably expect, except when you need to use **exponential notation**. You may have used exponential notation and called it scientific notation. In exponential notation, very large or very small numbers are represented with a fractional part (called the mantissa) and an exponent. Use an *e* to signify exponential notation. Just place an *e* in the number to separate the mantissa from the exponent. Below are some examples of statements that initialize floating-point variables.

```
x = 2.5;
ElectronGFactor = 1.0011596567;
Radius_of_Earth = 6.378164e6;    // radius of Earth at equator
Mass_of_Electron = 9.109e-31;    // 9.109 x 10-31 kilograms
```

Code List 3-3 shows a program that declares and initializes three floating-point variables.

CODE LIST 3-3

```cpp
// floatdec.cpp
// Example of floating-point variable declaration.

#include <iostream.h>

int main()
{
  float x;
  double Radius_of_Earth, Mass_of_Electron;
  x = 2.5;
  Radius_of_Earth = 6.378164e6;
  Mass_of_Electron = 9.109e-31;

  cout << x << '\n';
  cout << Radius_of_Earth << '\n';
  cout << Mass_of_Electron << '\n';
  return 0;
}
```

STEP-BY-STEP ▷ 3.5

1. Enter the program shown in Code List 3-3.

2. Save the source code as **floatdec.cpp**.

3. Compile and run the program. The three values should appear, as shown in Figure 3-2.

4. When the program runs successfully, save and close the program.

✓ **Note**

The format in which the floating-point values appear on your screen may differ from Figure 3-2, depending on the compiler you are using.

FIGURE 3-2

The program prints three floating-point values to the screen.

Boolean Variables

A ***Boolean variable*** is a variable that can have only two possible values. One of the values represents true (or some other form of the affirmative), and the other value represents false (or some other form of the negative). Boolean variables are very useful in programming to store information such as whether an answer is yes or no, whether a report has been printed or not, or whether a device is currently on or off.

 Did You Know?

Boolean variables are named in honor of George Boole, an English mathematician who lived in the 1800s. Boole created a system called *Boolean algebra*, which is a study of operations that take place using variables with the values true and false.

Some C++ compilers do not support a Boolean variable. Others have a data type bool, which can be used to declare Boolean variables. If your compiler does not support the bool data type, you can use the `bool.h` header file on your work disk to make the feature available in your programs. Your instructor can help you access this header file. Later in this course, you will use the bool data type and examine the header file that makes it work.

Constants

In C++, a constant holds data that remains the same as the program runs. Constants allow you to give a name to a value that is used several times in a program so that the value can be more easily used. For example, if you use the value of π (3.14159) several times in your program, you can assign the value 3.14159 to the name PI. Then, each time you need the value 3.14159, you need only use the name PI.

Constants are defined in a manner that is similar to the way you define a variable. You still must select a data type and give the constant a name. But you also tell the compiler that the data is a constant using the const keyword and assign a value all in the same statement.

The statement below declares PI as a constant.

```
const double PI = 3.14159;
```

Any valid identifier name can be used to name a constant. The same rules apply as with variables. Traditionally, uppercase letters have been used when naming constants. Lowercase letters are generally used with variable names. Therefore, uppercase letters help distinguish constants from variables. Some C++ programmers think lowercase letters should be used for constants as well as variables. In this book, we will use uppercase letters for constants because it will help you quickly identify constants in programs. Just be aware that you may see programs elsewhere that use lowercase letters for constants.

Code List 3-4 shows a complete program that uses a constant for PI. Notice that the identifier PI is used in the line that calculates the circumference of the circle. Because PI is a constant, you do not have to be concerned about the value of PI changing while the program runs. The double data type is used for at least two reasons. By using the larger data type, the floating-point values have more digits of accuracy. In addition, some compilers will give a warning if you use a constant of type float because of concern about losing digits of accuracy.

CODE LIST 3-4

```cpp
// circle.cpp
// Example of using a constant.

#include <iostream.h>

int main()
{
  const double PI = 3.14159;     // declare PI as a constant
  double circumference, radius;

  // Ask user for the radius of a circle
  cout << "What is the radius of the circle? ";
  cin  >> radius;

  circumference = 2 * PI * radius;  // calculate circumference

  // Output the circle's circumference
  cout << "The circle's circumference is ";
  cout << circumference << '\n';
  return 0;
}
```

STEP-BY-STEP ▷ 3.6

1. Enter the program shown in Code List 3-4. Save the source code as **circle.cpp**.

2. Compile and run the program. Enter 4 as the radius of the circle. The program will return 25.1327 as the circumference. The number of digits displayed after the decimal point may vary.

3. An error message is generated if you add the following line at the end of the program because you cannot change the value of a constant while the program is running. Add the line before the return line at the end of the program.

```
PI = 2.5;
```

4. Compile the program again to see the error generated.

5. Delete the line causing the error and compile the program again.

6. Save and close the program.

Concept Builder

C++ error messages are often not very helpful to beginning programmers. For example, when you attempted to reassign a value to the constant PI, you may have received an error such as "l-value specifies const object," which may not tell you much. If you get an error message that does not make sense and you cannot detect your error, try using the help system or your compiler's documentation to get a clearer explanation of the error.

The compiler prohibits the assignment of another value to a constant after the declaration statement. If you fail to initialize the constant in the declaration statement, however, whatever value is in the memory location remains assigned to the constant throughout the execution of the program.

A good reason to use constants in a large program is that they give you the ability to easily change the value of the constant in more than one place in the program. For example, suppose you have a program that needs the sales tax rate in several places. If you declare a constant named TAX_RATE, when the tax rate changes you have to change the constant only where it is declared. Every place in the program that uses the TAX_RATE constant will use the new value.

Summary

■ Computers store data in many complex arrangements called data structures.

■ Most data is stored in either variables or constants. Variables hold data that can change while the program is running. Constants are used to store data that remains the same throughout the program's execution.

■ Integer data types are selected based on the range of values you need to store. Some integer data types are unsigned, meaning they can store only positive numbers.

■ Variables must be declared before they are used. Variables should also be initialized to clear any random values that may be in the memory location. When a variable is declared, it must be given a legal name called an identifier.

- Characters are stored in the computer as numbers. The char data type can store one character of data.

- Floating-point data types are selected based on the range of values and the required precision.

- Boolean variables are variables that can have only two possible values: true or false.

- Constants are declared in a way similar to variables. The const keyword tells the compiler that the data is a constant. The constant must be assigned a value in the declaration statement.

VOCABULARY REVIEW

Define the following terms:

ASCII	floating-point number
Boolean variable	identifier
characters	initialize
constant	integer
data type	keyword
declaring	string
exponential notation	variable

LESSON 3 REVIEW QUESTIONS

TRUE/FALSE

Circle the T if the statement is true. Circle the F if it is false.

T F 1. An integer is a number with digits after the decimal point.

T F 2. The unsigned char data type has a range of values of 0 to 255.

T F 3. Each char variable can store one character.

T F 4. Variables must be declared before they are used.

T F 5. Identifiers must start with a letter or a numeral.

T F 6. Underscores are not allowed to be a part of an identifier.

T F 7. Variables must be initialized because they have an indeterminant value when declared.

T   F   8.   A constant is data that remains the same as the program runs.

T   F   9.   Constants do not have data types.

T   F   10.   Constants must be named with uppercase characters.

WRITTEN QUESTIONS

Write your answers to the following questions.

11.   Why is it important to use data types that store your data efficiently?

12.   What floating-point data type provides the most digits of precision?

13.   What is a string?

14.   What are words called that cannot be used as identifiers because they are part of the C++ language?

15.   Why can't "first name" be used as an identifier?

16.   What character is used to assign a value to a variable?

17.   What is a constant?

18.   What keyword is used to declare a constant in C++?

19.   When is it appropriate to use constants?

20.   When must the value of a constant be assigned?

PROJECT 3A

Write code statements for each of the following.

1. Write a statement to declare an integer named age as an unsigned short.

2. Write a statement that declares four int data type variables i, j, k, and 1 in a single statement.

3. Write a constant declaration statement to create a constant for the number of feet in a mile (5,280).

4. Write a statement that declares a variable of type double named MyDouble.

5. Write a statement that assigns the value 9.999 to the variable MyDouble.

PROJECT 3B

1. Enter, compile, and run the following program. Save the source code file as **datatype.cpp**.

```
// datatype.cpp
// Examples of variable declaration and
// initialization.

#include <iostream.h>

int main()
{
  // declare a constant for the square root of two
  const double SQUARE_ROOT_OF_TWO = 1.414214;

  int i;                // declare i as an integer
  long j;               // j as a long integer
  unsigned long k;      // k as an unsigned long integer
  float n;              // n as a floating-point number

  i = 3;                // initialize i to 3
  j = -2048111;         // j to -2,048,111
  k = 4000000001;       // k to 4,000,000,001
  n = 1.887;            // n to 1.887

  // output constant and variables to screen
  cout << SQUARE_ROOT_OF_TWO << '\n';
  cout << i << '\n';
  cout << j << '\n';
  cout << k << '\n';
  cout << n << '\n';
  return 0;
}
```

2. Add declarations using appropriate identifiers for the values below. Declare *e*, the speed of light, and the speed of sound as constants. Initialize the variables. Use any identifier you want for those values that give you no indication as to their purpose.

100	*e* (2.7182818)
–100	Speed of light (3.00 × 108 m/s)
–40,000	Speed of sound (340.292 m/s)
40,000	

3. Print the new values to the screen.

4. Save, compile, and run. Correct any errors you have made.

5. Close the program.

CRITICAL THINKING

1. Write a program that declares two constants (A and B).

2. Initialize A = 1 and B = 2.2.

3. Declare an int named C and a float named D.

4. Initialize C = A and D = B.

5. Write statements to print C and D to the screen.

6. Save the source code as **abcddec.cpp**.

7. Compile and run. Correct any errors you have made.

8. Close the program.

MATH OPERATIONS

OBJECTIVES

When you complete this lesson, you will be able to:

- Use the assignment operator.
- Use the arithmetic operators.
- Use operators in output statements.
- Explain the problem with division by zero.
- Increment and decrement variables.
- Explain the order of operations.

⏱ **Estimated Time: 2 hours**

VOCABULARY

++ operator
-- operator
arithmetic operators
assignment operator
decrementing
expression
incrementing
modulus operator
order of operations
quotient
remainder

Assignment Operator

Y ou have already used the assignment operator (=) to initialize variables, so you already know most of what there is to know about the assignment operator. The *assignment operator* changes the value of the variable to the left of the operator. Consider the statement below:

```
i = 25;
```

The statement i = 25; changes the value of variable i to 25, regardless of what it was before the statement.

S TEP-BY-STEP ▷ 4.1

1. Turn on your computer and access the C++ compiler's text editor. Enter the program in Code List 4-1 and save your source code file as **iassign.cpp**.

2. Compile and run the program. Notice the difference between the value of i when it is displayed after the first output statement and after the second.

3. Close the program.

 Note

When the instructions in this book direct you to close a program, close the entire project or workspace to prepare the compiler to work with another source code file.

```
#include <iostream.h> // necessary for cout command

int main()
{
  int i;        // declare i as an integer
  i = 10000;    // assign the value 10000 to i
  cout << i << '\n';
  i = 25;       // assign the value 25 to i
  cout << i << '\n';
  return 0;
}
```

Recall from Lesson 3 that you can declare more than one variable in a single statement. For example, instead of:

```
int i;
int j;
int k;
```

you can use:

```
int i,j,k;
```

You can use a similar shortcut when initializing multiple variables. If you have more than one variable that you want to initialize to the same value, you can use a statement such as

```
i = j = k = 25;
```

S TEP-BY-STEP ▷ 4.2

1. Enter the program in Code List 4-2 and save your source code file as **multinit.cpp**.

2. Compile and run the program. The program's output is:

```
10
10
10
```

3. Close the program.

 Hot Tip

You may want to create a source code file that consists of the #include statement, int main(), and the opening and closing braces and use it as a starting point every time you need to create a new source code file. Just open the template file and save it under a new name before compiling.

```
#include <iostream.h> // necessary for cout command

int main()
{
    int i,j,k;          // declare i, j, and k as integers

    i = j = k = 10;     // initialize all of the variables to 10
    cout << i << '\n';
    cout << j << '\n';
    cout << k << '\n';
    return 0;
}
```

Variables may also be declared and initialized in a single statement. For example, both of the following are valid C++ statements.

```
int i = 2;
float n = 4.5;
```

Arithmetic Operators

A specific set of **arithmetic operators** is used to perform calculations in C++. These arithmetic operators, shown in Table 4-1, may be somewhat familiar to you. Addition and subtraction are performed with the familiar + and − operators. Multiplication uses an asterisk (*), and division uses a forward slash (/). C++ also uses what is known as a modulus operator (%) to determine the integer remainder of division. A more detailed discussion of the modulus operator is presented later in this lesson.

TABLE 4-1
Arithmetic operators

Symbol	Operation	Example	Read as...
+	Addition	3 + 8	three plus eight
−	Subtraction	7 − 2	seven minus two
*	Multiplication	4 * 9	four times nine
/	Division	6 / 2	six divided by two
%	Modulus	7 % 3	seven modulo three

Using Arithmetic Operators

The arithmetic operators are used with two operands, as in the examples in Table 4-1. The exception to this is the minus symbol (–), which can be used to change the sign of an operand. Arithmetic operators are most often used on the right side of an assignment operator, as shown in the examples in Table 4-2. The portion of the statement on the right side of the assignment operator is called an *expression*.

TABLE 4-2
Examples of expressions

Statement	Result
cost = price + tax;	cost is assigned the value of price plus tax.
owed = total – discount;	owed is assigned the value of total minus discount.
area = l * w;	area is assigned the value of l times w.
one_eighth = 1 / 8;	one_eighth is assigned the value of 1 divided by 8.
r = 5 % 2;	r is assigned the remainder of 5 divided by 2 by using the modulus operator.
x = –y;	x is assigned the value of –y.

The assignment operator (=) functions differently in C++ from the way the equal sign functions in algebra. Consider the following statement:

```
x = x + 10;
```

This statement is invalid for use in algebra because the equal sign is the symbol around which both sides of an equation are balanced. The left side equals the right side. But your C++ compiler looks at the statement differently. The expression on the right side of the equal sign is evaluated, and the result is stored in the variable to the left of the equal sign. In the statement `x = x + 10;`, the value of x is increased by 10.

 Did You Know?

Did you know that C++ compilers ignore blank spaces in math operations? Both of the statements shown below are valid and produce the same result.

```
x=y+z;
x = y + z;
```

STEP-BY-STEP 4.3

1. Retrieve the file named **assign.cpp**. The program shown in Code List 4-3 appears.

2. Look at the source code and try to predict the program's output.

3. Run the program and see whether you were correct in your prediction.

4. Close the program.

```
// assign.cpp

#include <iostream.h>

int main()
{
 int i = 2;
 int j = 3;
 int k = 4;
 int l;
 float a = 0.5;
 float b = 3.0;
 float c;

 l = i + 2;
 cout << l << '\n';

 l = l - j;
 cout << l << '\n';

 l = i * j * k;
 cout << l << '\n';

 l = k / i;
 cout << l << '\n';

 c = b * a;
 cout << c << '\n';

 c = b / a;
 cout << c << '\n';

 return 0;
}
```

More About Modulus

The *modulus operator*, which may be used only for integer division, returns the remainder rather than the result of the division. As shown in Figure 4-1, integer division is similar to the way you divide manually.

When integer division is performed, any fractional part that may be in the answer is lost when the result is stored into the integer variable. The modulus operator allows you to obtain the fractional part of the result as an integer remainder.

Consider the program in Code List 4-4. The user is prompted for two integers. Notice the program calculates the *quotient* using the division operator (/) and the *remainder* using the modulus operator (%).

FIGURE 4-1

The division operator and the modulus operator return the quotient and the remainder.

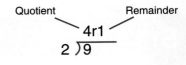

```
// remain.cpp

#include <iostream.h> // necessary for cin and cout commands

int main()
{
  int dividend, divisor, quotient, remainder;

  // Get the dividend and divisor from the user
  cout << "Enter the dividend ";
  cin >> dividend;
  cout << "Enter the divisor ";
  cin >> divisor;

  // Calculate the quotient and remainder
  quotient = dividend / divisor;
  remainder = dividend % divisor;

  // Output the quotient and remainder
  cout << "The quotient is " << quotient;
  cout << " with a remainder of " << remainder << '\n';
  return 0;
}
```

STEP-BY-STEP ▷ 4.4

1. Enter the program from Code List 4-4. Save the source file as **remain.cpp**.

2. Run the program several times using values that will produce different remainders. On

paper, record the inputs you used and the quotients and remainders produced.

3. Leave the source code file open for the next Step-by-Step exercise.

Using Operators in Output Statements

The program in Code List 4-4 required four variables and nine program statements. The program in Code List 4-5 accomplishes the same output with only two variables and seven statements. Notice in Code List 4-5 that the calculations are performed in the output statements. Rather than storing the results of the expressions in variables, the program sends the results to the screen as part of the output.

```
// remain2.cpp

#include <iostream.h> // necessary for cin and cout commands

int main()
{
  int dividend, divisor;

  // Get the dividend and divisor from the user.
  cout << "Enter the dividend ";
  cin >> dividend;
  cout << "Enter the divisor ";
  cin >> divisor;

  // Output the quotient and remainder
  cout << "The quotient is " << dividend/divisor;
  cout << " with a remainder of " << dividend % divisor << '\n';
  return 0;
}
```

Avoid including the calculations in the output statements if you need to store the quotient or remainder and use them again in the program. In situations like this, it is perfectly fine to use operators in the output statement.

STEP-BY-STEP ▷ 4.5

1. Modify the program on your screen to match Code List 4-5. Verify that you have changed each line that needs modification and removed the lines that are no longer necessary. Save the source file as **remain2.cpp**. Compile it and run it.

2. Test the program using the data you recorded on paper in Step-by-Step 4.4 to make sure you are still getting the same results.

3. Leave the source code file open for the next Step-by-Step exercise.

Dividing by Zero

In mathematics, division by zero is without a practical purpose. The same is true with computers. In fact, division by zero always generates some type of error.

S TEP-BY-STEP ▷ 4.6

1. Run the program on your screen again. Enter 0 for the divisor and see what error message is generated.

2. Close the program.

Most programs that have the potential of creating or allowing a division by zero include code that checks for this condition before the division occurs.

Incrementing and Decrementing

Adding or subtracting 1 from a variable is very common in programs. Adding 1 to a variable is called *incrementing,* and subtracting 1 from a variable is called *decrementing*. For example, you increment or decrement a variable when a program must execute a section of code a specified number of times or when you need to count the number of times a process has been repeated.

The ++ and -- Operators

C++ provides operators for incrementing and decrementing. In C++, you can increment an integer variable using the **++ *operator***, and decrement using the **-- *operator***, as shown in Table 4-3.

TABLE 4-3
Incrementing and decrementing

Statement	Equivalent to...
counter++;	counter = counter + 1;
counter--;	counter = counter – 1;

Earlier in this lesson you learned that spacing does not matter in math operations. The only time you must be careful with spacing is when using the minus sign to change the sign of a variable or number. For example, $x = y - -z$; is perfectly fine. The sign of the value in the variable z is changed and then it is subtracted from y. If you failed to include the space before the $-z$, you would have created a problem because two minus signs together (--) are interpreted as the decrement operator.

S TEP-BY-STEP ▷ 4.7

1. Retrieve the file **inc_dec.cpp**. The program shown in Code List 4-6 appears.

2. Compile and run the program.

3. Examine the output and leave the source code file open for the next Step-by-Step exercise.

```
// inc_dec.cpp

#include <iostream.h>

int main()
{
  int j;    // declare j as int

  j = 1;    // initialize j to 1
  cout << "j = " << j << '\n';
  j++;        // increment j
  cout << "j = " << j << '\n';
  j--;        // decrement j
  cout << "j = " << j << '\n';

  return 0;
}
```

Variations of Increment and Decrement

At first glance, the ++ and -- operators seem very simple. But there are two ways that each of these operators can be used. The operators can be placed either before or after the variable. The location of the operators affects the way they work.

Note

The ++ and -- operators can be used with any arithmetic data type, including all the integer and floating-point types.

Used in a statement by themselves, the ++ and -- operators can be placed before or after the variable. For example, both of the statements shown below increment whatever value is in j.

```
j++;
++j;
```

The difference in where you place the operator becomes important if you use the ++ or -- operator in a more complex expression, or if you use the operators in an output statement. First let us look at how the placement of the operators affects the following statement. Assume that j holds a value of 10.

```
k = j++;
```

In the case of this statement, k is assigned the value of the variable j before j is incremented. Therefore, the value of 10 is assigned to k rather than the new value of j, which is 11. If the placement of the ++ operator is changed to precede the variable j (for example k = ++j;), then k is assigned the value of j after j is incremented to 11.

STEP-BY-STEP ▷ 4.8

1. Add a statement to the file named **inc_dec.cpp** that declares `k` as a variable of type int.

2. Add the following lines to the program on your screen before the `return 0;` command line.

```
k = j++;
cout << "k = " << k << '\n';
cout << "j = " << j << '\n';
k = ++j;
cout << "k = " << k << '\n';
cout << "j = " << j << '\n';
```

3. Save the new source code file as **inc_dec2.cpp**.

4. Compile and run the program to see the new output. Remember, you may have to close the current project or workspace to compile and run **inc_dec2.cpp**.

5. Close the program.

Order of Operations

Y ou may recall the rules related to the order in which operations are performed from your math classes. These rules are called the *order of operations*. The C++ compiler uses a similar set of rules for its calculations. Calculations are processed in the following order:

1. Minus sign used to change sign (–)

2. Multiplication and division (* / %)

3. Addition and subtraction (+ –)

C++ lets you use parentheses to change the order of operations. For example, consider the two statements in Figure 4-2.

FIGURE 4-2
Parentheses can be used to change the order of operations.

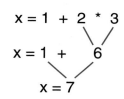

 Hot Tip

For a complete table of the order of operators, see Appendix D.

STEP-BY-STEP ▷ 4.9

1. Retrieve the file named **order.cpp**. The program in Code List 4-7 appears.

2. Look at the source code and try to predict the program's output.

3. Run the program and see whether your prediction is correct.

4. Close the program.

```
// order.cpp

#include <iostream.h>

int main()
{
 int answer;

 answer = 1 + 2 * 2 + 3;
 cout << answer << '\n';

 answer = (1 + 2) * (2 + 3);
 cout << answer << '\n';

 answer = 1 + 2 * (2 + 3);
 cout << answer << '\n';

 answer = (1 + 2) * 2 + 3;
 cout << answer << '\n';

 return 0;
}
```

Summary

- The assignment operator (=) changes the value of the variable to the left of the operator to the result of the expression to the right of the operator.

- You can initialize multiple variables to the same value in a single statement.

- The arithmetic operators are used to create expressions.

- The modulus operator (%) returns the remainder of integer division.

- Expressions can be placed in output statements.

- Dividing by zero generates an error in C++.

- Spaces can be placed around all operators but are not required in most cases.

- The ++ and -- operators increment and decrement arithmetic variables, respectively.

- The placement of the ++ and -- operators becomes important when the operators are used as part of a larger expression or in an output statement.

- C++ calculations follow an order of operations.

VOCABULARY REVIEW

Define the following terms:

++ operator

-- operator

arithmetic operators

assignment operator

decrementing

expression

incrementing

modulus operator

order of operations

quotient

remainder

LESSON 4 REVIEW QUESTIONS

TRUE/FALSE

Circle the T if the statement is true. Circle the F if it is false.

T   F   1.   Variables can be declared and initialized in the same statement.

T   F   2.   You can initialize multiple variables to the same value in the same statement.

T   F   3.   The * operator performs multiplication.

T   F   4.   The modulus operator is the @ sign.

T   F   5.   C++ allows you to divide by zero.

T   F   6.   Subtracting 1 from a variable is called incrementing.

T   F   7.   You can increment and decrement variables without the ++ and -- operators.

T   F   8.   The ++ and -- operators do not work on floating-point numbers.

T   F   9.   The ++ operator can appear before or after a variable.

T   F   10.   Addition and subtraction are performed before multiplication and division.

WRITTEN QUESTIONS

Write your answers to the following questions.

11. What is the assignment operator?

12. When using the assignment operator, on which side of the operator must you place the variable getting the new value?

13. What symbol is used to represent the division operation?

14. What symbol is used to represent the subtraction operation?

15. What does the modulus operator do?

16. When is it not a good idea to perform calculations in output statements?

17. Using the addition operator, write a statement that is equivalent to

```
x = x++;
```

18. If the value of i is 10 before the following statement is executed, what is the value of j after the statement?

```
j = i++;
```

19. If the value of i is 4 before the following statement is executed, what is the value of j after the statement?

```
j = --i;
```

20. What can be used to override the order of operations?

LESSON 4 PROJECTS

PROJECT 4A

1. Write a program that declares an integer named up_down and initializes it to 3.

2. Have the program print the value of up_down to the screen.

3. Have the program increment the variable and print the value to the screen.

4. Add statements to the program to decrement the variable and print the value to the screen again.

5. Save the source code as **updown.cpp**, compile it, and run it.

6. Close the program.

PROJECT 4B

1. Retrieve the file named **salestax.cpp**. The file is a complete program with the exception of one line of code.

2. Under the comment line that reads "Calculate sales tax due," enter a line of code that will calculate the amount of tax due. To calculate the tax due, you must divide the tax rate by 100 and then multiply that value by the cost of the item.

3. Save the modified source code and run the program.

4. Test the program several times before closing it.

PROJECT 4C

Write a program that evaluates the following expressions and prints the different values that result from the varied placement of the parentheses. Store the result in a float variable to allow for fractional values. Save the source code file as **paren.cpp**.

$2 + 6 / 3 + 1 * 6 - 7$

$(2 + 6) / (3 + 1) * 6 - 7$

$(2 + 6) / (3 + 1) * (6 - 7)$

PROJECT 4D

The volume of a box is calculated using the formula $V = abc$, where a, b, and c are the lengths of the box's sides. Write a program that calculates the volume of a box based on the input of the length of three sides by the user. Use the code from **salestax.cpp** as an example of using cin to get the input. Save the source code file as **volbox.cpp**. Compile, run, and test the program.

CRITICAL THINKING

Suppose you have a group of people who need to be transported on buses and vans. You can charter a bus only if you can fill it. Each bus holds 50 people. You must provide vans for the 49 or fewer people who will be left over after you charter the buses. Write a program that accepts a number of people and determines how many buses must be chartered and reports the number of people left over who must be placed on vans. *Hint*: Use the modulus operator to determine the number of people left over.

HOW DATA TYPES AFFECT CALCULATIONS

OBJECTIVES

When you complete this lesson, you will be able to:

- Properly mix data types in calculations.

- Avoid overflow in calculations.

- Avoid underflow in calculations.

- Explain floating-point rounding errors.

🕐 **Estimated Time: 1 hour**

VOCABULARY

"E" notation
overflow
promotion
truncate
typecast operator
typecasting
underflow

Mixing Data Types

C++ allows you to mix data types in calculations (for example, dividing a float value of 125.25 by an integer such as 5). Many programming languages do not allow the mixing of data types because it can lead to errors if you do not understand the proper way to deal with mixed data types and the consequences of mixing them.

You learned in Lesson 3 that each data type is able to hold a specific range of values. When you perform calculations, the capacity of your variables must be kept in mind. It is possible for the result of an expression to be too large or too small for a given data type.

C++ can automatically handle the mixing of data types (called *promotion*), or you can direct the compiler on how to handle the data (called *typecasting*).

Promotion

Consider the program in Code List 5-1. The variable `number_of_people` is an integer. The other variables involved in the calculation are floating-point numbers. Before you mix data types, you should understand the way the compiler is going to process the variables.

CODE LIST 5-1

```
// share.cpp

#include <iostream.h>

int main()
```

```
{
  int number_of_people;   // declare number_of_people as an integer
  float money;            // declare money as a float
  float share;            // declare share as a float

  cout << "How many people need a share of the money? ";
  cin >> number_of_people;
  cout << "How much money is available to share among the people? ";
  cin >> money;

  share = money / number_of_people;

  cout << "Give each person $" << share << '\n';

  return 0;
}
```

In cases of mixed data types, the compiler makes adjustments so as to produce the most accurate answer. In the program in Code List 5-1, for example, the integer value (`number_of_people`) is temporarily converted to a float so that the fractional part of the variable `money` can be used in the calculation. This is called ***promotion***. The variable called `number_of_people` is not actually changed. Internally, the computer treats the data as if it were stored in a float. But after the calculation, the variable is still an integer.

The reason that data types must match when a calculation is performed is because of the way that the microprocessor handles calculations. The values involved in the calculation must be of the same number of bytes and same format to ensure correct results. Converting all values in the calculation to the data type with the most precision before performing the calculation guarantees the most accurate results.

STEP-BY-STEP ▷ 5.1

1. Retrieve the file named **share.cpp**. The program from Code List 5-1 appears in your editor.

2. Compile and run the program and observe how the mixed data types function.

3. Close the program.

Promotion of the data type can occur only while an expression is being evaluated. Consider the program in Code List 5-2.

```
// losedata.cpp

#include <iostream.h>

int main()
{
  int answer, i;
  float x;

  i = 3;
  x = 0.5;
  answer = x * i;

  cout << answer << '\n';
  return 0;
}
```

The variable i is promoted to a float when the expression is calculated, which gives the result 1.5. But then the result is stored in the integer variable answer. You are unable to store a floating-point number in space reserved for an integer variable. The floating-point number is *truncated*, which means the digits after the decimal point are dropped. The number in answer is 1, which is not correct.

Concept Builder

Truncation is the equivalent of chopping off everything to the right of the decimal point. When a number is truncated, 1.00001 becomes 1 and 1.999999 also becomes 1.

STEP-BY-STEP ▷ 5.2

1. Retrieve the file **losedata.cpp**. The program in Code List 5-2 appears.

2. Compile the program. You may get a warning that points out the loss of data that will occur when the program is run.

3. Run the program and verify that the result is truncated.

4. Close the program.

Typecasting

Even though C++ handles the mixing of data types fairly well, unexpected results can occur. To give the programmer more control over the results when data types are mixed, C++ allows you to explicitly change one data type to another using operators called *typecast operators*. Using a typecast operator is usually referred to as *typecasting*.

Consider the program you ran in Step-by-Step 5.1 (share.cpp), shown again in Code List 5-3. The calculated value in the variable share is of type float. If you are interested only in round dollar amounts, you can force the compiler to interpret the variable money as an integer data type by typecasting.

```cpp
// share.cpp

#include <iostream.h>

int main()
{
  int number_of_people;   // declare number_of_people as an integer
  float money;            // declare money as a float
  float share;            // declare share as a float

  cout << "How many people need a share of the money? ";
  cin >> number_of_people;
  cout << "How much money is available to share among the people? ";
  cin >> money;

  share = money / number_of_people;

  cout << "Give each person $" << share << '\n';

  return 0;
}
```

To typecast a variable, simply supply the name of the data type you want to use to interpret the variable, followed by the variable placed in parentheses. The statement below, for example, typecasts the variable `diameter` to a float.

```cpp
C = PI * float(diameter);
```

In cases where the data type to which you want to typecast is more than one word (for example, long double), place both the data type and the variable in parentheses as shown in the following example.

```cpp
C = PI * (long double)(diameter);
```

STEP-BY-STEP ▷ 5.3

1. Retrieve the file **share.cpp** again.

2. Change the type of `share` to int.

3. Change the calculation statement to read as shown in Code List 5-4.

4. Compile and run the program again.

5. Save the source code file and close it.

```cpp
share = int (money) / number_of_people;
```

There are a number of ways to accomplish what was done in Step-by-Step 5.3. The purpose of the exercise is to show you how to use the typecast operator in case you ever need it.

Overflow

Overflow is the condition where a value becomes too large for its data type. The program in Code List 5-5 shows a simple example of overflow. The expression `j = i + 2000;` results in a value of 34000, which is too large for the short data type.

CODE LIST 5-5

```
// overflow.cpp

#include <iostream.h>

int main()
{
  short i,j;

  i = 32000;
  j = i + 2000; // The result (34000) overflows the short int type
  cout << j << '\n';
  return 0;
}
```

STEP-BY-STEP ▷ 5.4

1. Retrieve the file **overflow.cpp**. The program shown in Code List 5-5 appears.

2. Compile and run to see the result of the overflow.

3. Change the data type from short to long. Compile and run again. This time the result should not overflow.

4. Save and close the program.

Underflow

Underflow is similar to overflow. Underflow occurs with floating-point numbers when a number is too small for the data type. For example, the number 1.5×10^{-144} is too small to fit in a standard float variable. It is such a small number that the float data type considers it to be zero.

STEP-BY-STEP 5.5

1. Enter the program shown in Code List 5-6. Save the source code as **unflow.cpp**.

2. Compile and run the program to see that the small value underflows the variable, giving an incorrect output. You may get a compiler warning because of the potential for underflow.

3. Change the data type of x to double and run again. The value can now be successfully stored in the variable.

4. Change the data type of x back to float and run again. The value again underflows.

5. Save and close the program.

CODE LIST 5-6

```cpp
// unflow.cpp

#include <iostream.h>

int main()
{
  float x;

  x = 1.5e-144;

  cout << x << '\n';
  return 0;
}
```

Floating-Point Rounding Errors

Using floating-point numbers can produce incorrect results if you fail to take the precision of floating-point data types into account.

In Lesson 3, you assigned floating-point values to variables using statements such as the one below.

```cpp
Mass_of_Electron = 9.109e-31;   // 9.109 x 10-31 kilograms
```

The form of exponential notation used in the statement above is called **"E" notation**. "E" notation makes it possible to represent very large and very small floating-point numbers. For example, the number 3.5×10^{20} can be represented as 3.5e20 in your program.

You must keep the precision of your data type in mind when working with numbers in "E" notation. Look at the program in Code List 5-7.

```
// floaterr.cpp

#include <iostream.h>  // necessary for cout command

int main()
{
 float x,y;

 x = 3.9e10 + 500.0;
 y = x - 3.9e10;

 cout << y << '\n';
 return 0;
}
```

At first glance, the two calculation statements appear simple enough. The first statement adds 3.9×10^{10} and 500. The second one subtracts the 3.9×10^{10}, which should leave the 500. The result assigned to y, however, is not 500. Actual values vary depending on the compiler, but the result is incorrect whatever the case.

The reason is that the float type is not precise enough for the addition of the number 500 to be included in its digits of precision. If you converted 3.9×10^{10} to standard notation, the value would be represented as 39,000,000,000. Adding 500 to that number would result in 39,000,000,500. In exponential notation, that is $3.90000005 \times 10^{10}$.

In science you may have worked with the concept of *significant digits*. This concept states that the accuracy of the result of a calculation is only as good as the accuracy of your least accurate value. The accuracy of floating-point values in a computer must be treated in a similar way. Because the float type is precise to only about seven digits, the 5 gets lost after the string of zeros and is too insignificant to have ever been properly added to such a large number.

However, the double data type is accurate to about 15 digits, which is more than enough to properly include the addition of the 500 to the 39 billion.

STEP-BY-STEP ▷ 5.6

1. Enter, compile, and run the program in Code List 5-7. See that the result in the variable y is not 500.

2. Change the data type of x and y to double and run again. The increased precision of the double data type should result in the correct value in y.

3. Save the source code file as **floaterr.cpp** and close the source code file.

Summary

■ C++ allows data types to be mixed in calculations.

■ When C++ is allowed to handle mixed data types automatically, variables are promoted to other types.

■ You can explicitly change data types using typecasting.

■ When the digits after the decimal point are dropped from a value, it is said to have been truncated.

■ Overflow is a condition in which an integer becomes too large for its data type.

■ Underflow occurs when a floating-point number is so small that a data type interprets it as zero.

■ Floating-point rounding errors can occur if you are not aware of the data types used in calculations.

VOCABULARY REVIEW

Define the following terms:

"E" notation
overflow
promotion
truncate

typecast operator
typecasting
underflow

LESSON 5 REVIEW QUESTIONS

TRUE/FALSE

Circle the T if the statement is true. Circle the F if it is false.

T F 1. Many programming languages do not allow the mixing of data types in calculations.

T F 2. Promotion permanently changes the data type of a variable.

T F 3. The way C++ automatically converts data types is called typecasting.

T F 4. Assigning an integer value to a floating-point variable can result in truncation.

T F 5. Overflow can occur only with floating-point variables.

T F 6. Sometimes an overflow can be corrected by changing data types.

T F 7. Underflow occurs when a number is too small for a variable.

T F 8. Floating-point precision can affect calculations.

T F 9. "E" notation prevents variable overflow and underflow.

T F 10. The float and double data types have the same amount of precision.

WRITTEN QUESTIONS

Write your answers to the following questions.

11. When a variable of type int is multiplied by a variable of type float, which variable is promoted?

12. After a calculation in which a variable of type float is promoted to another type, what data type does the variable retain?

13. If a calculation results in the value 4.9, and that value is assigned to a variable of type short, what value will the variable of type short contain after the assignment is complete?

14. What is the term that means the numbers to the right of the decimal point are removed?

15. What operator is used to explicitly change one data type to another?

16. Write a statement that changes the contents of a variable named radius to type float, multiplies it by 2.5, and assigns the result to a variable named A.

17. Define overflow.

18. What floating-point data type is the most likely to have difficulty with underflow?

19. How would you write 6.9×10^8 in "E" notation?

20. How would you write -3.1×10^{-6} in "E" notation?

PROJECT 5A

1. Enter and compile the program that appears below. Save the source code as **datatest.cpp**.

```cpp
// datatest.cpp

#include <iostream.h>

int main()
{
  short x;

  cout << "Enter a value: ";
  cin >> x;

  cout << "The value you entered is: ";
  cout << x << '\n';
  return 0;
}
```

2. Run the program repeatedly. Enter increasing large values until you create an overflow. Try the following values: 290, 1000, 30000, 35000, 70000.

3. Refer to the documentation you gathered about your compiler in Step-by-Step 3.1 in Lesson 3. Test the limits of the short data type to see if the overflow occurs where expected.

4. Leave the program open for the next project.

PROJECT 5B

1. Change the data type of x in **datatest.cpp** to int.

2. Using the information you have about the range of a variable of type int, run the program several times to test the limits of the int data type. Test the range of the positive and negative ends.

3. Change the data type of x to unsigned int.

4. Test the range of the x by running the program several times. Test the largest positive value and verify that the data type will not hold negative values.

5. Leave the program open for the next project.

PROJECT 5C

1. Change the data type of x in **datatest.cpp** to float.

2. Run the program repeatedly. Use the following values for input and record the output on paper. *Note*: The format of the output will vary among compilers.

   3.14159

   2.9e38

   2.9e39

   5.1e-38

   5.1e-39

   0.0000000005

3. Close the program.

CRITICAL THINKING

Write a program similar to the **datatest.cpp** program you wrote in Projects 5A, 5B, and 5C. Name the source code file **floattst.cpp**. The program should declare a variable of each floating-point data type (x, y, and z). Have the program prompt the user for three values and output the values back to the screen. Run the program repeatedly. Each time you run the program, use the same value in all three variables and compare the three outputs.

Some values to try are:

3.4e38

3.4e100

1.7e308

1.7e309

4.6e1000

1.1e4932

1.1e4933

Data and Operations

REVIEW QUESTIONS

MATCHING

Write the letter of the description from Column 2 that best matches the term or phrase in Column 1.

Column 1

____ 1. assignment operator

____ 2. Boolean variable

____ 3. constant

____ 4. decrementing

____ 5. expression

____ 6. identifier

____ 7. incrementing

____ 8. initializi

____ 9. overflow

____10. variable

Column 2

A. Subtracting 1

B. A math statement made up of terms and operators

C. The process of assigning a value to a variable

D. Stores data that can change while the program runs

E. A variable that can have only two possible values: true or false

F. The condition in which a value becomes too large for its data type

G. Changes the value of the variable to the left of the operator

H. Names given to variables and constants

I. Adding 1

J. Stores data that remains the same throughout a program's execution

WRITTEN QUESTIONS

Write your answers to the following questions.

1. List three data types that can store floating-point values.

2. How many characters can be stored in a variable of type char?

3. What happens if you attempt to use a variable that has not been declared?

4. What is the operator symbol that performs multiplication?

5. What is the purpose of the modulus operator?

6. What is the operator that increments a variable?

7. In the order of operations, which is performed first, multiplication or addition?

8. What is the term that describes the feature where C++ automatically changes a data type of a value in order to perform a calculation?

9. Define overflow.

10. Which floating-point data type has the greatest chance of having a problem with precision?

APPLICATIONS

APPLICATION 2-1

1. Write a statement that declares a variable named `salary` of type float.

2. Write a statement to assign the value 42,000.00 to the variable named `salary`.

3. Write a statement that stores the remainder of dividing the variable `i` by `j` in a variable named `k`.

4. Write a statement that declares a constant named `SALES_TAX` of type double with the value 0.075.

5. Write a statement that calculates the sales tax for an item. Assign the cost of the item (use 19.99) to a variable named `item_cost`. Use the `SALES_TAX` constant you declared above as the tax rate. Store the result in a variable named `tax_due`. You do not have to declare types.

6. Write a statement that increments a variable `m` using the increment operator.

7. Write a statement that decrements a variable `n` using the decrement operator.

8. What will the value of j be after the following statement is executed?

```
= 3 + 4 / 2 + 5 * 2 - 3;
```

9. What will the value of j be after the following statement is executed?

```
= (3 + 4) / (2 + 5) * 2 - 3;
```

10. Suppose that you have a program in which x is experiencing overflow. Rewrite the following declaration statement to minimize the chance of an overflow when a value is assigned to x.

```
short x;
```

APPLICATION 2-2

In this application, you will create a program that calculates the area of an ellipse. The area of an ellipse is found by multiplying the length of the ellipse by the width of the ellipse and then multiplying by PI, as shown in the following statement.

Area of Ellipse = Length × Width × 3.14159

Write a program to calculate the area of an ellipse following these steps:

1. Begin a new source code file. Name the file **ellipse.cpp**.

2. Declare three variables named width, length, and area. Use an appropriate floating-point data type.

3. Enter the following lines to prompt the user for input.

```
cout << "Enter the width of the ellipse: ";
cin >> width;

cout << "Enter the length of the ellipse: ";
cin >> length;
```

4. Write a statement to calculate the area of the ellipse based on the formula above.

5. Enter the following statement to output the result of your calculation.

```
cout << "\nArea of ellipse: " << area << '\n';
```

6. Complete the program and save the source code.

7. Compile and run the program.

8. Enter 3.5 as the width and 7.0 as the length. The result should be approximately 76.969.

9. Try some other values before closing the program.

Boolean variables are named in honor of George Boole, an English mathematician who lived in the 1800s. Boole created a system called Boolean algebra, which is a study of operations using variables with the values true and false. In this activity, you will use the Internet to learn more about George Boole and Boolean algebra.

1. Open your Web browser.

2. Go to the Web address below.

    http://www.programcpp.com/basics

3. On the home page, click the link called **Internet Activities from the book**.

4. On the Internet Activities page, click the **Unit 2** link.

5. Read the information presented there about Boole and Boolean algebra. Follow the links provided there.

6. When you have read the information and visited the sites, answer the written questions on the Unit 2 Internet Activity Web page.

STRINGS AND SCREEN INPUT AND OUTPUT

UNIT 3

lesson 6 — 1 hr.
Strings and the String Class

lesson 7 — 2 hrs.
Input and Output

🕐 **Estimated Time for Unit: 3 hours**

STRINGS AND THE STRING CLASS

OBJECTIVES

When you complete this lesson, you will be able to:

- Define strings and literals.

- Explain classes and objects.

- Use the string class to store strings in your programs.

- Perform basic string operations.

⏱ **Estimated Time: 1 hour**

VOCABULARY

concatenation
containment
dot operator
instance
literals
message
method
object-oriented
  programming
string class
string object

Introduction to Strings and Literals

In Lesson 3, you learned about the character data type and that a group of characters put together to create text is called a *string*. Strings are one of the most useful kinds of data in a program. Strings help programs communicate with the user and allow computers to process data other than numbers. For example, when you prompt the user with a statement such as "Enter the cow's weight:" you are using a string. Or when you ask the user to enter the cow's name, the name the user enters is a string.

C++ does not have a data type specifically for strings. Many C++ programmers work with strings by manually manipulating groups of characters, called *character arrays*. Working with character arrays requires a thorough understanding of how the C++ language deals with strings. Character arrays provide programmers with considerable flexibility. However, as you will learn in this lesson, C++ also allows you to hide the details of the character array using a special set of code and data called a *string class*. In this lesson, you will learn a little about strings, and then use a string class for your own programs.

Recall that when you have worked with numeric values, some of the values are keyed directly into the source code and some values are calculated or are entered by the user. Values that are keyed directly into the source code are often called *hard-coded* values. Values or strings that are hard coded into the source code are called **literals**. A hard-coded numeric value is called a *numeric literal*. A string of text that is hard coded is called a *string literal*.

A single character can also be hard coded. A *character literal* appears in single quotation marks. A string literal appears in double quotation marks. Code List 6-1 shows examples of literals.

```
x = 6.3;          // 6.3 is a numeric literal
cout << "Hello"; // "Hello" is a string literal
MyChar = 'A';    // 'A' is a character literal
```

Obviously, literals do not change when the program runs. However, when a literal is used to initialize a variable, the value in the variable can change.

Just as you have used numeric literals when working with numeric data types and variables, you will use string literals and character literals when working with strings and characters.

Introduction to Classes and Objects

You may have heard that C++ is an *object-oriented programming language*. **Object-oriented programming (OOP)** is a way of programming that treats parts of a computer program as objects that are similar to real-world objects. The best way to understand object-oriented programming is to consider an example.

In the lessons you have completed in this book, you have used floating-point data types such as double to store data. You have also used the addition operator to add values together. The double data type and the addition operator are part of the C++ language. You don't have to know how they work. All you have to know is how to use them. When a line of code like the one below is executed, the addition takes place and the result is stored. You do not have to know exactly how the addition is achieved or exactly how the data is stored; those details have been taken care of for you.

```
x = x + 4.2;
```

As you learned in Lesson 1, the purpose of a high-level language is to hide the details and make programming a more rapid and dependable process. In that lesson, you saw how a simple statement like the one preceding is translated into many machine-language instructions.

Object-oriented programming takes the concept of a high-level language to a new level by allowing programmers to create their own operations and even data types, while hiding the details in a way similar to the built-in features of the language. For example, you learned earlier in this lesson that C++ has no built-in string data type. The object-oriented features of C++, however, allow you (or better yet, someone else) to create a string data type for you to use. And just as for the double data type, you will not have to know how the string data type works. You will just have to know how to use it.

When working with OOP, it is important to understand some basic object-oriented programming terms. To learn these terms, let us stick with the example of the object-oriented string data type. An object-oriented string data type is referred to as a ***string class***. A string class is actually a definition used to create a ***string object***.

The distinction between a *class* and an *object* is important. Think of a class as a generic definition from which an object is created. In the real world, dog would be an example of a class, while Rover would be an object based on the dog class. An object is said to be an ***instance*** of a class. Therefore, Rover is an instance of the dog class, or, in programming terms, a string object is an instance of a string class. In order to store an actual string, a programmer creates a string object using a string class.

This will make more sense once you have used a class yourself. In the Step-by-Step exercises to follow, you will use a string class that is provided with this textbook to store strings.

Using the String Class

Using the string class is a little more complicated than using the built-in data types. However, once you have mastered a few simple tasks, you will see how easy using the string class really is.

Preparing to Use the String Class

To use the string class, you must include a header file in your source code, in this case oostring.h. The string class used in this book consists of two files: oostring.h and oostring.cpp. Your compiler must also be set up properly to compile a program that uses the string class. For general tips on compilers and how to get more information on your specific compiler, see Appendix G.

To give the string class a try with your compiler, let us compile and run a program that uses the string class.

Hot Tip

If your compiler does not have the bool data type, you will receive an error message when you compile oostring.cpp. See the special instructions in Appendix E.

STEP-BY-STEP 6.1

1. Open **oostring.cpp** and **stringex.cpp** into a project in your compiler. The file **oostring.h** must also be available to your compiler.

2. Compile and run the program. The program creates a string object, assigns the string

"Hello World!" to the string object, and prints the string to the screen.

3. Leave the project open for the next Step-by-Step exercise.

Declaring a String Object

Now that you have successfully compiled and run a program that uses the string class, we can look at the features offered by the string class.

When you declare a string object, you can create an empty string object or you can initialize the object with a string. As the code in Code List 6-2 shows, the process of declaring a string object is similar to declaring other data.

CODE LIST 6-2

```
oostring MyString1;            // declare an empty string object
oostring MyString2("ABCDEF");  // initializing while declaring
```

Assigning Strings to String Objects

You can assign strings to string objects in one of three ways:

1. You can assign the contents of one string object to another string object.

2. You can assign a string literal to a string object.

3. You can assign a character literal to a string object.

Code List 6-3 shows an example of each of the three ways to assign a string to a string object.

CODE LIST 6-3

```
MyString1 = MyString2;
MyString1 = "string literal";
MyString1 = 'A';
```

Printing the Contents of a String Object to the Screen

You can use cout to display the contents of a string object. The statement below shows a typical line of code that outputs the contents of a string class.

```
cout << MyString1 << '\n';
```

STEP-BY-STEP 6.2

1. Modify the source code of **stringex.cpp** to match the program in Code List 6-4.

2. Save the source code. Compile and run the program. The program stores two strings using separate objects.

3. Leave the program open for the next Step-by-Step exercise.

```
// stringex.cpp

#include <iostream.h>
#include "oostring.h"

int main()
{
  oostring MyString1;
  oostring MyString2("ABCDEFGHIJKLMNOPQRSTUVWXYZ");

  MyString1 = "Hello World!";

  cout << MyString1 << '\n';
  cout << MyString2 << '\n';

  return 0;
}
```

Step-by-Step 6.2 is an example of how more than one object can be created from the same class. A program can include as many string objects as necessary. The name of the object is used to distinguish among them.

String Operations

Programs that use strings often need to perform a variety of operations on the strings it has stored. For example, to properly center a string, you may need to know the number of characters in the string. You may also need to add strings together.

One of the reasons that objects are especially useful is that they do more than hold data. Objects also perform operations on the data they hold. A string object is no exception. In fact, as you will see, a string object is a great example of an object that holds data and performs operations on that data.

String objects should be used to store numbers such as ZIP codes, Social Security numbers, and phone numbers. These kinds of numbers often include parentheses or hyphens, which are not allowed in numeric data types. In a string, however, characters other than numerals are allowed.

Concept Builder

The #include statements you have been using have placed angle brackets (<>) around the filename being included. These statements are pre-compiled libraries that are stored in a special directory when the compiler is installed. When you include oostring.h, you place it in double quotation marks to tell the compiler that it is not pre-compiled and to look for it in the current directory.

Messages

One of the important concepts behind the use of objects is the idea of **containment** (or *encapsulation*). These terms refer to the way an object hides the details of how data is stored and how operations work. The data, and the code required to work with that data, is contained or encapsulated within the object itself. To make the object do what we want it to do, we send the object a *message*.

For example, when you want to know the length of the string stored in a string object, you send the object a message that asks the object to report the string's length. How it calculates the length of the string does not matter. We just want an accurate answer. It is the object's job to provide that answer.

Did You Know?

Objects got their name because they have characteristics similar to real-world objects.

Obtaining the Length of a String

The message used to obtain the length of a string is simply *length*. The following statement shows an example of the code required to send the length message to a string object.

```
l = MyString2.length();
```

Let us look at the statement piece by piece. First, 1 is an integer variable that will store the length that the object reports. The assignment operator (=) assigns the value returned by the string object to the variable 1. MyString2 is the name of the string object to which we want to send the message. The period that follows the name of the object is called the **dot operator** (or *class-member operator*). The dot operator separates the name of the object from the message, in this case length.

The code inside the object that performs the length operation is called a **method**. Therefore, when you are sending the length message you could say that you are using the length method of the string class.

STEP-BY-STEP ▷ 6.3

1. Modify the source code of **stringex.cpp** to match the program in Code List 6-5. See whether you can predict the output of the program.

2. Save the source code. Compile and run the program to see if your prediction was correct.

3. Leave the program open for the next Step-by-Step exercise.

```
// stringex.cpp

#include <iostream.h>
#include "oostring.h"

int main()
{
  int len1, len2;
  oostring MyString1;
  oostring MyString2("ABCDEFGHIJKLMNOPQRSTUVWXYZ");

  MyString1 = "Hello World!";

  len1 = MyString1.length();
  len2 = MyString2.length();

  cout << MyString1 << '\n';
  cout << "Length = " << len1 << '\n';
  cout << MyString2 << '\n';
  cout << "Length = " << len2 << '\n';

  return 0;
}
```

String Concatenation

Concatenation is a big word that describes the operation of adding one string onto the end of another string. Suppose, for example, that you have one string object holding a first name and another string object holding a last name. To get both strings together in one string object, you need to concatenate the last name onto the first name. Actually, you would first concatenate a space onto the end of the first name to insert a space between the first and last names.

The string class includes the ability to perform concatenation. To make the concatenation process the most flexible, the string class makes use of an operator called a *compound operator*. The operator is +=. The += operator is specifically intended to provide a shorthand method for adding a value to an existing variable or object. For example, x +=1 is equivalent to x = x + 1. Table 6-1 gives some more examples.

To concatenate strings using the compound operator, use statements like the examples in Table 6-2.

TABLE 6-1
Concatenation examples

Shorthand Method	Long Method
j += 7;	j = j + 7;
k += n;	k = k + n;

TABLE 6-2
Concatenation statements

Statement	Description
`MyString1 += MyString2;`	Add MyString2 to the end of MyString1.
`MyString1 += "string literal";`	Add a string literal to the end of MyString1.
`MyString1 += Ch;`	Add a character to the end of MyString1.
`MyString1 += 'A';`	Add a character literal to the end of MyString1.

Consider the statements in Code List 6-6. The statements build a new string in MyString1 by performing three concatenations.

CODE LIST 6-6

```
MyString1 = "Tracy";
MyString2 = "Stewart";

MyString1 += ' ';          // add a space after the first name
MyString1 += MyString2;    // add the last name to MyString1
MyString1 += " was here."; // add a string literal to MyString1

cout << MyString1 << '\n';
```

STEP-BY-STEP ▷ 6.4

1. Add the code in Code List 6-6 to the end of the program on your screen (before the return 0;). Can you predict the output of the concatenated string?

2. Compile and run the program to see the result of the concatenation.

3. Close the program.

Summary

- Strings allow computers to process text as well as numbers.

- Hard-coded numeric values are called numeric literals. Hard-coded text is called a string literal.

- Object-oriented programming is a way of programming that treats parts of a computer program as objects that are similar to real-world objects.

- A class is a definition used to create an object. An object is said to be an instance of a class.

- Compiling a program that uses classes requires special setup.

- When declaring a string object, you can declare an empty object or initialize the object with a string.

- You can assign one string to another, a string literal to a string object, or a character literal to a string object.

- You can use cout to display the contents of a string object.

- Objects hold data and the operations you can perform on that data.

- To make an object perform an operation on itself, you send the object a message.

- The length method is used to determine the length of a string stored in a string object.

- Concatenation is the operation of adding one string onto the end of another string.

VOCABULARY REVIEW

Define the following terms:

concatenation	message
containment	method
dot operator	object-oriented programming
instance	string class
literals	string object

LESSON 6 REVIEW QUESTIONS

TRUE/FALSE

Circle the T if the statement is true. Circle the F if it is false.

T F 1. C++ has a built-in data type specifically for strings.

T F 2. A hard-coded string of text is called a string literal.

T F 3. A class is said to be an instance of an object.

T F 4. A string class must be initialized when it is declared.

T F 5. You can assign a character literal to a string object.

T F 6. A string object adjusts its length as necessary as the program runs.

T F 7. Each program can declare only one string object at a time.

T F 8. To make an object do what we want it to do, we send it a message.

T F 9. The dot operator separates the name of the object from the assignment operator.

T F 10. Concatenation refers to the process of disposing of a string object when you are done with it.

WRITTEN QUESTIONS

Write your answers to the following questions.

11. What kind of literal appears in single quotes?

12. Explain the distinction between a class and an object.

13. What are the names of the two files that make up the string class?

14. Write a statement that declares a string object named FirstName and initializes the string object with your first name.

15. Write a statement that assigns the contents of a string object named NewName to a string object named MyName.

16. Write a statement that displays the contents of the string object named MyName to the screen.

17. Explain the concept of encapsulation.

18. What is the method used to determine the length of a string in a string object?

19. Write a statement that assigns the length of the string named MyName to an integer variable named len.

20. What is the compound operator used to concatenate strings?

PROJECT 6A

1. Write a program that declares two string objects named FavoriteColor and FavoritePlace. Initialize FavoriteColor with the name of your favorite color at the time the object is declared. Leave FavoritePlace empty.

2. Use the assignment operator to assign the name of your favorite place to visit to the FavoritePlace object.

3. Write statements to produce output similar to the following lines. The statements should use the contents of your string objects to fill in the blanks.

    My favorite color is _____.
    My favorite place to visit is _____.

4. Save the source code as **favorite.cpp**, compile, and run the program.

5. Close the program.

PROJECT 6B

1. Write a program that declares a string object named MyString. Leave the object empty.

2. Use the assignment operator to assign the character 'A' to the string object.

3. Print the contents of the string to the screen.

4. Concatenate the character 'B' to the end of the string.

5. Print the contents of the string to the screen.

6. Print the length of the string to the screen using a statement like the one below.
   ```
   cout << MyString.length() << '\n';
   ```

7. Concatenate the string "CDEFG" to the end of the string.

8. Print the contents of the string to the screen.

9. Print the length of the string to the screen again.

10. Save the source code as **abc.cpp**, compile, and run the program.

11. Close the program.

CRITICAL THINKING

1. Write a program that declares a string object named *spacer* and initializes the object to hold nine blank spaces.

2. Declare a string object named *ruler*.

3. Use concatenation to build a string that matches the string shown below. The first character in the string should be a zero (0) and the last character should be a three (3). There should be nine spaces between each numeral. *Hint*: You can use multiple concatenation statements.

   0   1   2   3

4. Print the concatenated string to the screen.

5. Report the length of the concatenated string to the screen.

6. Name the source code file **spacer.cpp**.

INPUT AND OUTPUT

OBJECTIVES

When you complete this lesson, you will be able to:

- Use cin and cout.
- Use special characters.
- Use the cout format options.
- Use the I/O manipulators.
- Accept characters as input.
- Accept strings as input.

⏱ **Estimated Time: 2 hours**

VOCABULARY

console I/O
end-of-line character
extraction operator
field width
I/O manipulators
input stream
insertion operator
new line character
special character
standard input device
standard output device
stream

Using cin and cout

We have treated cin and cout (pronounced "see-in" and "see-out") as commands up to this point. You may be surprised, however, to learn that the << and >> symbols actually represent the action. Consider the following simple statements.

```
cout << j;
cin >> i;
```

The << and >> symbols are operators, as + and * are operators. The << symbol is the output operator, and >> is the input operator. As you know, the variable to the right of the << or >> operator is what is being input or output. So what are cout and cin? They are actually objects. The cout object is the destination of the output, and the cin object is the source of the input.

 Important

The `#include <iostream.h>` directive is required to use streams.

The >> operator is also referred to as the ***extraction operator*** because it extracts data from the stream. The << operator is also referred to as the ***insertion operator*** because it inserts data into the stream.

Streams

The cin and cout objects are known as streams. When you think of a stream, you probably think of water flowing from one place to another. In C++, a ***stream*** is data flowing from one place to another. You should think of C++ streams as channels that exist to provide an easy way to get data to and from devices. The stream that brings data from your keyboard is cin, and the stream that takes data to your screen is cout.

Some beginning programmers find it difficult to remember when to use << and when to use >>. There is a method you can use to help you remember: the symbols in the input and output operators point in the direction that the data is flowing. For example, in the statement `cout << j;`, the data is flowing from the variable `j` to the destination of the output (`cout`). When you use the input operator (as in `cin >> i;`), the data flows from the source of the input (`cin`) to the variable `i`.

For example, your monitor (screen) is a device. You do not have to understand exactly how output gets to the screen. You just have to know that the cout object is the stream that leads to your screen. When you use the output operator to place something in the cout stream, your screen is the destination.

The cin and cout objects may represent devices other than the keyboard and screen. The cin stream reads from what is called the ***standard input device***, and the cout stream leads to the ***standard output device***. By default, the standard input device is the keyboard and the standard output device is the screen. But they can be changed to other devices. There are other streams that you will learn about in later lessons.

Using Console I/O

The term *console I/O* refers to using the screen and keyboard for input and output (I/O is an abbreviation of input/output). In other words, the standard use of cin and cout is console I/O. Let us look at some examples of console I/O to make sure you understand the role of each part of the statements.

Figure 7-1 illustrates the general form of the << operator. The << operator indicates to the compiler that the statement is producing output. The destination of the output is the standard output device (the screen). The output can be any valid C++ expression.

Note

Remember, << is an operator. Therefore you can use it many times in the same output expression, just as you can use a mathematical operator multiple times in the same expression. For example, the statement `n = 2 + 4 + 5` uses the addition operator twice. In the same way, the output operator can appear more than once in a statement.

FIGURE 7-1
The << operator is used for output.

Output stream

Output expression

cout << expression;

Extraction operator

The examples in Code List 7-1 show how the output can be a string literal, a variable, or a mathematical expression. The figure also shows that more than one item can be output in a single statement by using multiple output operators.

```
cout << "This string literal will appear on the screen. \n";
cout << distance;
cout << length_of_room * width_of_room;
cout << "The room is " << area << " square feet.\n";
```

Figure 7-2 illustrates the general form of the >> operator. The >> operator tells the compiler that the statement is requesting input. The source of the input is the standard input device (the keyboard). The destination of the input must be a variable or variables.

FIGURE 7-2
The >> operator is used for input.

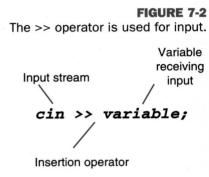

Input stream

Variable receiving input

cin >> variable;

Insertion operator

STEP-BY-STEP ▷ 7.1

1. Load, compile, and run **basicio.cpp** to review the basic use of input and output operators.

2. Close the program.

New Line and Other Special Characters

You have been including '\n' in output statements without a good explanation of what '\n' does. It is an important part of formatting output because it causes the cursor to return to the next line of the screen. The \n character is one of the special characters available in C++.

What Is \n?

The \n character is called the ***new line character*** or the ***end-of-line character***. Use it in any output statement that completes a line. The new line character has the same effect in an output statement as pressing the Return or Enter key in a word processor.

The \n character must appear in double quotation marks if it is used in conjunction with other characters or may be used with single quotation marks if it appears alone. See the examples in Code List 7-2.

```
cout << i << '\n';  // single quotes because it is a single character
cout << "String\n"; // double quotes because it is part of a string
```

Special Characters

The end-of-line character is called a *special character*. Although \n appears as two characters in the source code, the compiler interprets it as one character. The backslash (\) tells the compiler that a special character is being formed. The reason for this system is because there is no single keyboard character available to represent the end-of-line character.

Table 7-1 shows other special characters available for use in output statements. The first one generates a tab character. The others are used to print characters to the screen that would otherwise be unprintable because they have other meanings to the compiler. For example, because the backslash is used by the compiler to signify a special character, you must use a special character to print a backslash. There are also special characters for printing single and double quotation marks.

Hot Tip

The \n character can be enclosed in double quotation marks, even when it appears alone. The compiler will treat the character as a string because it is in double quotes. The statement will, however, produce the same result.

TABLE 7-1
Special characters used in output statements

Character Sequence	Result
\t	Generates a tab character to move the cursor to the next tab stop.
\\	Prints a backslash (\ ).
\'	Prints a single quotation mark (').
\"	Prints a double quotation mark (").

Using endl

There is an alternative to \n that you may find easier to enter and more readable. You can enter endl in the place of '\n'. For example, the two statements in Code List 7-3 are functionally identical.

CODE LIST 7-3

```
cout << i << '\n';
cout << i << endl;
```

You can use endl in place of the character '\n', but do not use endl as part of a larger string. Think of endl as a constant that holds the value '\n'. If used in a statement such as cout << "String endl";, the endl will be considered as part of the string, and no end-of-line character will be included. To use endl with string literals, use a statement similar to the following one.

```
cout << "How now brown cow." << endl;
```

1. Enter the program shown in Code List 7-4. Save the source code as **specchar.cpp**.

2. Compile and run the program. The output window should appear similar to Figure 7-3.

3. Compare the output on your screen to the statements in the source code to see that you understand the way the output was achieved.

4. Add the numbers 5 and 6 to the line of tab-separated numerals. Be sure to include the tab character in between the numbers.

5. Run the program again to verify that your modifications worked.

6. Add a statement before the first cout statement that prints your name to the screen in double quotation marks. For example, "Dale Lee".

7. Run the program again.

8. When you have the program producing the correct output, close the program.

FIGURE 7-3

The special characters allow you to print characters to the screen that you otherwise would not be able to display.

```cpp
// specchar.cpp
// Example of new line and special characters

#include <iostream.h>

int main()
{
  int i;

  i = 25;
  cout << i << '\n';  // single quotes because it is a single character
  cout << "String\n"; // double quotes because it is part of a string

  cout << "The numbers on the following line are separated by tabs.\n";
  cout << "1 \t 2 \t 3 \t 4 \n";

  // The following lines use endl
  cout << "In C++, you can output backslashes (\\)" << endl;
  cout << "You can also print single quotes (\') and" << endl;
  cout << "double quotes (\")." << endl;

  return 0;
}
```

Using setf and unsetf

The cout object has format options that can be changed. To change these options, you send a message to the object using setf and unsetf. Table 7-2 lists the options that can be used.

Hot Tip

The exact result of the format options may vary slightly among compilers.

TABLE 7-2
cout format options

Option	Description
left	Left-justifies the output
right	Right-justifies the output
showpoint	Displays decimal point and trailing zeros for all floating-point numbers, even if the decimal places are not needed
uppercase	Displays the "e" in E-notation as "E" rather than "e"
showpos	Displays a leading plus sign before positive values
scientific	Displays floating-point numbers in scientific ("E") notation
fixed	Displays floating-point numbers in normal notation

Now, examine how the format option *right* (indicating that the output is to be right-justified) is used in the expanded format statement below.

```
cout.setf(ios::right);
```

You will learn more about how to use statements like the preceding one later. What is important now is that you understand that the word *right* is the format option and the setf method is what changes the option in the cout object.

You can remove the options by replacing setf with unsetf, as in the following example.

```
cout.unsetf(ios::scientific);
```

 Did You Know?

If neither the scientific nor fixed option is set, most compilers decide the method to display floating-point numbers based on whether the number can be displayed more efficiently in scientific or fixed notation.

STEP-BY-STEP ▷ 7.3

1. Enter the program in Code List 7-5 and save the source code file as **coutsetf.cpp**.

2. Run the program to see how the format options change the output. Your compiler's results may vary slightly from the predictions made in the program's comments.

3. Close the program.

CODE LIST 7-5

```cpp
// coutsetf.cpp

#include <iostream.h>

int main()
{
  float x = 24.0;

  cout << x << endl;              // displays 24

  cout.setf(ios::showpoint);
  cout << x << endl;              // displays 24.0000

  cout.setf(ios::showpos);
  cout << x << endl;              // displays +24.0000

  cout.setf(ios::scientific);
  cout << x << endl;              // displays +2.400000e+001

  cout.setf(ios::uppercase);
  cout << x << endl;              // displays +2.400000E+001

  cout.unsetf(ios::showpoint);
  cout << x << endl;              // displays +2.400000E+001
```

```
   cout.unsetf(ios::showpos);
   cout << x << endl;              // displays 2.400000E+001

   cout.unsetf(ios::uppercase);
   cout << x << endl;              // displays 2.400000e+001

   cout.unsetf(ios::scientific);
   cout << x << endl;              // displays 24

   return 0;
}
```

Using the I/O Manipulators

Another set of format options is available in C++: the *I/O manipulators*. The most common of these are setprecision and setw. They may be placed directly in the output statement.

Using setprecision

When used in conjunction with the fixed format option, the setprecision I/O manipulator sets the number of digits that are to appear to the right of the decimal point. This is very convenient when printing amounts when a specific number of digits is important—for example, when printing dollars and cents.

Look at the example in Code List 7-6. First the fixed format option is set. Then in the output statement, the desired precision is set. The setprecision manipulator sets the number of digits displayed to the number provided in the parentheses. The setprecision manipulator affects all floating-point numbers that follow it in the statement. It also affects any floating-point numbers output to the cout stream until setprecision is called again to set another precision.

Hot Tip

In order to use I/O manipulators, you must use the directive `#include <iomanip.h>` to include the necessary code to make the manipulators available.

If you do not set the fixed option before using setprecision, the results will vary, depending on your compiler. Some compilers will set the number of digits to the right of the decimal point anyway. Others will set the overall number of digits on both sides of the decimal point. To be safe, you should set the fixed option.

CODE LIST 7-6

```
cout.setf(ios::fixed);
cout << setprecision(2) << price << '\n';
```

1. Retrieve the source code file named **iomanip.cpp**. The program shown in Code List 7-7 appears. Notice that the program uses two new line characters in a row to cause the output to skip a line.

2. Compile and run the program to see the difference that the formatting makes.

3. Change the line that includes the setprecision I/O manipulator to match Code List 7-8. The new line includes text to print a dollar sign as part of the output. Notice that the dollar sign appears in single quotation marks because it is a single character.

4. Run the program again to see the dollar sign display.

5. Leave the program open for the next Step-by-Step exercise.

CODE LIST 7-7

```
// iomanip.cpp

#include <iostream.h>
#include <iomanip.h>

int main()
{
  double cost = 34.99;
  double total;

  total = cost + (cost * 0.07875);  // add tax to cost to get total

  // Display total without formatting
  cout << "Total with no formatting:\n";
  cout << total << "\n\n"; // use two new line characters to skip line

  // Display total with fixed precision
  cout << "Total with formatting:\n";
  cout.setf(ios::fixed);
  cout << setprecision(2) << total << "\n\n";

  return 0;
}
```

CODE LIST 7-8

```
cout << setprecision(2) << '$' << total << "\n\n";
```

Using setw

The setw manipulator can be used to change the number of spaces the compiler uses when it displays a number. The amount of space used to display a number is called the *field width*. You can use setw to set a minimum field width or use it to format numbers.

For example, if i = 254, j = 44, and k = 6, the statement `cout << i << j << k << '\n';` produces the output 254446 because only the space necessary to output the numbers is used. The statement below, however, adds spaces to the left of each number to give formatted output.

```
cout << setw(10) << i << setw(10) << j << setw(10) << k << endl;
```

The output of the statement above appears as shown below.

```
254        44          6
```

The best way to see the difference is to try it yourself in the next Step-by-Step exercise.

STEP-BY-STEP ▷ 7.5

1. Add the declarations in Code List 7-9 to the top of the program on your screen.

2. Add the code in Code List 7-10 before the `return` statement at the end of the program.

3. Compile and run to see how the setw manipulators affect the output of the integers.

4. Save and close the program.

CODE LIST 7-9

```
int i = 1499;
int j = 618;
int k = 2;
```

CODE LIST 7-10

```
// Output with no field widths
cout << "Output of i, j, and k with no field widths specified:\n";
cout << i << j << k << "\n\n";

// Output with field widths set
cout << "Output of i, j, and k with field widths specified:\n";
cout << setw(10) << i << setw(10) << j << setw(10) << k << "\n\n";
```

Inputting Characters

The >> operator can be used to input characters. If the user enters more than one character, only the first character will be stored in the variable.

STEP-BY-STEP 7.6

1. Retrieve the source code file named **inchar.cpp**. The program shown in Code List 7-11 appears.

2. Run the program to see how inputting a character works. Run the program several times. Try entering a variety of characters and more than one character at a time.

3. Close the program.

 Did You Know?

When you enter a number such as 4 into a character variable, the character '4' is stored rather than the integer 4. Therefore, you perform mathematical operations on numbers when they are stored as characters.

CODE LIST 7-11

```cpp
// inchar.cpp

#include <iostream.h>

int main()
{
  char c;

  cout << "Enter a single character: ";
  cin >> c;
  cout << "You entered " << c << '\n';
  return 0;
}
```

Inputting Strings

In Lesson 6, you assigned strings to string objects at the time of declaration and later, using the assignment operator. You may have been thinking, "How do I enter a string provided by the user into a string object?" As you might have guessed, the string object has a method for doing just that. It is called getline.

Consider the statement below. The getline method is used somewhat differently from the other object methods you have used. When using getline, the parentheses are used to specify the input stream object and the string object you want to input the string into.

```
getline(cin, MyString);
```

When you use getline, you can use it just like the preceding statement. Just change MyString to the name of your string object.

STEP-BY-STEP ▷ 7.7

1. Retrieve the source code file named **instring.cpp**. The program shown in Code List 7-12 appears.

2. Compile and run the program. As an object is supposed to do, the string object hides the

details of the operation, making getline easy to use.

3. Close the program.

CODE LIST 7-12

```cpp
// instring.cpp

#include <iostream.h>
#include "oostring.h"

int main()
{
  oostring FirstName;
  oostring LastName;

  cout << "Enter your first name: ";
  getline(cin, FirstName);

  cout << "Enter your last name: ";
  getline(cin, LastName);

  cout << "Your name is " << FirstName << " " << LastName << ".\n";

  return 0;
}
```

Flushing the Input Stream

The cin object is often referred to as the *input stream*. Think of the input stream as a line at a checkout stand. Characters are lined up in the input stream as keys are pressed on the keyboard. Each character, however, must wait its turn to be processed. Therefore, if a prompt for input does not use every character in the input stream, the remaining characters wait in the input stream for the next prompt.

Using statements such as `cin >> x;` for inputting numbers and getline for inputting strings works well—until you try to use them together. The problem arises because after you have input a number using a statement like the preceding one, the new line character that is generated when you press Enter stays in the input stream. That character stays in the stream until the program requests something else from the stream. In other words, statements such as `cin >> x;` do not clean up after themselves very well.

This is not a problem if the next input from the user is another number, because C++ will ignore the new line character that is still waiting in the stream and wait for a number to come down the stream. When the next input is a string, however, you have a problem. The problem arises because the getline method is looking for any sequence of characters ending in a new line character. If a new line character, or any other characters for that matter, is waiting in the input stream, that is what you get in your string.

Let's see the problem first hand.

STEP-BY-STEP ▷ 7.8

1. Retrieve the source code file named **flush.cpp**. The program asks for a numeric value and then asks for a string.

2. Compile and run the program. Enter **12** for the quantity and press **Enter**. Notice that the program rushes to the end without stopping to

   ask for the description. The new line character left over from the input of the integer was accepted as input by the getline method.

3. Leave the program open for the next Step-by-Step exercise.

To remedy this problem, you must remove the extra characters from the input stream before the getline method is executed. This operation is called flushing the input stream. To flush the input stream, insert the line below after the statement where the number was input.

```
cin.ignore(80, '\n');
```

The `80` tells the program to ignore the next 80 characters in the stream. The `'\n'` tells the function to stop ignoring characters when it gets to a new line character. You could use a number smaller than 80 in most cases. The function will usually stop ignoring after only a few characters because it will find a new line character. Most programmers use 80 to play it safe.

Code List 7-13 shows the **flush.cpp** program with the addition of the flush statement.

It is a good idea to flush the input stream after all numeric input statements in programs where strings are also used.

```
// flush.cpp

#include <iostream.h>
#include "oostring.h"

int main()
{
  int quantity;
  oostring desc;

  cout << "Enter the quantity desired: ";
  cin >> quantity;
  cin.ignore(80, '\n'); // Flush the input stream

  cout << "Enter the description of the item: ";
  getline(cin, desc);

  cout << "You requested " << quantity << " of item described as \n";
  cout << desc << ".\n";

  return 0;
}
```

S TEP-BY-STEP ▷ 7.9

1. Add the line required to flush the input stream. Use Code List 7-13 as a reference.

2. Compile and run the program again. The prompt for description now works properly.

3. Close the program.

Using Descriptive Prompts

When writing programs that interact with the user, be sure to output prompts that clearly explain the input the program is requesting. For example, if prompting the user for his or her name, use a descriptive prompt like the one below.

```
Please enter your last name:
```

If prompting for a telephone number or some other formatted data, you may want to use the prompt to give an example.

```
Please enter your phone number using the format (555) 555-5555:
```

The more descriptive and clear your prompts are, the more likely the user is to enter the information in the form your program is expecting.

Clearing the Screen and Printing a Hard Copy

Now that you have learned more about screen I/O, you may be interested in learning how to clear the screen or print to a printer. The techniques required to clear the screen and print to a printer vary, depending on the compiler and operating system you are using. Your compiler may have a function available for clearing the screen, or you may have to use another technique. Modern operating systems sometimes require special programming in order to send output to a printer. You may want to send output to a text file on disk and then use a text editor to print the contents of the file.

The specific instructions for use with your compiler can be found on the **www.programcpp.com/basics** Web site.

Summary

■ The << and >> symbols are actually operators. The cin and cout keywords are actually objects.

■ The cin and cout objects are streams. A stream is data flowing from one place to another.

■ The cin object brings data from the standard input device. The cout object takes data to the standard output device.

■ Console I/O refers to using the screen and keyboard for input and output.

■ The \n character is a special character called the new line character or end-of-line character.

■ There are special characters for printing characters such as tab, the backslash, and quotation marks.

■ You can use endl in place of the character '\n'.

■ The cout object has format options that can be changed with the setf and unsetf methods.

■ The setprecision I/O manipulator is used to set the number of digits that will appear to the right of the decimal point.

■ The setw I/O manipulator is used to set a field width for numbers that are output to the screen.

■ The >> operator can be used to input characters.

■ To input strings, use the getline method of the string class.

■ When a program includes numeric and string input, it is necessary to flush the input stream after each numeric entry to remove characters left in the input stream.

■ Programs should use prompts that clearly explain the input that the program is requesting.

■ The process for clearing the screen and printing a hard copy varies among compilers and operating systems.

VOCABULARY REVIEW

Define the following terms:

console I/O

end-of-line character

extraction operator

field width

I/O manipulators

input stream

insertion operator

new line character

special character

standard input device

standard output device

stream

LESSON 7 REVIEW QUESTIONS

TRUE/FALSE

Circle the T if the statement is true. Circle the F if it is false.

T F 1. The << and >> symbols are actually objects.

T F 2. A stream is data flowing from one place to another.

T F 3. The cin stream reads from the standard output device.

T F 4. The new line character is represented as \l.

T F 5. The special character for generating a tab character is \t.

T F 6. The forcepoint format option displays decimal point and trailing zeros for all floating-point numbers, even if the decimal places are not needed.

T F 7. The setprecision I/O manipulator sets the field width for output.

T F 8. The >> operator can be used to input characters.

T F 9. The getline method is part of the string object.

T F 10. Flushing the input stream removes all characters from the stream.

Write your answers to the following questions.

11. What is the name of the standard output stream object?

12. What is another name for the input operator (>>)?

13. What is another name for the output operator (<<)?

14. What is the special character used to print a backslash?

15. What is the alternative to entering \n to generate a new line character?

16. What format option displays floating-point numbers in E-notation?

17. What I/O manipulator sets the number of digits to be displayed after the decimal point?

18. What two pieces of information must be provided when using getline?

19. Write the statement used to flush the input stream.

20. Why is it important to use descriptive prompts when prompting for data?

LESSON 7 PROJECTS

PROJECT 7A

Write a program that asks the user for three floating-point numbers. Print the numbers back to the screen with a precision of one decimal point. Use a field width for the output that places the three numbers across the screen as in the following example. Save the source code as **float3.cpp**.

```
123.4      33.2       1.9
```

PROJECT 7B

Write a program that asks the user for a name, address, city, state, ZIP code, and phone number and stores each in appropriate string objects. Use descriptive prompts for each input. After the strings are stored, print the information back to the screen in the following format. Save the source code as **address.cpp**.

Name

Address

City, State ZIP Code

Phone Number

PROJECT 7C

Write a program that prompts the user for the names of three colors and stores the responses in three string objects. Use descriptive prompts for each input. After the strings are stored, print the information back to the screen on one line, separated by tabs. Save the source code as **tabs.cpp**.

CRITICAL THINKING

ACTIVITY 7A

Write a program that uses the special characters to print the following line of code to the screen. The code should appear on the screen exactly as shown below, including backslashes, single quotation marks, and double quotation marks. Save the source code as **special.cpp**.

```
cout << "The answer is: " << Answer << '\n';
```

ACTIVITY 7B

Write a program that asks the user for two floating-point numbers. The program should multiply the numbers together and print the product to the screen. Next, have the program ask the user how many digits to display to the right of the decimal point and print the product again with the new precision. Save the source code as **setprec.cpp**.

Strings and Screen Input and Output

REVIEW QUESTIONS

MATCHING

Write the letter of the description from Column 2 that best matches the term or phrase in Column 1.

Column 1

_____ 1. class

_____ 2. concatenation

_____ 3. encapsulation

_____ 4. extraction operator

_____ 5. insertion operator

_____ 6. literal

_____ 7. message

_____ 8. new line character

_____ 9. object

_____ 10. stream

Column 2

A. Takes data from a stream

B. Tells an object what to do

C. Causes the cursor to move to the next line of text

D. The definition for an object

E. Describes the way an object hides data and operations

F. An instance of a class

G. Adding one string to another

H. Data flowing from one place to another

I. Hard-coded data

J. Puts data into a stream

WRITTEN QUESTIONS

Write your answers to the following questions.

1. What is a hard-coded string of text called?

2. Which comes first, a class or an object?

3. What happens if you assign a string to an object and that string is longer than the existing object's length?

4. When working with objects, what is the purpose of a message?

5. Define concatenation.

6. Where does the cout stream lead?

7. What are two ways to represent a new line character in source code?

8. In source code, what character generates a tab?

9. What option displays the decimal point and trailing zeros for all floating-point numbers, even if the decimal places are not needed?

10. When is it necessary to flush the input stream?

APPLICATIONS

APPLICATION 3-1

1. Write a statement that declares a string object named `City` and initializes it with the name of your city.

2. Write a statement that changes the string stored in `City` to *Grand Rapids*.

3. Write a statement that prints the content of the `City` string object to the screen.

4. Write a statement that assigns the length of the `City` string object to an integer named `CityLength`.

5. Write statements necessary to append a comma and *Michigan* to the `City` string.

6. Write a statement that gets a number from the keyboard and stores it in a variable i.

7. Write a statement that prints the letters A, B, and C to the screen, separated by tabs.

8. Write a statement that uses setf to display a leading plus sign before positive values.

9. Write the statements necessary to output the variable cost with two decimal places.

10. Write a statement that inputs a line of text into a string object named address.

APPLICATION 3-2

1. Open **instring.cpp**.

2. Add a declaration for a string object named FullName.

3. Add a statement that assigns FirstName, a space, and LastName to the FullName object.

4. Modify the current output statement to output the FullName object instead of outputting first and last name separately.

APPLICATION 3-3

SCANS

Write a program that asks the user for the diameter of a circle and returns the circumference of the circle. First, store the user's input (diameter) in a floating-point variable. Next, the program should calculate PI * diameter using a declared constant for PI of 3.14159. Output the result of PI * diameter in normal notation with a precision of four digits to the right of the decimal point. Save the source code file as **circumfr.cpp**.

APPLICATION 3-4

SCANS

Write a program that takes in the name, opening value, closing value, and number of shares owned of a publicly traded stock. Have the program print the stock name, opening value, closing value, and the amount of value gained or lost that day in one formatted line. Save the source code file as **stocks.cpp**.

INTERNET ACTIVITY

In this activity, you will use the Internet to find a conversion factor on which to base a program.

1. Open your Web browser.

2. Go to the Web address below.

   http://www.programcpp.com/basics

3. On the home page, click the link called **Internet Activities from the book**.

4. On the Internet Activities page, click the **Unit 3** link.

5. Follow the links provided there to find conversion factors for converting among different units of measurement.

6. Select one of these conversion factors and write a program that prompts the user to enter the measurement in the initial units. The program should convert the measurement to the new unit of measure.

7. Apply proper formatting and set the precision of the output.

8. Save the source code as **convert.cpp**.

AIRLINE FLIGHT ANALYSIS

⏱ **Estimated Time: 1 hour**

SCANS

Overview

In this case study, you will examine a program that analyzes the cost of an airline flight. The program asks for the number of passengers on the flight, the length of the flight, and the average ticket price. The program then calculates and outputs several values, including the time required for the flight, the cost of the flight, total fares collected from ticket sales, and the profit for the flight.

Obviously, there is much more to take into consideration when calculating the profit an airline makes on a specific flight. The program, however, demonstrates many of the topics covered in the first three units.

Let us begin by loading, compiling, and running the program. Then we will analyze the source code.

S TEP-BY-STEP ▷ CSI.1

1. Retrieve the source code file **airline.cpp**. The program makes use of the string class. Therefore you need to set up your project or workspace to use the string class the way you did in Lesson 6.

2. Compile and run the program. The program is configured for the Boeing 747-400 jet.

3. Enter 300 for the number of passengers, 2500 for the length of the flight, and 349.25 as the average ticket price. The program's output will appear similar to Figure CSI-1.

4. Leave the source code file open.

The program's output appears similar to the output shown here.

```
Airline                                                    _ □ ×
Auto                 A

AIRLINE FLIGHT ANALYSIS
Airplane name: Boeing 747-400
Enter the number of passengers on the flight (maximum 398): 300
Enter the distance (in miles) of the flight (maximum 4331): 2500
Enter the average ticket price: 349.25

Analysis for Boeing 747-400

The flight will take approximately 4.69 hours.
The cost of the flight will be $32546.90, with a
cost per passenger of $108.49.
The total fares collected from ticket sales is $104775.00,
resulting in a profit of $72228.09.
Press any key to continue
```

Analyzing the Program

The complete source code for the program appears in Code List CSI-1. Spend a few minutes looking over the complete source code before reading the analysis that follows.

CODE LIST CSI-1

```cpp
// Airline Flight Cost Analysis

#include <iostream.h>   // necessary for input/output
#include <iomanip.h>    // necessary for setprecision manipulator
#include "oostring.h"   // necessary for string object

// main function
int main ()
{
 // Specifications for a Boeing 747-400
 // Source: The World Almanac and Book of Facts 1995
 oostring plane_name("Boeing 747-400");
 int const plane_speed = 533;
 int const number_of_seats = 398;
 int const max_flight_length = 4331;
 int const cost_per_hour = 6939;

 int num_pass;              // number of passengers on the plane
 float num_miles;           // flight distance
```

(continued on next page)

```
float avg_ticket_price;   // average ticket price for flight
float flight_cost;        // cost for the flight
float cost_per_pass;      // cost per passenger
float total_fares;        // total fares collected for the flight
float profit;             // profit for the flight
float hours;              // length of flight in hours

cout << "\nAIRLINE FLIGHT ANALYSIS\n";
cout << "Airplane name: " << plane_name << endl;
cout << "Enter the number of passengers on the flight (maximum "
    << number_of_seats << "): ";
cin >> num_pass;
cout << "Enter the distance (in miles) of the flight (maximum "
    << max_flight_length << "): ";
cin >> num_miles;
cout << "Enter the average ticket price: ";
cin >> avg_ticket_price;

hours = num_miles / plane_speed;  // calculate flight time
flight_cost = hours * cost_per_hour; // calculate cost of flight
cost_per_pass = flight_cost / num_pass; // cost per passenger
total_fares = num_pass * avg_ticket_price; // calculate total fares
profit = total_fares - flight_cost; // calculate flight profit

cout.setf(ios::showpoint);  // force decimal point to be displayed
cout.setf(ios::fixed);      // prevent scientific notation
cout << "\nAnalysis for " << plane_name << endl;
cout << "\nThe flight will take approximately " << setprecision(2)
    << hours << " hours.\n";
cout << "The cost of the flight will be $" << flight_cost
    << ", with a \n";
cout << "cost per passenger of $" << cost_per_pass << ".\n";
cout << "The total fares collected from ticket sales is $"
    << total_fares << ",\n";
cout << "resulting in a profit of $" << profit << ".\n";
return 0;
}
```

The program begins with three compiler directives that include `iostream.h`, `iomanip.h`, and `oostring.h`. The first two are necessary to make the input and output functions available. The `oostring.h` include is necessary to use the string class.

Next, the main function begins. The remainder of the program is contained in the main function. Notice that the `#include` directives must appear before the main function.

The first set of statements in the main function (shown again in Code List CSI-2) define the specifications for a particular aircraft. Currently, the values are based on a particular model of the Boeing 747. The name of the aircraft is stored in a string object. The other values are stored in constants. These values will be used in calculations later in the program.

```
// Specifications for a Boeing 747-400
// Source: The World Almanac and Book of Facts 1995
oostring plane_name("Boeing 747-400");
int const plane_speed = 533;
int const number_of_seats = 398;
int const max_flight_length = 4331;
int const cost_per_hour = 6939;
```

The next step is to declare variables (see Code List CSI-3). The variable that holds the number of passengers on the flight is declared as an integer; the others are floating-point variables. All the constants and variables could have been declared as floating-point types to avoid the mixing of data types. Here, we will use integers where appropriate and allow the integer data types to be promoted during calculation.

```
int num_pass;            // number of passengers on the plane
float num_miles;         // flight distance
float avg_ticket_price;  // average ticket price for flight
float flight_cost;       // cost for the flight
float cost_per_pass;     // cost per passenger
float total_fares;       // total fares collected for the flight
float profit;            // profit for the flight
float hours;             // length of flight in hours
```

You should always clarify the use for each variable using comments, as was done in the declarations in Code List CSI-3.

The next group of statements (shown in Code List CSI-4) gets the required input from the user. Remember, \n or endl can be used to force the cursor to the next line of the screen. To give the user more information about the range of possible input, the number of seats and maximum flight length for the particular aircraft are part of the prompt for the input.

```
cout << "\nAIRLINE FLIGHT ANALYSIS\n";
cout << "Airplane name: " << plane_name << endl;
cout << "Enter the number of passengers on the flight (maximum "
     << number_of_seats << "): ";
cin >> num_pass;
cout << "Enter the distance (in miles) of the flight (maximum "
     << max_flight_length << "): ";
cin >> num_miles;
cout << "Enter the average ticket price: ";
cin >> avg_ticket_price;
```

After the input is gathered, the calculations must be performed. First, the time required for the flight is calculated using the statement below.

```
hours = num_miles / plane_speed;  // calculate flight time
```

The constant `plane_speed` is an integer, but `num_miles` and `hours` are both floating-point variables. Therefore, `plane_speed` is promoted to a floating-point type for the calculation, and the result, also a floating-point value, is stored in hours.

A similar promotion of an integer type occurs in the other calculations that follow. In each case, the result is a floating-point value. As shown in the statements in Code List CSI-5, the cost of the flight is calculated by multiplying the time required by the cost of operating the aircraft for an hour. That flight cost is divided by the number of passengers to get a cost per passenger. The total number of dollars collected from ticket sales is estimated by multiplying the average ticket price by the number of passengers. Finally, the projected profit for the flight is calculated by subtracting the cost of the flight from the dollars collected from ticket sales.

CODE LIST CSI-5

```
flight_cost = hours * cost_per_hour; // calculate cost of flight
cost_per_pass = flight_cost / num_pass; // cost per passenger
total_fares = num_pass * avg_ticket_price; // calculate total fares
profit = total_fares - flight_cost; // calculate flight profit
```

The only task remaining is printing the output to the screen. The statements shown in Code List CSI-6 format the output in paragraph form. The first two statements below are necessary to have the numbers appear in the desired format. The showpoint format option causes the decimal point to be displayed, even if a nonfractional value is being printed. The fixed option prevents numbers from appearing in scientific or "E" notation. In the fourth statement, the setprecision manipulator is used to specify that only two digits should be displayed to the right of the decimal point.

CODE LIST CSI-6

```
cout.setf(ios::showpoint);  // force decimal point to be displayed
cout.setf(ios::fixed);      // prevent scientific notation
cout << "\nAnalysis for " << plane_name << endl;
cout << "\nThe flight will take approximately " << setprecision(2)
     << hours << " hours.\n";
cout << "The cost of the flight will be $" << flight_cost
     << ", with a \n";
cout << "cost per passenger of $" << cost_per_pass << ".\n";
cout << "The total fares collected from ticket sales is $"
     << total_fares << ",\n";
cout << "resulting in a profit of $" << profit << ".\n";
```

Modifying the Program

As an additional exercise, modify the program to analyze another aircraft. Choose one of the four airplanes in the following table.

Aircraft	Seats	Speed	Flight Length	Cost per Hour
L-1011	288	496	1498	4564
DC-10-10	281	492	1493	4261
B737-500	113	408	532	1594
F-100	97	366	409	1681

Source: The World Almanac and Book of Facts 1995.

When you run the program with specifications from an airplane other than the 747-400, notice how the input prompts change to provide you with the allowable range of values.

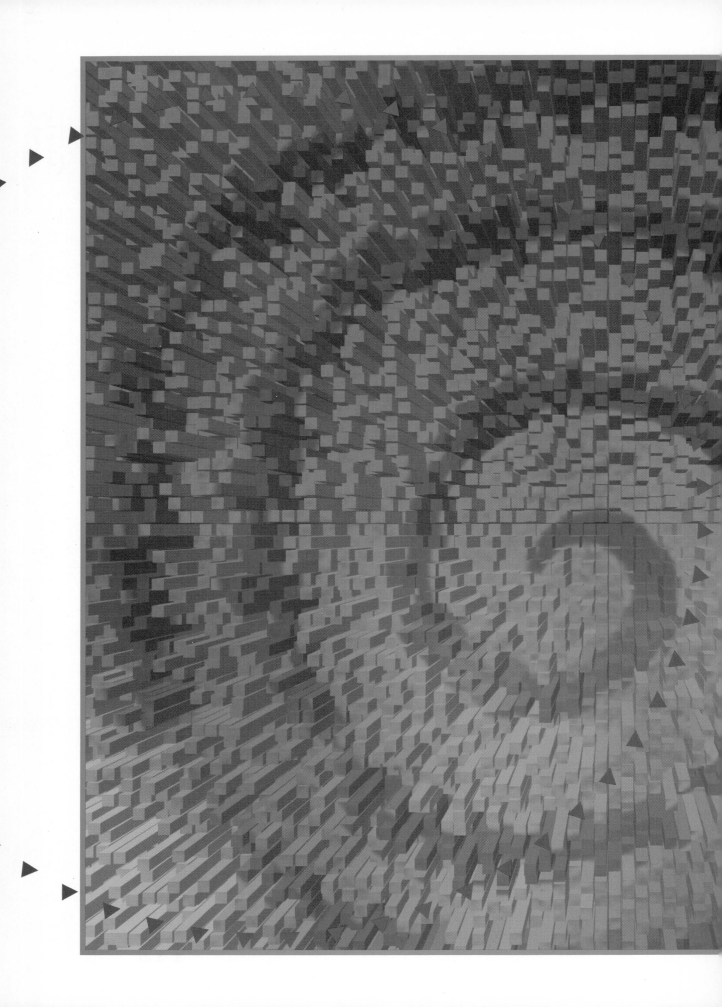

DECISION MAKING AND LOOPS

BUILDING BLOCKS OF DECISION MAKING

OBJECTIVES

When you complete this lesson, you will be able to:

■ Describe how decisions are made in programs.

■ Describe how true and false are represented in C++.

■ Use relational operators.

■ Use logical operators.

■ Describe short-circuit evaluation.

⏱ **Estimated Time: 1 hour**

VOCABULARY

flowchart
fuzzy logic
logical operators
relational operators
short-circuit evaluation
truth tables

Decision Making in Programs

When you make a decision, your brain goes through a process of comparisons. For example, when you shop for clothes you compare the prices with those you previously paid. You compare the quality with other clothes you have seen or owned. You probably compare the clothes to what other people are wearing or what is in style. You might even compare the purchase of clothes to other possible uses for your available money.

Although your brain's method of decision making is much more complex than what a computer is capable of, decision making in computers is also based on comparing data. In this section, you will learn to use the basic tools of computer decision making.

Almost every program that is useful or user-friendly involves decision making. Although some algorithms progress sequentially from the first to the last instruction, most algorithms branch out into more than one path. At the point at which the branching takes place, a decision must be made as to which path to take.

It often helps to illustrate the flow of a program with a special drawing called a *flowchart*. A flowchart maps the decisions a program is to make and the path down which each decision leads. The flowchart in Figure 8-1 is part of an algorithm in which the program is preparing to output a document to the printer. The user enters the number of copies he or she wants to print. To make sure the number is valid, the program verifies that the number of copies is not less than zero. If the user enters a negative number, a message is printed and the user is asked to reenter the value. If the user's input passes the test, the program simply goes on to the next step.

 Did You Know?

Each shape used in a flowchart has a special meaning. The shapes are connected with arrows that show the direction of the flow of the program. Rectangles represent processing or action. Diamonds represent a decision. Parallelograms like those in Figure 8-1 represent input or output.

118

FIGURE 8-1
The decision-making part of this flowchart prevents
the program from proceeding with invalid data.

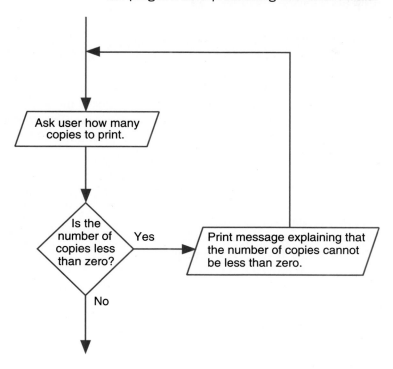

FIGURE 8-2
The path a program takes may be dictated by the user.

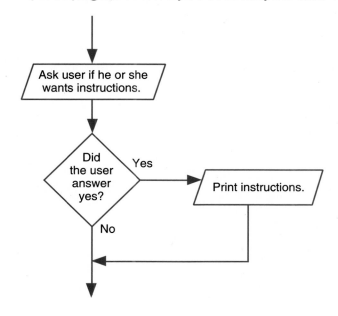

Decisions may also have to be made based on the wishes of the user. The flowchart in Figure 8-2 shows how the response to a question changes the path the program takes. If the user wants instructions printed on the screen, the program displays the instructions. Otherwise, that part of the program is bypassed.

119

The examples in Figures 8-1 and 8-2 show two common needs for decisions in programs. There are many other instances in which decisions must be made. As you do more and more programming, you will use decision making in countless situations.

Representing True and False in C++

The way computers make decisions is very primitive. Even though computers make decisions in a way similar to the way the human brain does, computers do not have intuition or "gut" feelings. Decision making in a computer is based on performing simple comparisons. The microprocessor compares two values and "decides" whether they are equivalent. Clever programming and the fact that computers can do millions of comparisons per second sometimes make computers appear to be "smart."

In Lesson 3 you learned about the Boolean data type, which provides a convenient way to store true and false values. Internally, however, true and false are represented as numbers. When the computer makes a comparison, the comparison results in a value of either 0 or 1. If the resulting value is 0, it means the comparison proved false. If the result is 1, the comparison proved true. So in C++, the Boolean value of false is represented by the integer 0 and true is represented by the integer 1.

Relational Operators

To make comparisons, C++ provides a set of *relational operators*, shown in Table 8-1. They are similar to the symbols you have used in math when working with equations and inequalities.

TABLE 8-1
Relational operators

Operator	Meaning	Example
==	equal to	i == 1
>	greater than	i > 2
<	less than	i < 0
>=	greater than or equal to	i >= 6
<=	less than or equal to	i <= 10
!=	not equal to	i != 12

The relational operators are used to create expressions like the examples in Table 8-1. The result of the expression is 1 (true) if the data meets the requirements of the comparison. Otherwise, the result of the expression is 0 (false). For example, the result of 2 > 1 is 1 (true), and the result of 2 < 1 is 0 (false).

The program in Code List 8-1 demonstrates how expressions are made from relational operators. The result of the expressions is to be displayed as either a 1 or 0.

 Important

Do not confuse the relational operator (==) with the assignment operator (=). Use == for comparisons and = for assignments.

CODE LIST 8-1

```cpp
// relate.cpp

#include <iostream.h>

int main()
{
  int i = 2;
  int j = 3;
  bool true_false;

  cout << (i == 2) << endl; // displays a 1 (true)
  cout << (i == 1) << endl; // displays a 0 (false)
  cout << (j > i) << endl;
  cout << (j < i) << endl;  // Can you predict
  cout << (j <= 3) << endl; // the output of
  cout << (j >= i) << endl; // these statements?
  cout << (j != i) << endl;

  true_false = (j < 4); // The result can be stored
                        // to a Boolean variable.
  cout << true_false << endl;
  return 0;
}
```

S TEP-BY-STEP ▷ 8.1

1. Enter the program from Code List 8-1 into a blank editor screen. Save the source code file as **relate.cpp**. Can you predict its output?

2. Compile, link, and run the program.

3. After you have analyzed the output, close the program.

Logical Operators

Sometimes it takes more than two comparisons to obtain the desired result. For example, if you want to test to see whether an integer is in the range 1 to 10, you must do two comparisons. In order for the integer to fall within the range, it must be greater than 0 *and* less than 11.

C++ provides three *logical operators*. Table 8-2 shows the three logical operators and their meaning.

Note

The key used to enter the two vertical lines of the or operator (||) is usually located near the Enter or Return key. It is usually on the same key with the back-slash (\\).

TABLE 8-2
Logical operators

Operator	Meaning	Example
&&	and	(j == 1 && k == 2)
||	or	(j == 1 || k == 2)
!	not	result = !(j == 1 && k == 2)

Figure 8-3 shows three diagrams called *truth tables*. They will help you understand the result of comparisons with the logical operators and, or, and not.

FIGURE 8-3
Truth tables illustrate the results of logical operators.

AND

A	B	A && B
false (0)	false (0)	false (0)
false (0)	true (1)	false (0)
true (1)	false (0)	false (0)
true (1)	true (1)	true (1)

OR

A	B	A || B
false (0)	false (0)	false (0)
false (0)	true (1)	true (1)
true (1)	false (0)	true (1)
true (1)	true (1)	true (1)

NOT

A	!A
false (0)	true (1)
true (1)	false (0)

Consider the following C++ statement.

```
in_range = (i > 0 && i < 11);
```

The variable `in_range` is assigned the value 1 if the value of `i` falls into the defined range, and 0 if the value of `i` does not fall into the defined range.

The not operator (!) turns true to false and false to true. For example, suppose you have a program that catalogs old movies. Your program uses an integer variable named `InColor` that has the value 0 if the movie was filmed in black and white and the value 1 if the movie was filmed in color. In the statement below, the variable `Black_and_White` is set to 1 (true) if the movie is not in color. Therefore, if the movie is in color, `Black_and_White` is set to 0 (false).

```
Black_and_White = !InColor;
```

S TEP-BY-STEP ▷ 8.2

1. Retrieve the source code file named **logical.cpp**. The program shown in Code List 8-2 appears. Look closely at the statements that include the logical operators.

2. Compile and run the program to see the output.

3. After you have analyzed the output, close the source code file.

CODE LIST 8-2

```cpp
// logical.cpp

#include <iostream.h>

int main()
{
  int i = 2;
  int j = 3;
  bool true_false;

  true_false = (i < 3 && j > 3);
  cout << "The result of (i < 3 && j > 3) is "
       << true_false << '\n';

  true_false = (i < 3 && j >= 3);
  cout << "The result of (i < 3 && j >= 3) is "
       << true_false << '\n';

  cout << "The result of (i -- 1 || i == 2) is "
      << (i == 1 || i == 2) << '\n';

  true_false = (j < 4);
  cout << "The result of (j < 4) is "
       << true_false << '\n';

  true_false = !true_false;
  cout << "The result of !true_false is "
       << !true_false << '\n';

  return 0;
}
```

Combining More Than Two Comparisons

You can use logical operators to combine more than two comparisons. Consider the following statement, which decides whether it is okay for a person to ride a roller coaster.

```
ok_to_ride = (height_in_inches > 45 && !back_trouble
              && !heart_trouble);
```

In the preceding statement, `back_trouble` and `heart_trouble` hold the value 0 or 1 depending on whether the person being considered has the problem. For example, if the person has back trouble, the value of `back_trouble` is set to 1. The not operator (!) is used because it is okay to ride if the person does not have back trouble and does not have heart trouble. The entire statement says that it is okay to ride if the person's height is greater than 45 inches and the person has no back trouble and no heart trouble.

Order of Logical Operations

You can mix logical operators in statements as long as you understand the order in which the logical operators will be applied. The not operator (!) is applied first, then the and operator (&&), and finally the or operator (||). Consider the following statement.

```
dog_acceptable = (white || black && friendly);
```

This example illustrates why it is important to know the order in which logical operators are applied. At first glance it may appear that the statement would consider a dog to be acceptable if the dog is either white or black and also friendly. But in reality, the statement above considers a white dog that wants to chew your leg off to be an acceptable dog. Why? Because the and operator is evaluated first and then the result of the and operation is used for the or operation. The statement can be corrected with some additional parentheses, as shown below.

```
dog_acceptable = ((white || black) && friendly);
```

C++ evaluates operations in parentheses first just as in arithmetic statements. The program in Code List 8-3 demonstrates the difference that the parentheses make. Also notice that the Boolean variables `white` and `black` are initialized using the `true` and `false` keywords. These keywords provide a more readable way to assign one and zero to the Boolean variables.

CODE LIST 8-3

```cpp
// logical2.cpp

#include <iostream.h>

int main()
{
 bool white, black, friendly, acceptable;

 white = true;      // dog is white
 black = false;     // dog is not black
 friendly = false;  // dog is not friendly

 // The following statement produces incorrect results due to the
 // order of operations.
 acceptable = (white || black && friendly);
 cout << acceptable << endl;
```

```
// The parentheses in the following statement override the
// order of operations and the statement produces the correct result.
acceptable = ((white || black) && friendly);
cout << acceptable << endl;

return 0;
}
```

STEP-BY-STEP ▷ 8.3

1. Open **logical2.cpp**. The program shown in Code List 8-3 appears.

2. Compile, link, and run the program to see the effect of the parentheses.

3. Close the source code file.

Short-Circuit Evaluation

Suppose you have decided you want to go to a particular concert. You can only go, however, if two conditions can be met: You must get tickets and you must get off work the night of the concert. Before you check whether you can get off work, you find out that the concert is sold out and you cannot get a ticket. There is no longer a need to check whether you can get off work because you do not have a ticket anyway.

C++ has a feature called *short-circuit evaluation* that allows the same kind of determinations in your program. For example, in an expression such as `in_range = (i > 0 && i < 11);`, the program first checks to see whether `i` is greater than 0. If it is not, there is no need to check any further because regardless of whether `i` is less than 11, `in_range` will be false. So the program sets `in_range` to false and goes to the next statement without evaluating the right side of the &&.

Concept Builder

Compilers often have an option to disable short-circuit evaluation.

Short-circuiting also occurs with the or (||) operator. In the case of the or operator, the expression is short-circuited if the left side of the || is true, because the expression will be true, regardless of the right side of the ||.

Summary

■ Computers make decisions by comparing data.

■ A flowchart is an illustration that helps show the flow of a program.

- In C++, true is represented by 1 and false is represented by 0.

- Relational operators are used to create expressions that result in a value of 1 or 0.

- Logical operators can combine relational expressions.

- Parentheses can be used to control the order in which logical expressions are evaluated.

- Short-circuit evaluation allows the evaluation of a logical expression to be stopped early if the ultimate result of the expression is already determined.

VOCABULARY REVIEW

Define the following terms:

flowchart

fuzzy logic

logical operators

relational operators

short-circuit evaluation

truth tables

LESSON 8 REVIEW QUESTIONS

TRUE/FALSE

Circle the T if the statement is true. Circle the F if it is false.

T F 1. Decision making in computers is based on comparing data.

T F 2. A flowchart is a special drawing used to illustrate the flow of a program.

T F 3. Internally, true and false are represented by characters.

T F 4. The result of an expression that includes relational operators is either true or false.

T F 5. The equal to relational operator is represented by =.

T F 6. There are four different logical operators available.

T F 7. The not operator turns a result to false regardless of its previous value.

T F 8. Parentheses can be used to change the order of logical operations.

T F 9. The and operator is applied before the or operator.

T F 10. Compilers often have an option to disable short-circuit evaluation.

WRITTEN QUESTIONS

Write your answers to the following questions.

11. What flowchart symbol represents processing or action?

12. What flowchart symbol represents a decision?

13. What is the value that represents the Boolean condition false?

14. What is fuzzy logic?

15. What is the relational operator that performs the "not equal to" operation?

16. What do you call the tables that show the combination of results of logical operators?

17. What logical operator performs the or operation?

18. Why is the order of logical operations important?

19. In the order of logical operations, what operator is applied first?

20. What is short-circuit evaluation?

LESSON 8 PROJECTS

PROJECT 8A

In the blanks beside the statements in the program below, write a T or F to indicate the result of the expression. Fill in the answers beginning with the first statement and follow the program in the order the statements would be executed in a running program.

```
int main()
{
 int i = 4;
 int j = 3;
 bool true_false;

 true_false = (j < 4);                    _____
```

```
true_false = (j < 3);                                   _____

true_false = (j < i);                                   _____

true_false = (i < 4);                                   _____

true_false = (j <= 4);                                  _____

true_false = (4 > 4);                                   _____

true_false = (i != j);                                  _____

true_false = (i == j || i < 100);                       _____

true_false = (i == j && i < 100);                       _____

true_false = (i < j || true_false && j >= 3);           _____

true_false = (!(i > 2 && j == 4));                      _____

true_false = !1;                                        _____

return 0;
}
```

PROJECT 8B

1. Retrieve the file named **truth.cpp**.

2. Compile, link, and run the program. The program displays a truth table for the AND operation.

3. Duplicate the code that displays the AND truth table and modify it to display an OR truth table.

4. Save and close the program.

CRITICAL THINKING

Modify the **truth.cpp** program from Project 8B to also display a truth table for the NOT operation. Use Figure 8-3 as a reference.

SELECTION STRUCTURES

Introduction to Selection Structures

Programs consist of statements that solve a problem or perform a task. Up to this point, you have been creating programs with sequence structures. *Sequence structures* execute statements one after another without changing the flow of the program. Other structures, such as the ones that make decisions, *do* change the flow of the program. The structures that make decisions in C++ programs are called *selection structures*. When a decision is made in a program, a selection structure controls the flow of the program based on the decision. In this lesson, you will learn how to use selection structures to make decisions in your programs. The three selection structures available in C++ are the if structure, the if/else structure, and the switch structure.

Using if

Many programming languages include an *if structure*. Although the syntax varies among programming languages, the if keyword is usually part of every language. If you have used if in other programming languages, you should have little difficulty using if in C++. The if structure is one of the easiest and most useful parts of C++.

The expression that makes the decision is called the *control expression*. Look at the code segment in Code List 9-1. First the control expression (i == 3) is evaluated. If the result is true, the code in the braces that follow the if statement is executed. If the result is false, the code in the braces is skipped.

Concept Builder

When only one statement appears between the braces in an if structure, the braces are not actually necessary. It is, however, a good idea to always use braces in case other statements are added later.

```
if (i == 3)
    {
      cout << "The value of i is 3\n";
    }
```

You can place more than one line between the braces, as shown in Code List 9-2.

Figure 9-1 shows the flowchart for an if structure. The if structure is sometimes called a ***one-way selection structure*** because the decision is whether to go "one way" or just bypass the code in the if structure.

 Important

Remember to be careful not to confuse the == operator with the = (assignment) operator. Entering if (i = 3) will cause i to be assigned the value 3, and the code in the braces that follow will be executed regardless of what the value of i was before the if structure.

CODE LIST 9-2

```
if (YesNo == 'Y')
    {
      cout << "Enter the title: ";
      getline(cin, title);
    }
```

FIGURE 9-1
The if structure is sometimes called
a one-way selection structure.

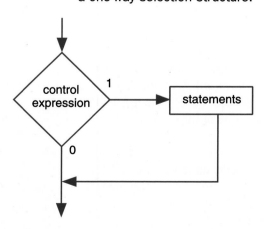

Analyze the program in Code List 9-3. The program declares a string object and an unsigned long integer. The user is asked for the name of his or her city or town and for the population of the city or town. The if structure compares the population to a value that would indicate whether the city is among the 100 largest U.S. cities. If the city is one of the 100 largest U.S. cities, the program prints a message saying so.

```cpp
// city.cpp

#include <iostream.h>
#include "oostring.h"

int main()
{
 oostring city_name;
 unsigned long population;

 cout << "What is the name of your city or town? ";
 getline(cin, city_name);

 cout << "What is the population of the city or town? ";
 cin >> population;
 cin.ignore(80,'\n');

 if (population >= 185086)
 {
   cout << "According to estimated population figures, "
        << city_name << endl
        << "is one of the 100 largest U.S. cities.\n";
 }

 return 0;
}
```

Accidentally putting a semicolon at the end of the control expression will end the if structure, causing unexpected results. For example, in the code below, the semicolon at the end of the control expression ends the if structure. Therefore, the statement that follows in braces is executed regardless of the value of i. The compiler thinks the statement in braces is just the next statement after the if structure.

```cpp
if (i == 3);          // don't do this!!
  { cout << "The value of i is 3\n"; }
```

1. Open **city.cpp**. The program from Code List 9-3 appears without the if structure.

2. Add the if structure shown in Code List 9-3 to the program. Enter the code carefully.

3. Compile, link, and run the program. Enter your city or town to test the program.

4. If your city or town is not one of the 100 largest cities, or if you do not know your city or town's population, enter Albuquerque, a city in New Mexico with a population of about 420,000. *Warning*: Do not enter the comma when entering populations.

5. Leave the source code file open for the next Step-by-Step exercise.

Using if/else

The *if/else structure* is sometimes called a *two-way selection structure*. Using if/else, one block of code is executed if the control expression is true and another block is executed if the control expression is false. Consider the code fragment in Code List 9-4.

Concept Builder

Notice how the braces in Code List 9-4 are on the same line as the code they enclose. Some programmers prefer this more compact way of entering code.

CODE LIST 9-4

```
if (i < 0)
   {cout << "The number is negative.\n";}
else
   {cout << "The number is zero or positive.\n";}
```

The else portion of the structure is executed if the control expression is false. Figure 9-2 shows a flowchart for a two-way selection structure.

FIGURE 9-2
The if/else structure is a
two-way selection structure.

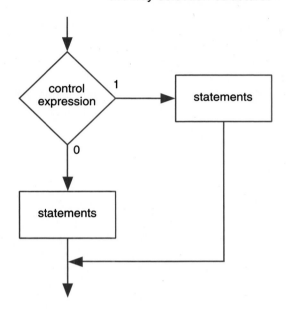

The code shown in Code List 9-5 adds an else clause to the if structure in the program in Step-by-Step 9.1. Output is improved by providing information on whether the city's population qualifies it as one of the 100 largest U.S. cities. If the population is 185,086 or more, the first output statement is executed; otherwise, the second output statement is executed. In every case, one or the other output statement is executed.

Concept Builder

Many programmers make the mistake of using > or < when they really need >= or <=. In the code segment in Code List 9-5, using > rather than >= would cause Glendale, California, the 100th largest city, to be excluded because its population is 185086, not greater than 185086.

CODE LIST 9-5

```
if (population >= 185086)
 {
   cout << "According to estimated population figures, "
        << city_name << endl
        << "is one of the 100 largest U.S. cities.\n";
 }
else
 {
   cout << "According to estimated population figures, "
        << city_name << endl
        << "is not one of the 100 largest U.S. cities.\n";
 }
```

1. Add the else clause shown in Code List 9-5 to the if structure in the program on your screen. Save the new program as **cityelse.cpp**.

2. Compile, link, and run the program.

3. Enter the city of Gary, Indiana (population 108,469). The program reports that Gary is not one of the 100 largest cities in the United States.

4. Run the program again using Lubbock, Texas (population 190,974). Lubbock is among the 100 largest U.S. cities.

5. Close the program.

Nested if Structures

You can place if structures within other if structures. When an if or if/else structure is placed within another if or if/else structure, the structures are said to be *nested*. The flowchart in Figure 9-3 decides whether a student is exempt from a final exam based on grade average and days absent.

FIGURE 9-3

This flowchart can be programmed using nested if structures.

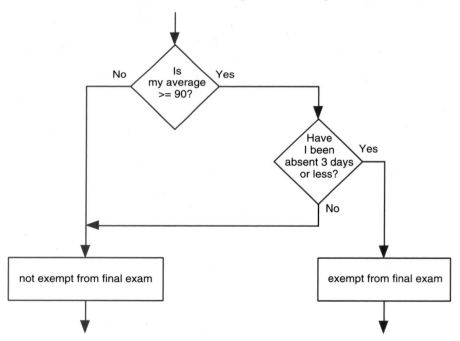

To be exempt from the final, a student must have a 90 average or better and cannot have missed more than three days of class. The algorithm first determines if the student's average is greater than or equal to 90. If the result is false, the student must take the final exam. If the result is true, the number of days absent is checked to determine if the other exemption requirement is met. Code List 9-6 shows the algorithm as a C++ code segment.

The code in Code List 9-6 is written to initially assume that the student is not exempt from the final exam. If the requirements are met, as determined by the nested if structures, the exemption will be granted.

```
exempt_from_final = false;

if (my_average >= 90)
  {                                    // If your average is 90 or better
    if (my_days_absent <= 3)           // and you have missed three days
    { exempt_from_final = true; }      // or less, you are exempt.
  }
```

Algorithms involving nested if structures can get more complicated than the one in Code List 9-6. Figure 9-4 shows the flowchart from Figure 9-3 expanded to include another way to be exempted from the final exam. In this expanded algorithm, students can also be exempted if they have an 80 or higher average, as long as they have been present every day or missed only one day.

FIGURE 9-4

This algorithm provides two paths to exemption from the final exam.

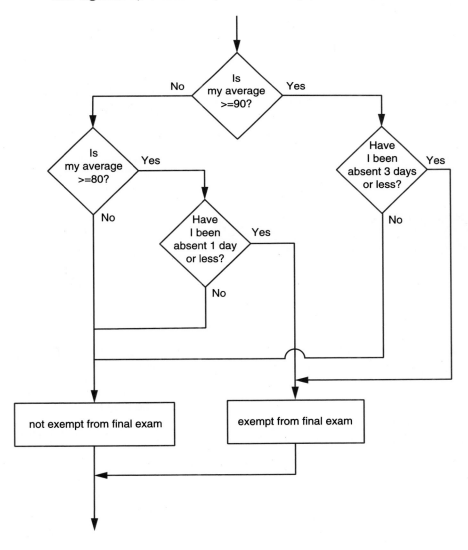

As you can probably imagine, programming the algorithm in Figure 9-4 will require careful construction and nesting of if and if/else structures. Code List 9-7 shows you how it is done.

Concept Builder

Earlier you learned that it is a good idea to always use braces with if structures. Code List 9-7 illustrates another reason you should do so. Without the braces, the compiler may assume that the else clause goes with the nested if structure rather than the first if.

CODE LIST 9-7

```
exempt_from_final = false;

if (my_average >= 90)
  {                                    // If your average is 90 or better
   if (my_days_absent <= 3)           // and you have missed three days
   { exempt_from_final = true; }      // or less, you are exempt.
  }
else  // If you don't have a 90+ average, you still have a chance.
  { if (my_average >= 80)
    {                                  // If your average is 80 or better
     if (my_days_absent <= 1)         // and you have missed one day or
       { exempt_from_final = true; }  // less, you are exempt.
    }
  }
```

STEP-BY-STEP 9.3

1. Open **final.cpp**.

2. Compile, link, and run the program.

3. Enter 90 as your grade average and 3 as your days absent. The program reports that you are exempt from the final exam.

4. Run the program again. Enter 88 as your grade average and 1 as your days absent. You are still exempt.

5. Run the program again. Enter 89 as your grade average and 2 as your days absent. The program reports that you must take the final.

6. Run the program again using values of your own choice.

7. Close the program.

Code List 9-8 shows a simple program that includes a nested if structure. The program asks the user to input the amount of money he or she wants to deposit in order to open a new checking account. Based on the value provided by the user, the program recommends a type of account.

CODE LIST 9-8

```
// deposit.cpp

#include <iostream.h>

int main()
{
  float amount_to_deposit;

  cout << "How much do you want to deposit to open the account? ";
  cin  >> amount_to_deposit;

  if(amount_to_deposit < 1000.00 )
   {
    if(amount_to_deposit < 100.00 )
      { cout << "You should consider the EconoCheck account.\n"; }
    else
      { cout << "You should consider the FreeCheck account.\n"; }
   }
  else
    { cout << "You should consider an interest-bearing account.\n"; }
  return 0;
}
```

S TEP-BY-STEP ▷ 9.4

1. Open **deposit.cpp**. The program in Code List 9-8 appears.

2. Compile, link, and run the program. Run the program several times, using values that are less than $100, between $100 and $1000, and greater than $1000.

3. Close the program.

The switch Structure

You have studied one-way (if) and two-way (if-else) selection structures. C++ has another method of handling multiple options known as the *switch structure*. The switch structure has many uses but may be most often used when working with menus. A *menu* is a set of options presented to the user of a program. Code List 9-9 displays a menu of choices and asks the user to enter a number that corresponds to one of the choices. Then a case statement is used to handle each of the options.

137

```
cout << "How do you want the order shipped?\n";
cout << "1 - Ground\n";
cout << "2 - 2-day air\n";
cout << "3 - Overnight air\n";
cout << "Enter the number of the shipping method you want: ";
cin >> shipping_method;

switch(shipping_method)
 {
   case 1:
     shipping_cost = 5.00;
     break;
   case 2:
     shipping_cost = 7.50;
     break;
   case 3:
     shipping_cost = 10.00;
     break;
   default:
     shipping_cost = 0.00;
     break;
 }
```

Let's analyze the switch structure in Code List 9-9. It begins with the keyword switch, followed by the control expression (the variable shipping_method) to be compared in the structure. Within the braces of the structure are a series of case keywords. Each one provides the code that is to be executed in the event that shipping_method matches the value that follows case. The default keyword tells the compiler that if nothing else matches, execute the statements that follow.

The break keyword, which appears at the end of each case segment, causes the flow of logic to jump to the first executable statement after the switch structure.

Note

In C++, only integer or character types may be used as control expressions in switch statements.

STEP-BY-STEP ▷ 9.5

1. Open **shipping.cpp**. The program includes the segment from Code List 9-9.

2. Compile, link, and run the program. Choose shipping method 2. The cost of shipping by second-day air appears.

3. Add a fourth shipping option called Carrier Pigeon to the menu.

4. Add the code below to the switch structure, before the default keyword.

   ```
   case 4:
     shipping_cost = 99.99;
     break;
   ```

5. Compile, link, and run to test your addition to the options.

6. Save the source code and close.

Nested if/else structures could be used in the place of the switch structure. But the switch structure is easier to use and a programmer is less prone to making errors that are related to braces and indentations. Remember, however, that an integer or character data type is required in the control expression of a switch structure. Nested ifs must be used if you are comparing floating-point values.

When using character types in a switch structure, enclose the characters in single quotation marks as in any other character literal. The code segment in Code List 9-10 is an example of using character literals in a switch structure.

CODE LIST 9-10

```cpp
switch(character_entered)
  {
    case 'A':
      cout << "The character entered was A, as in albatross.\n";
      break;
    case 'B':
      cout << "The character entered was B, as in butterfly.\n";
      break;
    default:
      cout << "Illegal entry\n";
      break;
  }
```

STEP-BY-STEP ▷ 9.6

1. Open **chswitch.cpp**. The program includes the segment from Code List 9-10.

2. Compile, link, and run the program. Enter **A** as input. The appropriate output is generated.

3. Run the program again. Enter **B** as input. The second case is executed.

4. Run the program again. Enter **C** as input. The input is reported to be illegal.

5. Close the program.

Concept Builder

C++ allows you to place your case statements in any order. You can, however, increase the speed of your program by placing the more common choices at the top of the switch structure and less common ones toward the bottom. The reason is that the computer makes the comparisons in the order they appear in the switch structure. The sooner a match is found, the sooner the computer can move on to other processing.

139

Summary

■ Selection structures are how C++ programs make decisions.

■ The if structure is a one-way selection structure. When a control expression in an if statement is evaluated to be true, the statements associated with the structure are executed.

■ The if/else structure is a two-way selection structure. If the control expression in the if statement evaluates to true, one block of statements is executed; otherwise, another block is executed.

■ It is possible to nest if structures and if/else structures.

■ The switch structure is a multiway selection structure that executes one of many sets of statements, depending on the value of the control expression. The control expression must evaluate to an integer or character value.

VOCABULARY REVIEW

Define the following terms:

control expression   selection structures

if structure   sequence structures

if/else structure   switch structure

menu   two-way selection structure

one-way selection structure

LESSON 9 REVIEW QUESTIONS

TRUE/FALSE

Circle the T if the statement is true. Circle the F if it is false.

T F 1. Selection structures execute statements one after another without changing the flow of the program.

T F 2. The expression that makes the decision in an if structure is called a control expression.

T F 3. The if keyword is unique to C++.

T F 4. If the condition in an if structure is true, the code in the braces that follow the if statement is executed.

T F 5. The = operator and the == operator are interchangeable.

T F 6. The if/else structure is a two-way selection structure.

T F   7.   Placing if structures within if structures is called stacking if structures.

T F   8.   The operation of a switch structure can be replaced by if/else structures.

T F   9.   The switch structure includes an `else` keyword.

T F   10.   The control expression of a switch structure works only with integers and characters.

WRITTEN QUESTIONS

Write your answers to the following questions.

11.   What are the three selection structures available in C++?

12.   What are sequence structures?

13.   When are the braces in an if structure not necessary?

14.   When is the else portion of an if/else structure executed?

15.   Write an if structure that prints the word *complete* to the screen if the variable named `percent_complete` is equal to 100.

16.   Write an if structure that assigns the value 100 to the variable named `percent_complete` if the character in the variable named `Done` equals *Y*.

17.   Write an if/else structure that prints the word *complete* to the screen if the variable named `percent_complete` is equal to 100, and prints the phrase *not complete* to the screen otherwise.

18.   What structure is often used when working with menus?

19.   What keyword in a switch structure tells the compiler what statements to execute if none of the options match?

20.   What does the `break` keyword in a switch structure do?

PROJECT 9A

Write a program that uses the if/else structure in Code List 9-4 to report whether an integer entered by the user is positive or negative. Save the source code file as **sign.cpp**.

PROJECT 9B

SCANS

Rewrite **final.cpp** so that it begins with the assumption that the student is exempt and makes comparisons to see whether the student must take the test. Save the revised source code as **final2.cpp**.

PROJECT 9C

SCANS

1. Open **lengths.cpp** and analyze the source code.

2. Compile and link the program. *Note*: The program requires the string class.

3. Run the program several times and try different conversions and values.

4. Add a conversion for miles to the program. Use 0.00018939 for the conversion factor.

5. Test the program to ensure that your addition is working properly.

PROJECT 9D

SCANS

1. Obtain the exchange rates for at least three foreign currencies. Currency exchange rates can be found in most newspapers or on the Internet at the Web sites of major banks and financial services companies. You can also call a local bank to obtain the information you need.

2. Write a program similar to **lengths.cpp** that asks the user for an amount of money in dollars and then prompts the user to select the currency into which the dollars are to be converted.

3. Save the program as **currency.cpp**.

CRITICAL THINKING

Write a program that asks for an integer and reports whether the number is even or odd. *Hint*: Use if/else and the modulus operator. Save the source code file as **evenodd.cpp**.

LOOPS

OBJECTIVES

When you complete this lesson, you will be able to:

- Describe the purpose of loops.
- Use for loops.
- Use while loops.
- Use do while loops.
- Use the break and continue statements.
- Nest loops.

⏱ **Estimated Time: 2 hours**

VOCABULARY

do while loop
for loop
infinite loop
iteration
iteration structures
loop
parameters
while loop

Introduction to Loops

You have probably noticed that much of the work a computer does is repeated many times. For example, a computer can print a personalized letter to each person in a database. The basic operation of printing the letter repeats for each person in the database. When a program repeats a group of statements a given number of times, the repetition is accomplished using a *loop*.

In Lesson 9, you learned about sequence structures and selection structures. In this lesson, you will learn about another category of structures: *iteration structures*. Loops are iteration structures. Each loop or pass through a group of statements is called an *iteration*. A condition specified in the program controls the number of iterations performed. For example, a loop may iterate until a specific variable reaches the value 100.

The for Loop

The *for loop* repeats one or more statements a specified number of times. A for loop is difficult to read the first time you see one. Like an if statement, the for loop uses parentheses. In the parentheses are three items called *parameters*, which are needed to make a for loop work. Each parameter in a for loop is an expression. Figure 10-1 shows the format of a for loop.

FIGURE 10-1

A for loop repeats one or more statements a specified number of times.

```
for (initializing expression; control expression; step expression)
   { statements to execute }
```

Look at the program in Code List 10-1. The variable i is used as a counter. The counter variable is used in all three of the for loop's expressions. The first parameter, called the *initializing expression*, initializes the counter variable. The second parameter is the expression that will end the loop, called the *control expression*. As long as the control expression is true, the loop continues to iterate. The third parameter is the step expression. It changes the counter variable, usually by adding to it.

Concept Builder

As with if structures, you are not required to use braces in for loops when there is only one statement in the loop.

CODE LIST 10-1

```cpp
// forloop.cpp

#include <iostream.h>

int main()
{
 int i; // counter variable
 for(i = 1; i <= 3; i++)
     { cout << i << endl; }
 return 0;
}
```

In Code List 10-1, the statements in the for loop will repeat three times. The variable i is declared as an integer. In the for statement, i is initialized to 1. The control expression tests to see if the value of i is still less than or equal to 3. When i exceeds 3, the loop will end. The step expression increments i by 1 each time the loop iterates.

Important

Placing a semicolon after the closing parenthesis of a for loop will prevent any lines from being iterated.

STEP-BY-STEP ▷ **10.1**

1. Key the program from Code List 10-1 into a blank editor screen.

2. Save the source code file as **forloop.cpp**.

3. Compile and run the program. The program counts to 3.

4. Close the source file.

Counting Backward and Other Tricks

A counter variable can also count backward by having the step expression decrement the value rather than increment it. The program in Code List 10-2 counts backward from 10 to 1. The counter is initialized to 10. With each iteration, the decrement operator subtracts 1 from the counter.

CODE LIST 10-2

```
// backward.cpp

#include <iostream.h>

int main()
{
  int i; // counter variable
  for(i = 10; i >= 0; i--)
    { cout << i << endl; }
  cout << "End of loop.\n";
  return 0;
}
```

STEP-BY-STEP ▷ 10.2

1. Enter the program in Code List 10-2 into a blank editor screen.

2. Save the source file as **backward.cpp**.

3. Compile and run the program. Figure 10-2 shows the output you should see.

4. Close the source code file.

FIGURE 10-2
A for loop can decrement the counter variable.

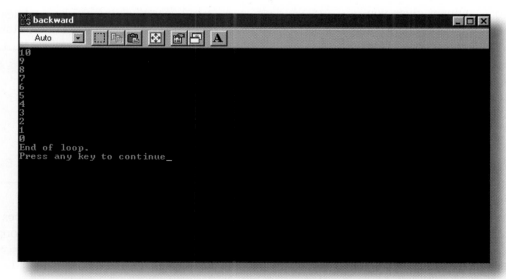

The output prints numbers from 10 to 0 because i is being decremented in the step expression. The phrase "End of loop." is printed only once because the loop ends with the semicolon that follows the first cout statement.

The counter variable can do more than step by 1. In the program in Code List 10-3, the counter variable is doubled each time the loop iterates.

CODE LIST 10-3

```
// dblstep.cpp

#include <iostream.h>

int main()
{
 int i;    // counter variable
 for(i = 1; i <= 100; i = i + i)
    { cout << i << endl; }
 return 0;
}
```

STEP-BY-STEP ▷ 10.3

1. Enter the program from Code List 10-3 into a blank editor screen.

2. Save the source file as **dblstep.cpp**. Can you predict the program's output?

3. Compile and run the program to see whether your prediction was right.

4. Close the program.

The for statement gives you a lot of flexibility. As you have already seen, the step expression can increment, decrement, or count in other ways. Some more examples of for statements are shown in Table 10-1.

Using a Statement Block in a for Loop

If you need to include more than one statement in the loop, place all the statements that are to be part of the loop inside braces. The statements in the braces will be repeated each time the loop iterates. The statements that follow the braces are not part of the loop.

TABLE 10-1
Examples of for statements

for Statement	Count Progression
for (i = 2; i <= 10; i = i + 2)	2, 4, 6, 8, 10
for (i = 1; i < 10; i = i + 2)	1, 3, 5, 7, 9
for (i = 10; i <= 50; i = i + 10)	10, 20, 30, 40, 50

In Code List 10-4, an output statement has been added inside the loop of the **backward.cpp** program. The phrase *Inside Loop* will appear with each iteration of the loop.

```cpp
// backward.cpp

#include <iostream.h>

int main()
{
  int i; // counter variable
  for(i = 10; i >= 0; i--)
  {
      cout << i << endl;
      cout << "Inside Loop\n";
  }
  cout << "End of loop.\n";
  return 0;
}
```

S TEP-BY-STEP ▷ 10.4

1. Open **backward.cpp** and edit the source code to match the Code List 10-4.

2. Compile and run the program to see that the phrase *Inside Loop* prints on every line. The

second cout statement is now part of the loop because it is within the braces.

3. Close the source file without saving changes.

while Loops

A *while loop* is similar to a for loop. Actually, while loops are sometimes easier to use than for loops and are better suited for many loops. With a for loop, the parameters in the parentheses control the number of times the loop iterates, and the statements in the loop structure are just along for the ride. In a while loop, something inside the loop triggers the loop to stop.

For example, a while loop may be written to ask a user to input a series of numbers until the number 0 is entered. The loop would repeat until the number 0 is entered.

There are two kinds of while loops: the standard while loop and the do while loop. The difference between the two is where the control expression is tested. Let us begin with the standard while loop.

The while Loop

The while loop repeats a statement or group of statements as long as a control expression is true. Unlike a for loop, a while loop does not use a counter variable. The control expression in a while loop can be any valid expression. The program in Code List 10-5 uses a while loop to repeatedly divide a number by 2 until the number is less than or equal to 1.

```
// while1.cpp

#include <iostream.h>

int main()
{
 float num;

 cout << "Please enter the number to divide: ";
 cin >> num;
 while (num > 1.0)
   {
    cout << num << endl;
    num = num / 2;
   }
 return 0;
}
```

In a while loop, the control expression is tested before the statements in the loop begin. Figure 10-3 shows a flow chart of the program in Code List 10-5. If the number provided by the user is less than or equal to 1, the statements in the loop are never executed.

 Important

As with the for loop, placing a semicolon after the closing parenthesis of a while loop will prevent any lines from being iterated.

FIGURE 10-3

A while loop tests the control expression before the loop begins.

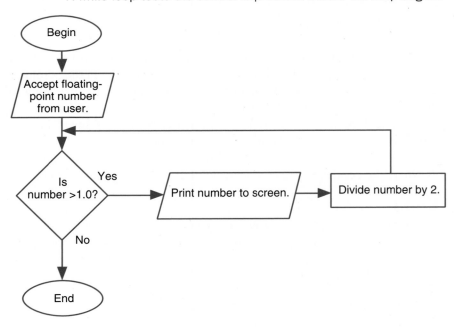

1. Enter the program shown in Code List 10-5 into a blank editor screen.

2. Save the source file as **while1.cpp**.

3. Compile and run the program. Run the program

several times. Try the following numbers as input: 8, 21, 8650, 1, 2.1, 0.5.

4. Close the program.

In order for a while loop to come to an end, the statements in the loop must change a variable used in the control expression. The result of the control expression must be false for a loop to stop. Otherwise, iterations continue indefinitely in what is called an *infinite loop*. In the program you compiled in Step-by-Step 10.5, the statement num = num / 2; divides the number by 2 each time the loop repeats. Even if the user enters a large value, the loop will eventually end when the number becomes less than 1.

A while loop can be used to replace any for loop. So why have a for loop in the language? Because sometimes a for loop offers a better solution. Figure 10-4 shows two programs that produce the same output. The program using the for loop is better in this case because the counter variable is initialized, tested, and incremented in the same statement. In a while loop, a counter variable must be initialized and incremented in separate statements.

FIGURE 10-4

Although both of these programs produce the same output, the for loop gives a more efficient solution.

```
#include <iostream.h>

int main()
{
  int j;
  for(j = 1; j <= 3; j++)
    { cout << j << endl; }
  return 0;
}
```

```
#include <iostream.h>

int main()
{
  int j;
  j = 1;
  while(j <= 3)
    {
      cout << j << endl;
      j++;
    }
  return 0;
}
```

The do while Loop

The last iteration structure in C++ is the *do while loop*. A do while loop repeats a statement or group of statements as long as a control expression is true at the end of the loop. Because the control expression is tested at the end of the loop, a do while loop is executed at least one time. Code List 10-6 shows an example of a do while loop.

```
// dowhile.cpp

#include <iostream.h>

int main()
{
 double num, squared;
 do
  {
    cout << "Enter a number (Enter 0 to quit): ";
    cin >> num;
    squared = num * num;
    cout << num << " squared is " << squared << endl;
  }
 while (num != 0);
 return 0;
}
```

To help illustrate the difference between a while and a do while loop, compare the two flowcharts in Figure 10-5. Use a while loop when you need to test the control expression before the loop is executed the first time. Use a do while loop when the statements in the loop need to be executed at least once.

FIGURE 10-5
The difference between a while loop and a do while loop is where the control expression is tested.

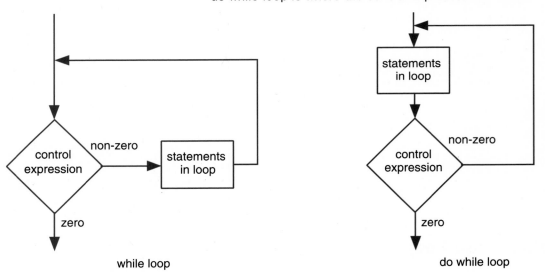

1. Enter the program from Code List 10-6 into a blank editor screen.

2. Save the source file as **dowhile.cpp**.

3. Compile and run the program. Enter several

numbers greater than 0 to cause the loop to repeat. Enter 0 to end the program.

4. Leave the program open for the next Step-by-Step exercise.

Stopping in the Middle of a Loop

The keyword break, also used with switch statements, can be used to end a loop before the conditions of the control expression are met. Once a break terminates a loop, the execution begins with the first statement following the loop. In the program you ran in Step-by-Step 10.6, entering 0 caused the program to end. But the program squares 0 before it ends, even though the step is unnecessary. The program in Code List 10-7 uses a break statement to correct the problem.

CODE LIST 10-7

```
// dowhile.cpp

#include <iostream.h>

int main()
{
 double num, squared;
 do
  {
   cout << "Enter a number (Enter 0 to quit): ";
   cin >> num;
   if (num == 0.0) // Break out of loop if
   { break; }       // number entered is zero.
   squared = num * num;
   cout << num << " squared is " << squared << endl;
  }
while (1); // Create an infinite loop and allow the
          // break statement to end the loop.
 return 0;
}
```

In the program in Code List 10-7, the value entered by the user is tested with an if statement as soon as it is input. If the value is 0, the break statement is executed to end the loop. If the value is any number other than 0, the loop continues.

The while loop's control expression can remain num != 0 without affecting the function of the program. In this case, however, the break statement will stop the loop before the control expression is reached. Therefore, the control expression can be changed to 1 to create an infinite loop. The 1 creates an infinite loop because the loop continues to iterate as long as the control expression is true, which is represented by the value 1. The loop will repeat until the break statement is executed.

S TEP-BY-STEP ▷ 10.7

1. Modify the program on your screen to match Code List 10-7.

2. Save the source file.

3. Compile and run the program. Enter several numbers greater than 0 to cause the loop to repeat. Enter 0 to end the program. Notice that the program now ends without squaring the zero.

4. Close the program.

Concept Builder

You should allow the control expression to end an iteration structure whenever practical. Whenever you are tempted to use a break statement to exit a loop, make sure that using the break statement is the best way to end the loop.

The continue statement is another way to stop a loop from completing each statement. But instead of continuing with the first statement after the loop, the continue statement skips the remainder of a loop and starts the next iteration of the loop. Code List 10-8 shows an example of how the continue statement can be used to cause a for loop to skip an iteration.

CODE LIST 10-8

```
// continue.cpp

#include <iostream.h>

int main()
{
 int i;
 for(i = 1; i <= 10; i++)
  {
    if (i == 5)
    { continue; }
    cout << i << endl;
  }
 return 0;
}
```

The continue statement in Code List 10-8 causes the statements in the for loop to be skipped when the counter variable is 5. The continue statement also can be used in while and do while statements.

1. Open **continue.cpp**. The program shown in Code List 10-8 appears.

2. Compile and run the program. Notice that the

number 5 does not appear in the output because of the continue statement.

3. Close the program.

Nesting Loops

You have already learned how to nest if structures. Loops can also be nested. In fact, loops within loops are very common. You must, however, trace the steps of the program carefully to understand how nested loops behave. The program in Code List 10-9 provides output that will give you insight into the behavior of nested loops.

CODE LIST 10-9

```cpp
// nestloop.cpp

#include <iostream.h>

int main()
{
 int i,j;
 cout << "BEGIN\n";
 for(i = 1; i <= 3; i++)
   {
    cout << " Outer loop: i = " << i << endl;
    for(j = 1; j <= 4; j++)
      { cout << "      Inner loop: j = " << j << endl;}
   }
 cout << "END\n";
 return 0;
}
```

The important thing to realize is that the inner for loop (the one that uses j) will complete its count from 1 to 4 every time the outer for loop (the one that uses i) iterates. That is why in the output, for every loop the outer loop makes, the inner loop starts over.

1. Open **nestloop.cpp**.

2. Compile and run the program.

3. Close the source file.

Hot Tip

If you know how to use your compiler's debugger, step through the program to trace the flow of logic.

Nesting may also be used with while loops and do while loops, or in combinations of loops. In the upcoming Unit Review, you will run a program that nests a do while loop in a for loop.

Summary

- A loop is used to cause a program to repeat a group of statements a given number of times.

- Loops are iteration structures.

- Each loop through a group of statements is called an iteration.

- A for loop repeats one or more statements a specified number of times.

- A for loop uses three parameters to control the loop.

- A for loop can count backward by having the step expression decrement the value rather than increment it. The step expression can also count by values other than 1.

- Braces group the statements in a loop.

- A while loop repeats a statement or group of statements as long as a control expression is true. The control expression is tested at the top of the loop.

- A do while loop repeats a statement or group of statements as long as a control expression is true at the end of the loop.

- The `break` keyword ends a loop before the conditions in the control expression are met.

- The `continue` keyword skips the remainder of the statements in the loop and continues with the next iteration of the loop.

- Loops may be nested to have loops inside loops.

VOCABULARY REVIEW

Define the following terms:

do while loop	iteration structures
for loop	loop
infinite loop	parameters
iteration	while loop

LESSON 10 REVIEW QUESTIONS

TRUE/FALSE

Circle the T if the statement is true. Circle the F if it is false.

T   F   1.   A loop is a sequence structure.

T   F   2.   A for loop repeats a group of statements a specified number of times.

T   F   3.   The items in the parentheses of a for loop are called parameters.

T   F   4.   Counting backward in a for loop is accomplished by the initializing expression.

T   F   5.   In a while loop, the control expression is tested at the end of the loop.

T   F   6.   In order for a while loop to come to a natural end, the statements in the loop must change a variable used in the control expression.

T   F   7.   The statements in a while loop are always executed at least once.

T   F   8.   A do while loop allows the program to do other things while the statements in the loop repeat.

T   F   9.   The `break` keyword ends a loop before the conditions of the control expression are met.

T   F   10.   Only for loops may be nested in programs.

WRITTEN QUESTIONS

Write your answers to the following questions.

11.   What is each "loop" or pass through a group of statements in a loop called?

12.   What are the three expressions in the parentheses of a for loop?

13.   Describe the purpose of the counter variable in a for loop.

14.   What is the count progression of the following for loop?

```
for (j = 5; j <= 40; j = j + 5)
```

15. What is wrong with the following while loop?

```
while (num > 1.0);
  {
   cout << num << endl;
   num = num - 2.0;
  }
```

16. What term describes a loop that loops indefinitely?

17. Explain the difference between a while loop and a do while loop.

18. What is the result of using a control expression of 1 in a do while loop?

19. What effect does the continue statement have on a loop?

20. In the code below, what message will be printed to the screen the most times, "Red" or "Blue"?

```
for(j = 1; j <= 3; j++)
  {
   cout << "Red\n";
   for(k = 1; k <= 3; k++)
    { cout << "Blue\n"; }
  }
```

LESSON 10 PROJECTS

PROJECT 10A

Write a program that uses a for loop to print the odd numbers from 1 to 21. Save the source code file as **oddloop.cpp**.

PROJECT 10B

Write a program that implements the flowchart in Figure 10-6. Save the source code file as **sumitup.cpp**.

FIGURE 10-6

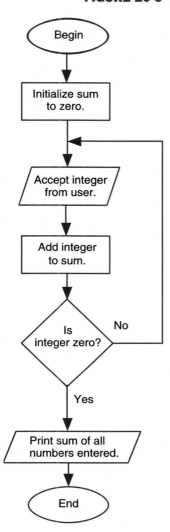

PROJECT 10C

Write a program that prints the numbers 1 to 20, but skips the numbers 3, 11, and 16. Save the source code file as **skipthem.cpp**.

CRITICAL THINKING

ACTIVITY 10A

Write a program that uses nested loops to produce the following output. Save the source code file as **abbb.cpp**.

A1B1B2B3A2B1B2B3

ACTIVITY 10B

W rite a program that asks the user for a series of integers one at a time. When the user enters the integer 0, the program displays the following information:

■   the number of integers in the series (not including zero)

■   the average of the integers

■   the largest integer in the series

■   the smallest integer in the series

■   the difference between the largest and smallest integer in the series

Save the source file as **ints.cpp**.

7. Complete the switch structure below. Add a case that prints the message "The character entered was C, as in cow." when C is entered. Also enter a default case that prints the message "Illegal entry" if no other case applies.

```
switch(character_entered)
  {
  case 'A':
    cout << "The character entered was A, as in albatross.\n";
    break;
  case 'B':
    cout << "The character entered was B, as in butterfly.\n";
    break;
```

8. Write a for loop that produces the count progression 4, 8, 12, 16, 20. The counter should be printed to the screen on each iteration.

9. Write a while loop that repeats a number of statements until a counter variable becomes less than 10. The counter variable should be initialized before the loop as 100. Each iteration of the loop should divide the counter by 3 and then print the value of the counter variable.

10. Write a do while loop that asks the user to enter a number in the range of 1 to 10. The loop should cause the prompt to repeat if the user enters an invalid number. When a valid number is entered, the loop should exit.

APPLICATION 4-2

Write a program that determines your weight on another planet. The program should ask for the user's weight on Earth, then present a menu of the other planets in our solar system. The user should choose one of the planets from the menu and use a switch statement to calculate the weight on the chosen planet. Use the following conversion factors for the other planets. Save the program as **planets.cpp**.

Planet	Multiply by	Planet	Multiply by
Mercury	0.37	Saturn	1.15
Venus	0.88	Uranus	1.15
Mars	0.38	Neptune	1.12
Jupiter	2.64	Pluto	0.04

APPLICATION 4-3

Modify the **planets.cpp** program from Application 4-2 to ask for the user's weight once and then repeatedly ask the user to choose a planet for which to calculate the weight until the user enters a menu selection directing the program to exit.

APPLICATION 4-4

In Lesson 10, you added a break statement to the do while loop in the program named **dowhile.cpp** to cause the loop to end if the user entered 0. Modify that program to use an if structure instead of the break keyword. The program should use an if structure to test the value of num. The statements that square num and print the output should execute only if num is not 0. Save the new version of this program as **ifskip.cpp**.

APPLICATION 4-5

Write a program that asks the user to think of a number between 1 and 100, and then attempts to guess the number. The program should make an initial guess of 50. The program should then ask the user whether 50 is the number the user has in mind, or if 50 is too high or too low. Based on the response given by the user, the program should make another guess. Your program must continue to guess until the correct number is reached. The program should report the number of guesses it made in order to guess the number. Save the source file as **hi-lo.cpp**.

INTERNET ACTIVITY

1. Open **reps.cpp**.

2. Study the program carefully before you run it. The program asks the user for the number of U.S. Representatives in his or her state. A for loop is used to ask the user to identify the political party of each representative. The do while loop is used to repeat the prompt if the user enters an invalid party choice.

3. Compile and run the program. Enter some invalid data to cause the nested loop to iterate. If you have trouble understanding the program, study the source code and run it again.

4. Open your Web browser and go to **http://www.programcpp.com/basics**.

5. On the home page, click the link called **Internet Activities from the book** and then go to the **Unit 4** link.

6. On that page, you will find a link to a Web page that will allow you to search for your state's U.S. Representatives. Gather the information for your state.

7. Run the program again, using the actual data for your state.

8. Modify the program to calculate the percentage of your state's representatives who belong to each party.

9. Run and test the program with the data from your state.

10. Save and close the program.

FUNCTIONS

11 BUILDING PROGRAMS WITH FUNCTIONS

OBJECTIVES

When you complete this lesson, you will be able to:

- Build structured programs that are divided into functions.

- Describe the flow of execution in a program with multiple functions.

- Describe what is meant by the phrase "scope of variable."

⏱ **Estimated Time: 1 hour**

VOCABULARY

automatic variables
bottom-up design
external variables
global variable
local variable
prototype
scope
top-down design

How to Build Programs with Functions

Examine the source code in Code List 11-1. The program consists of one function, `main()`. You may have difficulty, however, quickly determining what the program accomplishes.

CODE LIST 11-1

```cpp
// series.cpp

#include <iostream.h>

int main()
{
 int choice;  // variable for user input
 int i;       // variable for loops and output

 do  // loop until a valid choice is entered
  {
    cout << "Which series do you wish to display?\n";
    cout << "1 - Odd numbers from 1 to 30\n";
    cout << "2 - Even numbers from 1 to 30\n";
    cout << "3 - All numbers from 1 to 30\n";
    cin >> choice;  // get choice from user
```

```
  if ((choice < 1) || (choice > 3))  // if invalid entry, give message
   {
    cout << "Choice must be 1, 2, or 3\n";
   }
} while ((choice < 1) || (choice > 3));

switch (choice)
   {
    case 1:
      for (i = 1; i <= 30; i = i + 2)
      cout << i << ' ';
      cout << endl;
      break;
    case 2:
      for (i = 2; i <= 30; i = i + 2)
      cout << i << ' ;';
      cout << endl;
      break;
    case 3:
      for (i = 1; i <= 30; i++)
      cout << i << ' ';
      cout << endl;
      break;
   }
  return 0;
}
```

When the program is run, the user is prompted from a menu to choose to view a series of numbers. Depending on the user's choice, the program displays a series of odd numbers, even numbers, or all integers from 1 to 30.

Let us run the program to see its output.

S TEP-BY-STEP ▷ 11.1

1. Retrieve the source file **series.cpp**.

2. Compile and run the program to see the program's output.

3. Close the source code file.

The program you just executed could have been better built using more than one function. The diagram in Figure 11-1, known as a Visual Table of Contents (VTOC), illustrates the point. The lines represent connections between functions. Each function can be accessed by the function above it as long as a line connects them.

FIGURE 11-1
A diagram that shows the functions of a program is
sometimes called a Visual Table of Contents.

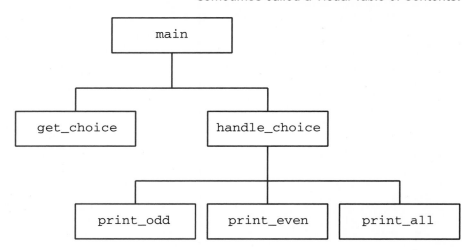

In this case, the `main` function "calls" the `get_choice` function to ask the user to choose the series to display. Next, the `handle_choice` function is called to direct the program flow to one of the three functions under it—one for each series. The source code for Figure 11-1 is presented in the next lesson.

Guidelines for Building a Program with Functions

Using functions helps the programmer develop programs that can be easily coded, debugged, and maintained. Keep the following guidelines in mind when building programs of more than one function.

1. **Organization**. A large program is easier to read and modify if it is logically organized into functions. It is easier to work with a program in parts, rather than one large chunk. A well-organized program, consisting of multiple functions, is easier to read and debug. Once a single function is tested and performs properly, you can set it aside and concentrate on problem areas.

2. **Autonomy**. Programs should be designed so that they consist mainly of stand-alone functions or modules. Each function is autonomous, meaning the function does not depend on data or code outside the function any more than necessary.

3. **Encapsulation**. The term *encapsulation* refers to enclosing the details of a function within the function itself, so that those details do not have to be known in order to use the function.

4. **Reusability**. Because functions typically perform a single and well-defined task, they may be reused in the same program or even in other programs.

Functions may be written for any purpose. For example, you could create a function that converts Fahrenheit temperatures to Celsius or a function that gets input from the user. A function can also be a go-between for other parts of the program, as illustrated in the `handle_choice` function of Figure 11-1.

There are two popular methods of designing programs. The first method, called ***top-down design***, begins with the functions at the top of the VTOC and works toward the functions at the bottom of the VTOC. In other words, the general organization and flow of the program is decided before the details are coded.

Bottom-up design involves beginning with the bottom of the VTOC and working your way up. Some programmers prefer to work out the details of how the program will perform specific tasks and then bring the details together to create the overall organization and flow.

Whether you use top-down or bottom-up design, it is important to take an organized approach to writing a multifunction program.

The Syntax of Functions

With each program you have written, you have created a main function. You can use a similar syntax to create other functions. But before we look at other functions, let us take another look at the main function. The main function in the programs shown in this book have looked like the one in Code List 11-2.

CODE LIST 11-2

```
int main()
{
 // body of program
 return 0;
}
```

When the program reaches the return 0; statement, the value 0 is returned to the operating system. This value tells the operating system that the program ended normally. The value returned is a standard integer because we specified an int data type when the main function was declared.

There are times when a function has no reason to return a value. To prevent a value from being returned, the void keyword is used in place of a data type. You may have seen programs with a main function like the one in Code List 11-3.

CODE LIST 11-3

```
void main()
{
 // body of program
}
```

In a void function, no value is returned; therefore, no return statement is included. Newer operating systems are more likely to take advantage of the value returned by the main function. Therefore, you should get into the habit of creating main functions that return a zero when they terminate normally. The void main functions are used less frequently now than in the past.

As mentioned earlier, creating other functions in C++ programs is similar to creating the main function. Code List 11-4 shows a simple function that prints a message to the screen.

CODE LIST 11-4

```
void print_title()
 {
  cout << "Soccer Tournament Scheduler Program\n";
  cout << "By Ben and Conrad McCue\n";
 }
```

The name of the function is `print_title`. The `void` keyword indicates that no value is returned. The parentheses after the name let the compiler know that `print_title` is a function. The statements between the braces are executed when the function `print_title` is "called." The `main` function in Code List 11-5 includes an example of a call to the `print_title` function.

CODE LIST 11-5

```
int main()
 {
  print_title(); // call to print_title

  // insert the rest of the program here

  return 0;
 }
```

Function Prototypes

There is one more thing you have to do to make your own functions work. At the top of your program, you must tell the compiler that your function exists. You do this by creating a *prototype*. Basically, a prototype defines the function for the compiler. Code List 11-6 shows the functions from Code Lists 11-4 and 11-5 assembled into a working program, including the required function prototype.

CODE LIST 11-6

```
// 1stfunct.cpp

#include <iostream.h>

void print_title();  // prototype for print_title function

int main()
{
  print_title(); // call to print_title

  // insert the rest of the program here

  return 0;
} // end of main function

  // function to print program title to the screen
  void print_title()
  {
    cout << "Soccer Tournament Scheduler Program\n";
    cout << "By Ben and Conrad McCue\n";
  } // end of print_title
```

The function prototype is identical to the first line of the function itself. There is, however, a semicolon at the end of the prototype.

To understand why a function prototype is necessary, consider the way a compiler works. A program is compiled one line at a time. As the compiler works its way down the program, it interprets the source code it reads and compiles that source code into machine code. The function prototypes at the top of the program inform the compiler that later in the source code it will find references to a custom-made function.

For example, in Code List 11-6, the function prototype for `print_title` tells the compiler to be expecting a call to a function named `print_title`. It also tells the compiler important information such as the fact that `print_title` is a void function. With this information, the compiler will know whether `print_title` is being called correctly. The compiler is content to wait for the bottom of the program before learning what the `print_title` function actually does.

Concept Builder

The compiler itself does not care whether it finds an actual function to match the prototype at the top of the program. It is the linker's job to link all the pieces together and find the functions referred to in a prototype. Often, a function prototype exists in C++ source code and the actual function is in another file or in a precompiled library. For example, when you include iostream.h in your programs, you are basically including function prototypes for the iostream features. The linker takes care of linking your program to those actual functions.

S TEP-BY-STEP ▷ 11.2

1. Carefully enter the program in Code List 11-6 into a blank editor screen. Save the program as **1stfunct.cpp**.

2. Compile, link, and run the program. The `main`

function calls the `print_title` function and prints the message to the screen.

3. Leave the program open for the next Step-by-Step exercise.

Functions and Program Flow

In Step-by-Step 11.1, the `main` function began executing when the program was run. The first statement in the `main` function called the `print_title` function. The call caused execution to jump to the `print_title` function. When a function is called, the computer executes the statements in the function beginning with the first statement. When the end of the function is reached, program execution resumes with the statement that follows the call to the function.

Suppose you are washing a car and you hear the phone ring. You leave the car for a moment and answer the phone. When you complete the phone call, you return to the car and begin washing where you left off. That is basically how the flow of a program works. Programs execute one statement at a time. Functions are just another way of controlling the flow of a program to make the program more efficient and better organized.

Figure 11-2 shows the sequence of execution in a simple three-function example.

FIGURE 11-2
The numbers next to the statements show the order of execution.

```
  int main()
  {  ◄─────────────────────────────     Program
①  print_title(); // call to print_title     Begins

     // insert the rest of the program here

④  print_goodbye();

     return 0;
⑥ } // end of main function  ◄──────     Program
                                          Ends


  // Function to print program title to the screen.
  void print_title()
  {
②    cout << "Soccer Tournament Scheduler Program\n";
③    cout << "By Ben and Conrad McCue\n";
  } // end of print_title


  // Function to print closing message
  void print_goodbye()
  {
⑤    cout << "Thank you for using the Soccer Tournament Scheduler.\n";
  } // end of print_goodbye
```

The program begins with the first statement of the main function (1), which is a call to the `print_title` function. The flow of logic goes to the `print_title` function, which includes two statements (2 and 3), and they are executed next. When the last statement (3) in the `print_title` function is executed, the flow of logic returns to the statement (4) that follows the previous function call in `main()`. The statement in the `print_goodbye` function (5) is then executed. The flow of logic then returns to `main()`, where the program ends (6).

Hot Tip

Notice that a function's prototype is just like the first line of the function, except for the semicolon. An error will result if you forget to include the semicolon at the end of a prototype.

CODE LIST 11-7

```
// 1stfunct.cpp

#include <iostream.h>

void print_title();    // prototype for print_title function
void print_goodbye(); // prototype for print_goodbye function
```

```
int main()
{
 print_title(); // call to print_title

 // insert the rest of the program here

 print_goodbye();

 return 0;
} // end of main function


// function to print program title to the screen
 void print_title()
 {
    cout << "Soccer Tournament Scheduler Program\n";
    cout << "By Ben and Conrad McCue\n";
 } // end of print_title


// function to print closing message
 void print_goodbye()
 {
    cout << "Thank you for using the Soccer Tournament Scheduler.\n";
 } // end of print_goodbye
```

STEP-BY-STEP ▷ 11.3

1. Modify **1stfunct.cpp** to match the program shown in Code List 11-7. Don't forget to add the new function prototype.

2. Compile, link, and run the program.

3. When you have run the program successfully, close the program.

Scope of Variables

When building a program that consists of functions, you must be concerned with how data is made available to the functions. In this section, you will learn about the accessibility of variables in functions and how to get data to and from functions.

As programs get larger, it is important to keep tight control over variables to prevent errors in your programs. One of the ways to do this is to make the data in variables accessible only in the areas where that data is needed. When data is needed in another part of the program, it is better to send that data and that data only to the part of the program that needs it.

You have been working primarily with programs that have only one function: main(). Within main(), you declared variables. These variables, however, would be inaccessible outside of main(). The "availability" of a variable is known as its *scope*. While this may sound difficult, in C++ the scope of variables is easy to understand.

171

Variables in C++ can either be local or global. A ***local variable*** is declared within a function and is accessible only within that function. A ***global variable*** is declared before the main function. Global variables are accessible by any function.

Consider the program in Code List 11-8. One variable (i) is declared before the main function, making it a global variable. Because j and k are declared in the main function, they are local to the main function. Therefore, j and k cannot be used outside of the main function. Within the function named myfunction, the variable l is declared. It too is local and accessible only within myfunction. After the last statement in myfunction is executed, the variable l is gone from memory.

CODE LIST 11-8

```
// scope.cpp

#include <iostream.h>

int i = 3;      // global variable

void myfunction();

int main()
 {
   int j,k; // variables local to the main function
           // j and k are not accessible outside of the main function
   j = 2;
   k = i + j;
   cout << "j = " << j << " and k = " << k << '\n';
   cout << "i = " << i << " before the call to myfunction.\n";
   myfunction(); // call to myfunction
   cout << "i = " << i << " after the call to myfunction.\n";
   return 0;
 }

void myfunction()
 {
   int l;    // local variable
   l = ++i; // the variable i is accessible because i is global
           // the variable i is changed globally
   cout << "l = " << l << '\n';
   cout << "The variable l is lost as soon as myfunction exits.\n";
 }
```

Because the variable i is accessible from the entire program, changes made to i while in myfunction will be made to the global variable. Therefore, those changes will still be in effect when the program returns to the main function.

If a statement were added to `myfunction` that attempted to access the variable `k`, located in `main`, an error would result. The variable `k` is accessible only from within the `main` function. In a similar manner, the variable `l` is inaccessible outside of `myfunction` because it is local to `myfunction`.

STEP-BY-STEP ▷ 11.4

1. Open **scope.cpp**. The program from Code List 11-8 appears on your screen.

2. Compile and run the program as it appears. Study the source code to get clear in your mind where each variable is available.

3. Enter the following statement at the end of `myfunction`.

   ```
   k = i + j;
   ```

4. Compile the program to see the errors the new statement generates. Your compiler wiill probably generate an error telling you that the variables `j` and `k` are not defined. The error is generated because `j` and `k` are available only in the main function.

5. Delete the erring statement and close the program.

Why have local variables if they are inaccessible to other parts of the program? One reason is that they exist only while the function is executing and memory is released when the function terminates. If a variable is needed only within a particular function, you save memory by creating and disposing of the variable within the function.

Using local variables could limit the number of errors that occur in a program. If all variables were global, an error made in a variable and used by various functions could cause multiple errors. However, if you use local variables, any errors are limited to the function in which the variable is declared.

Use local variables whenever possible. Even a large program should have very few global variables. Using local variables keeps a tighter control over your program's data, resulting in fewer bugs and programs that are easier to maintain.

You may be wondering how data can get to other functions if everything is local. As you will learn in the next lesson, when a function is created, you can choose what data you want to send to the function.

Summary

■ Designing a program that consists of functions results in code that is better organized, reusable, and easier to debug.

■ The syntax of functions you create is very similar to that of the `main` function. The parentheses after the function name tell the compiler that you are defining a function.

■ You must create a prototype for your functions to let the compiler know your function exists. Prototypes are placed at the top of the program.

■ A local variable is created within a function and is accessible only from within that function. A global variable is declared outside of all functions and is accessible from any function.

Define the following terms:

automatic variables   local variable

bottom-up design   prototype

external variables   scope

global variable   top-down design

TRUE/FALSE

Circle the T if the statement is true. Circle the F if it is false.

T F   1.   When a program jumps from one function to another, we say that the first function *called* the second.

T F   2.   Dividing a program into functions can improve the organization of a program.

T F   3.   A drawback to dividing a program into functions is that it makes it more difficult to debug.

T F   4.   Encapsulation refers to protecting programs from being copied.

T F   5.   In a top-down design, the `main` function is written first.

T F   6.   When the end of a function is reached, the next statement to be executed is the first statement of the `main` function.

T F   7.   A prototype of a function tells the compiler that your function exists.

T F   8.   The scope of a variable refers to the way the variable is passed to another function.

T F   9.   A local variable is sometimes called an automatic variable.

T F 10.   A variable that is available anywhere in your program is called a global variable.

WRITTEN QUESTIONS

Write your answers to the following questions.

11.   What is an advantage of dividing a program into multiple functions?

12. What is the name of the diagram that shows the functions that make up a program?

13. What are two guidelines that you can use to decide what code is a good candidate for being made into a function?

14. Briefly describe top-down and bottom-up design.

15. Why is a `return` statement unnecessary in a void function?

16. Suppose a program includes a function with the prototype shown below. What is the line of code necessary to call the function?

```
void print_message();
```

17. What is meant by the scope of a variable?

18. What is one advantage to using local variables?

19. Where must a variable be declared in order for it to be local?

20. Where must a variable be declared in order for it to be global?

LESSON 11 PROJECTS

PROJECT 11A

1. Open **gascheck.cpp**. An incomplete program appears. To complete the program, you will add two functions and an if structure that calls the new functions.

2. Add a void function called `print_warning` that warns the program has calculated that the user will run out of gas before the next available gas station. Do not forget to add the necessary function prototype.

3. Add a void function called `print_okay` that tells the user he or she will make it to the next gas station. Do not forget to add the necessary function prototype.

4. Add an if/else structure to the `main` function that calls `print_warning` if `fuel_miles` is less than `miles_remaining`. Otherwise, `print_okay` should be called.

5. Save and run the program.

6. Close the program.

PROJECT 11B

Write a program that asks the user for an integer. The program should call one of three functions, based on the value entered. If the value is negative, call a function that prints a message indicating the value is negative. Create similar functions to call when the value is 0 and positive. Save the source code as **valtest.cpp**.

PROJECT 11C

Write a program source code template that you can use as a starting point for programs you create in the future. Include comments at the top that give your name and provide places for you to fill in the date and description of the program. Set aside a place for `#include` directives, prototypes, constants, and global variables. Create an empty `main` function. Save the source code file as **newprog.cpp** and close the file.

CRITICAL THINKING

Write a program that meets the following requirements. Save the program as **scopex.cpp**. The program should:

1. Declare a global integer variable named x and initialize it to zero.

2. Declare a local integer variable within `main` named y.

3. From within `main`, prompt the user for a value for y.

4. Include a loop that calls a function named incx y number of times.

5. Include the function incx to increment the value of x by 1.

6. Print the value of x after each iteration of the loop.

PASSING DATA AND USING LIBRARY FUNCTIONS

OBJECTIVES

When you complete this lesson, you will be able to:

- Pass data to functions.

- Get values from functions using `return`.

- Describe and use library functions.

- Use common math functions.

- Use character manipulation functions.

⏱ **Estimated Time: 1 hour**

VOCABULARY

argument
header file
library functions
parameter
pass
passing by reference
passing by value

Getting Data to and from Functions

You have learned that the parentheses following a function's name let the compiler know that it is a function. The parentheses can serve another purpose as well. That is, parentheses can be used to *pass* data to a function and in some cases to return data from a function.

When a function is called, the data in the parentheses (called the *argument*) is passed into the receiving function. There are two ways to pass data to functions: *passing by value* and *passing by reference*.

Concept Builder

Getting data to and from functions is called *passing data*. Programmers talk about passing data to a function and the function passing a value back.

Passing by Value

When you pass a variable to a function by value, a copy of the value in the variable is given to the function for it to use. If the variable is changed within the function, the original copy of the variable in the calling function remains the same. Code List 12-1 is an example of a function that accepts data using the passing by value technique.

```
void print_true_or_false(bool True_False)
{
  if True_False          // If True_False is true,
   {                     // display the word TRUE.
    cout << "TRUE\n";
   }
  else                   // If True_False is false,
   {                     // display the word FALSE.
    cout << "FALSE\n";
   }
}
```

A value comes into the function through the parentheses, and the copy of the value will be placed in the variable `True_False`. The variable `True_False` is called a ***parameter***.

When you write a call to a function, you can put any variable or literal in the parentheses to be passed to the function as long as the data types do not conflict. For example, the statements in Code List 12-2 are all legal calls to the `print_true_or_false` function.

In Code List 12-2, as long as the variable named `complete` is a Boolean variable, the first line is legal. The second line is legal because `true` is actually a Boolean literal. The third line is legal because the expression in the parentheses evaluates to a Boolean value.

 Did You Know?

Many people use the terms *argument* and *parameter* interchangeably, but there is a difference. An argument is a value or expression passed to a function through the parentheses when a function is called. A parameter is the variable that receives the value or any other identifier in the parentheses of the function declaration. In other words, an argument is passed to a function, but once in the function, the argument is a parameter.

```
print_true_or_false(complete);        // passes a variable
print_true_or_false(true);            // passes a literal
print_true_or_false(j == 3 && k == 2); // passes the result
                                      // of an expression
```

The program in Code List 12-3 illustrates how a value passed to the function named `print_value` does not pass back to the `main` function. Notice that the `print_value` function uses a variable named `j`, even though the `main` function passes a variable named `i`. The data types must match, but the names are often different.

```
// passval.cpp

#include <iostream.h>

void print_value(int j);   // function prototype

int main()
 {
  int i = 2;
  cout << "The value before the function is " << i << endl;
  print_value(i);
  cout << "The value after the function exits is " << i << endl;
  return 0;
 }

void print_value(int j)
 {
  cout << "The value passed to the function is " << j << endl;
  j = j * 2; // the value in the variable i is doubled
  cout << "The value at the end of the function is " << j << endl;
 }
```

STEP-BY-STEP ▷ 12.1

1. Enter the program shown in Code List 12-3. Save the source code as **passval.cpp**.

2. Compile and run the program to see that the value passed to the `print_value` function is not passed back to the `main` function.

3. Leave the source code file open for the next Step-by-Step exercise.

Passing by Reference

Functions that pass variables by reference will pass any changes you make to the variables back to the calling function. For example, suppose you need a function that gets input from the user. The function in Code List 12-4 uses passing by reference to get two values from the user and pass them back through parentheses.

```
void get_values(float &income, float &expense)
 {
  cout << "Enter this month's income amount: $";
  cin >> income;
  cout << "Enter this month's expense amount: $";
  cin >> expense;
 }
```

To pass a variable by reference, simply precede the variable name with an ampersand (&) in the function definition. But even though it is easy to pass by reference, you should do so sparingly. You should write functions that pass variables by value whenever possible because passing variables by value is safer. When you pass a variable by value, you know it cannot be changed by the function you call. When you pass a variable by reference, a programming error in the function could cause a problem throughout the program.

As a general rule, you should use passing by reference only when data needs to be passed back to the calling function. In the preceding example, the data entered by the user must be passed back to the calling function.

The program you ran in Step-by-Step 12.1 passed a variable by value. Let us modify the program to make it pass the variable by reference.

STEP-BY-STEP ▷ 12.2

1. Add an ampersand (&) before the identifier j in both the prototype and the function declaration. Save the source code as **passref.cpp**.

2. Compile and run the program again to see the difference passing by reference makes.

3. Close the source code file.

Returning Values Using `return`

As you learned earlier in this lesson, unless a function is declared with the keyword `void`, the function will return a value. In the case of the `main` function, it returns a value to the operating system. Other functions, however, return a value to the calling function. The value to be returned is specified using the `return` statement.

The function in Code List 12-5 is an example of a function that returns a value of type double. The temperature in Celsius is passed into the function by value and the temperature in Fahrenheit is returned using the `return` statement.

CODE LIST 12-5

```
double celsius_to_fahrenheit(double celsius)
 {
  double fahr;  // local variable for calculation
  fahr = celsius * (9.0/5.0) + 32.0;
  return(fahr);
 }
```

Any function that is not declared as void should include a `return` statement. The value or expression in the `return` statement is returned to the calling function. In the `celsius_to_fahrenheit` function, the value stored in `fahr` is returned to the calling function.

The program in Code List 12-6 shows how you can use this function. The statement `fahrenheit = celsius_to_fahrenheit(celsius);` calls the `celsius_to_fahrenheit` function and passes the value in the variable `celsius` to the function. The function returns the temperature in Fahrenheit degrees, and the calling statement assigns the Fahrenheit temperature to the variable `fahrenheit`.

CODE LIST 12-6

```
// ctof.cpp

#include <iostream.h>

int main()
 {
  double fahrenheit;
  double celsius = 22.5;

  fahrenheit = celsius_to_fahrenheit(celsius);

  cout << celsius << " C = " << fahrenheit << " F\n";
  return 0;
 }
```

The `celsius_to_fahrenheit` function could be rewritten as shown in Code List 12-7 to include only one statement and return the same result. Any valid expression can appear in the parentheses of the `return` statement. In this case, performing the calculation in the `return` statement eliminates the local variable `fahr`.

Concept Builder

You can use any data type when declaring a function.

CODE LIST 12-7

```
double celsius_to_fahrenheit(double celsius)
 {
  return(celsius * (9.0/5.0) + 32.0);
 }
```

When using the `return` statement, keep the following important points in mind.

1. The `return` statement does not require that the value being returned be placed in parentheses. You may, however, want to get into the habit of placing variables and expressions in parentheses to make the code more readable.

2. A function can return only one value using `return`. Use passing by reference to return multiple values from a function.

3. When a `return` statement is encountered, the function will exit and return the value specified, even if other program lines exist below the `return`.

4. A function can have more than one `return` statement to help simplify an algorithm. For example, a `return` statement could be in an if structure allowing a function to return early if a certain condition is met.

5. The calling function is not required to use or even to capture the value returned from a function it calls.

STEP-BY-STEP ▷ 12.3

1. Open **ctof.cpp**. The complete Celsius to Fahrenheit program appears.

2. Compile, link, and run the program.

3. Leave the program open for the next Step-by-Step exercise.

One additional important note: When the last line of a function is reached, or when a `return()` statement is executed, the function ends and the program returns to the calling function and begins executing statements from where it left off. Do not end functions with a call back to the original function or the function will not terminate properly. Continually calling functions without returning from them will eventually cause the program to crash.

If you call the `main` function at the end of a function you wrote, the `main` function will begin with the first statement, rather than beginning with the statement following the call to your function.

More about Function Prototypes

A function prototype consists of the function's return type, name, and argument list. In this lesson, the function prototypes specified the parameter names in the argument list. However, this is not necessary as long as the type is specified. For example, the prototype for the `celsius_to_fahrenheit` function could be written as:

```
double celsius_to_fahrenheit(double);
```

The prototype for the `get_values` function could be written as:

```
void get_values(float &, float &);
```

STEP-BY-STEP ▷ 12.4

1. Change the function prototype in **ctof.cpp** to specify the data type only, as shown in the examples above.

2. Compile, link, and run the program. The program still functions normally. After you have seen it work, close the program.

Dividing the Series Program into Functions

Now that you have practiced creating functions and moving data to and from them, let us take another look at the program from Step-by-Step 11.1. In Lesson 11, you studied a VTOC of the program divided into functions. That VTOC appears again in Figure 12-1.

FIGURE 12-1
This Visual Table of Contents shows the
series program divided into functions.

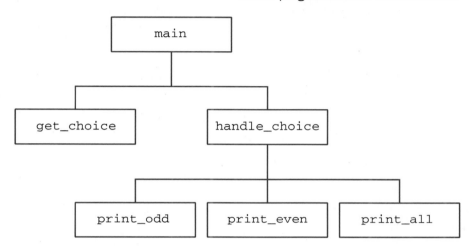

STEP-BY-STEP ▷ 12.5

1. Retrieve the source code file **series2.cpp**. Analyze the source code to see that the program is divided into functions.

2. Compile and run the program to see that it has the same result as the single-function version you ran in Step-by-Step 11.1.

3. Close the program.

Using Library Functions

C++ compilers include prewritten, ready-to-use functions to make programming easier. The number and type of functions available to you will vary depending on your compiler. The functions that come with your compiler are called *library functions*. This section shows you how to use some of the more common library functions.

Library functions are just like functions you create and may be used in the same way. The difference is that the source code for library functions does not appear in your program. The prototypes for library functions are provided to your program using the #include compiler directive.

Let us examine a common C++ library function, `pow()`, which is used to raise a value (x) by a designated power (y). The `pow()` function prototype is shown below.

```
double pow(double x, double y);
```

The function `pow` receives two values or expressions of type double and returns the result as a double. Below is an example of a call to the `pow` function.

```
z = pow(x, y); // z equals x raised to the y power
```

In order to use the `pow` function, you must include the math.h header file using the compiler directive below. A ***header file*** is a text file that provides the prototypes of a group of library functions. The linker uses the information in the header file to properly link your program with the function you want to use.

```
#include <math.h>
```

The program in Code List 12-8 is a simple example of the use of the `pow` function.

CODE LIST 12-8

```cpp
// power.cpp

#include <iostream.h>
#include <math.h>

int main()
  {
    double base;
    double exponent;
    double answer;

    cout << "Enter the base: ";      // prompt user for base
    cin >> base;
    cout << "Enter the exponent: "; // prompt user for exponent
    cin >> exponent;

    answer = pow(base, exponent);    // calculate answer

    cout << "The answer is " << answer << endl;

    return 0;
  }
```

STEP-BY-STEP ▷ 12.6

1. Enter the program in Code List 12-8 into a blank editor screen. Save the program as **power.cpp**.

2. Compile, run, and test your program.

3. Close the program.

Popular Math Functions

Many C++ compilers provide basic math functions, such as the one you used to calculate x^y. Table 12-1 describes some basic math functions and shows their prototypes and their purpose.

Note

All the functions in Table 12-1 require that math.h be included in the calling program.

TABLE 12-1
Basic math functions

Function	Prototype	Description
abs	int abs(int x);	Returns the absolute value of an integer
labs	long int labs(long int x);	Returns the absolute value of a long integer
fabs	double fabs(double x);	Returns the absolute value of a floating-point number
ceil	double ceil(double x);	Rounds up to a whole number
floor	double floor(double x);	Rounds down to a whole number
hypot	double hypot(double a, double b);	Calculates the hypotenuse (c) of a right triangle, where $c^2 = a^2 + b^2$
pow	double pow(double x, double y);	Calculates x to the power of y
pow10	double pow10(int x);	Calculates 10 to the power of x
sqrt	double sqrt(double x);	Calculates the positive square root of x

STEP-BY-STEP ▷ 12.7

1. Open **math.cpp** and analyze the source code to see the usage of the `ceil` and `floor` functions.

2. Compile and run the program. Be sure to enter a value with a fractional part, such as 2.4.

3. Add the line shown in Code List 12-9 to the program, below the other output statements.

4. Save, compile and run the program again. Run the program several times, entering both positive and negative numbers.

5. Close the program.

CODE LIST 12-9

```
cout << "The absolute value of " << x << " is " << fabs(x) << endl;
```

185

Functions for Working with Characters

C++ compilers also include many functions for analyzing and changing characters. The header file ctype.h must be included for a calling program to use the functions listed in Table 12-2. The conditional functions in the table return a nonzero integer if the condition is true and zero if the condition is false.

In addition to the math functions covered in this lesson, C++ compilers also include many trigonometric and logarithmic library functions. The Web site at http://www.programcpp.com/basics includes a C++ language reference that lists some of these functions.

TABLE 12-2
Character functions

Function	Prototype	Description
isupper	int isupper(int c);	Determines if a character is uppercase
islower	int islower(int c);	Determines if a character is lowercase
isalpha	int isalpha(int c);	Determines if a character is a letter (a–z, A–Z)
isdigit	int isdigit(int c);	Determines if a character is a digit (0–9)
toupper	int toupper(int c);	Converts a character to uppercase
tolower	int tolower(int c);	Converts a character to lowercase

The program in Code List 12-10 demonstrates the use of the isalpha, isupper, and isdigit functions. The program asks for a character and then reports to the user whether the character is uppercase or lowercase. If the user enters a numeral, the program detects and reports that as well. Finally, the program detects and reports if the character is neither a letter nor a number.

CODE LIST 12-10

```
// charfun.cpp

#include <iostream.h>
#include <ctype.h>

int main()
{
   char c;
```

```
cout <<"Enter a character\n";
cin >> c;

if(isalpha(c))
  {
   if(isupper(c))
      { cout << c <<" is an uppercase letter\n";}
   else
      { cout << c <<" is a lowercase letter\n";}
  }

if(isdigit(c))
  { cout << c <<" is a number\n";}

if(!(isdigit(c)||isalpha(c)))
  {cout << c <<" is neither a letter nor a number\n";}

return 0;
}
```

S TEP-BY-STEP ▷ 12.8

1. Open **charfun.cpp**. The program in Code List 12-10 appears, without the three if structures.

2. Enter the missing if structures using Code List 12-10 as a reference.

3. Save, compile, and run the program. Run it several times, trying uppercase and lowercase letters, numbers, and symbols.

4. Close the program.

Summary

■ Getting data to and from functions is called passing data.

■ Data can be passed to functions by value or by reference.

■ When possible, you should pass by value. Passing by value passes a copy of the data, and the original data cannot be changed from within the function.

■ Data passed by reference brings back changes made to it within a function.

■ A value can be passed to the calling function using `return`.

■ A void function does not return a value.

■ In a function prototype, you are only required to provide the data types of the parameters.

■ Library functions are functions that come with the compiler.

■ A header file provides the prototypes for library functions.

■ C++ includes common math functions and functions for working with characters.

Define the following terms:

argument

header file

library functions

parameter

pass

passing by reference

passing by value

TRUE/FALSE

Circle the T if the statement is true. Circle the F if it is false.

T   F   1.   Passing by value gives the function a copy of the passed variable.

T   F   2.   An @ symbol signifies a variable is to be passed by reference.

T   F   3.   The data in parentheses when a function is called is the argument.

T   F   4.   Use passing by value to return two values from a function.

T   F   5.   You should pass data by reference whenever possible.

T   F   6.   Any function that is not void should include a `return` statement.

T   F   7.   Any valid expression can appear in the parentheses of a `return` statement.

T   F   8.   A function can have only one `return` statement.

T   F   9.   The source code for a library function appears in your program.

T   F   10.   The `ceil` function rounds a floating-point number up to the next whole number.

WRITTEN QUESTIONS

Write your answers to the following questions.

11.   What is the difference between an argument and a parameter?

12.   What happens when a variable is passed by value?

13. What happens when a variable is passed by reference?

14. What data types can be used when declaring a function?

15. What happens when a `return` statement is encountered?

16. What happens in a void function after the last line in a function is executed?

17. What do you call the functions that come with the compiler?

18. What header file is required to use the `pow` function?

19. What function returns the absolute value of a floating-point number?

20. What function determines whether a character is uppercase?

LESSON 12 PROJECTS

PROJECT 12A

1. Open the version of **ctof.cpp** that you saved in Step-by-Step 12.4.

2. Add the following function to the program.

```
double get_celsius()
  {
   double celsius_in;

   cout << "Enter the temperature in Celsius: ";
   cin >> celsius_in;
   return celsius_in;
  }
```

3. Add the appropriate function prototype for the new function.

4. Add the following line to the `main` function, immediately following the variable declarations.

```
celsius = get_celsius();
```

5. Change the declaration of the variable `celsius` to remove the initialization.

6. Save, compile, and run the program.

PROJECT 12B

Write a program that uses the `sqrt` function to calculate the circumference of a circle, given its area. Use the formula $2\sqrt{\pi} * area$. Save the program as **circ.cpp** and close the source code when you have completed the exercise.

PROJECT 12C

Write a program that prompts the user for a single character that must be either an uppercase or lowercase letter. The program should use a do while loop to repeat the prompt if the character entered is not a letter. Once the user has entered a letter, the program should change the case of the letter. If the letter was entered as uppercase, the program should change the character to lowercase, and vice versa. The changed letter should be output, along with the original character entered by the user. *Hint*: The syntax for converting a character's case is shown in the example below.

```
c = tolower(c);
```

Save the source code as **charchng.cpp**.

PROJECT 12D

Modify **series2.cpp** so that the call to `get_choice` and `handle_choice` are in a do while loop. Add an item to the menu numbered 0 (zero) that exits the program. Have the loop continually redisplay the menu until zero is chosen. *Note*: Make sure you change the do while loop in the `get_choice` function so that zero is a valid input. Save the source code as **series3.cpp**.

CRITICAL THINKING

Modify the `get_celsius` function in the program you saved in Project 12A to use passing by reference to return the temperature to the `main` function.

Functions

MATCHING

Write the letter of the description from Column 2 that best matches the term or phrase in Column 1.

Column 1

_____ 1. bottom-up design

_____ 2. global variable

_____ 3. header file

_____ 4. library function

_____ 5. local variable

_____ 6. passing by reference

_____ 7. passing by value

_____ 8. prototype

_____ 9. scope

_____ 10. top-down design

Column 2

A. A variable accessible only within a function

B. The availability of a variable

C. A method of passing that allows the passed variable to be changed by the receiving function

D. Designing functions at the bottom of the VTOC first

E. Designing functions at the top of the VTOC first

F. A method of passing that sends a copy to the receiving function

G. Defines a function for the compiler

H. A variable accessible to any function

I. Provides function prototypes for functions that exist outside your program

J. Functions that come with the compiler

WRITTEN QUESTIONS

Write your answers to the following questions.

1. What effect does dividing a program into functions have on the ease of debugging? Why?

2. In a top-down design, what function is written first?

3. When the last line in a function is executed, what line is executed next?

4. What kind of variable is sometimes called an automatic variable?

5. What is the scope of a variable declared within the `main` function?

6. Where are global variables declared?

7. What symbol signifies that a variable is to be passed by reference?

8. When a function is called, what term is used to describe the items in the parentheses?

9. What method of passing data should be used whenever possible?

10. What function rounds a decimal value up to the next whole number?

APPLICATIONS

APPLICATION 5-1

Given the following prototypes and instructions, write the statement necessary to call the function.

1. Use the `floor` function to round down the value in `x` and store the result in `y`. The prototype appears below.

   ```
   double floor(double x);
   ```

2. Use the `pow` function to calculate 4 raised to the power of 7 and store the value in a variable called `four_to_the_seventh`. The prototype appears below.

   ```
   double pow(double x, double y); // raises x to the y
   ```

3. Use the `abs` function to return the absolute value of the integer named `amount` and store it in the same variable.

   ```
   int abs(int x);
   ```

4. Use the `toupper` function to change the character stored in the variable `MyChar` to uppercase.

   ```
   int toupper(int c);
   ```

5. Use the `islower` function in an if structure that executes the statement you wrote in question 4 above if the character stored in `MyChar` is lowercase.

```
int islower(int c);
```

APPLICATION 5-2

Modify the program you wrote in Application 4-3 (**planets.cpp**) that determines your weight on another planet. Divide the program into three functions. The `main` function should call a function that prompts the user for his or her weight on Earth and return the value using the return statement. The menu should remain in the `main` function. However, the user's selection should be passed to a function that uses the switch statement to calculate the user's weight on the chosen planet and print the results. *Note*: You may have to use passing by reference.

APPLICATION 5-3

Use the template you created in Project 11C as a starting point to write a program that will function as a point-of-sale system at a rodeo snack bar. The snack bar sells only six different items: a sandwich, chips, pickle, brownie, regular drink, and a large drink. All items are subject to sales tax. Set prices for the products.

The program should repeatedly display the menu below until the sale is totaled. The program should keep a running total of the amount of the sale based on costs that you place in constants for each of the food items. The running total should be displayed somewhere on the screen each time the menu is displayed again.

S = Sandwich
C = Chips
P = Pickle
B = Brownie
R = Regular drink
L = Large drink
X = Cancel sale and start over
T = Total the sale

If the sale is canceled, clear your running total and display the menu again. When the sale is totaled, calculate the sales tax based on your local tax rate (use 6% if you have no sales tax in your area). Print the final total due on the screen.

You can use your own functions to design a solution to the problem. You are required to use a function to calculate the sales tax. Other use of functions is up to you. Save the source code as **rodeo.cpp**.

APPLICATION 5-4

Steel measuring tapes vary in length slightly depending on the temperature. When they are manufactured, they are standardized for 20° Celsius (68° Fahrenheit). As the temperature varies above or below 20°C, the tape becomes slightly inaccurate, which must be taken into consideration. The formula below will produce a length correction given the length measured by the tape and the temperature in Celsius. (T = temperature, L = measured length)

$$C = 0.0000116 * (T - 20) * L$$

193

The adjusted length can be calculated using the following formula.

new length = $L + C$

Write a program that asks the user for a measured length and temperature in Celsius and outputs an adjusted length using the formulas above. The program should include a function that accepts the measured length and temperature and returns the adjusted length. Save the source code as **adjlen.cpp**.

Source of formulas: Brinker & Wolf, *Elementary Surveying,* 7th Edition, Harper & Row, 1984.

INTERNET ACTIVITY

SCANS

1. Open the program you wrote in Application 3-4 called **stocks.cpp**.

2. Modify the program to include a function named `Calculate_Value` that calculates the change in value based on the opening price, closing price, and number of shares.

3. Open your Web browser and go to **http://www.programcpp.com/basics**.

4. One the home page, click the link called **Internet Activities from the book** and then go to the **Unit 5** link. On that page, you will find links to sites that provide stock price information.

5. Use values of real stocks to test your program. Some suggested stocks are listed on the Unit 5 Web page.

COMPOUND INTEREST

🕐 **Estimated Time: 1 hour**

CANS

Overview

Although there are many approaches to writing programs, many programmers develop programs by following the steps below. These steps are called the programming process.

1. Define the problem.

2. Develop an algorithm.

3. Code the program.

4. Test and debug the program.

5. Document and maintain the program.

In this case study, you will follow the steps of the programming process to develop a program that calculates the growth of money using compound interest. When money is placed in an interest-bearing account, the bank adds the interest earned at a regular interval, often monthly. Each month, you earn interest on a larger amount of money because you are also earning interest on the interest you earned in previous months.

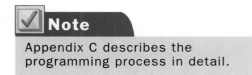

☑ **Note**

Appendix C describes the programming process in detail.

Defining the Problem

We will begin by defining the problem. As input, the program will ask for several pieces of data.

1. The amount of money placed in the savings account.

2. The interest rate the money will earn in the account.

3. The year that the money is placed in the account.

4. The month that the money is placed in the account.

5. The number of months the money is to remain in the account.

The output will be a table that shows the month and year and the amount of money by which the account has grown by that month.

Developing an Algorithm

The flow of the program is fairly simple. First, it must ask the user for the needed values. Then the program will use a loop as it calculates the new principal amount for each month. The flowchart in Figure CSII-1 illustrates the flow of logic necessary for the program.

FIGURE CSII-1
A flowchart helps a programmer
visualize the flow of logic in a program.

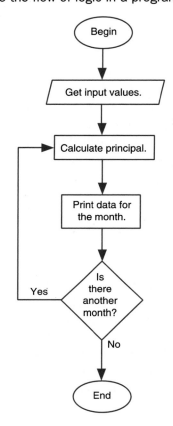

The next step would be to develop a Visual Table of Contents (VTOC) to decide what functions must be written. Functions would need to be written that get the input from the user, that calculate the new account balance, and that print a line of the table, as shown in the VTOC in Figure CSII-2.

FIGURE CSII-2
A Visual Table of Contents shows the functions of the program.

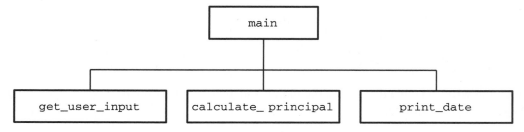

Coding the Program

Atop-down approach to coding the program is followed. We begin by writing the `main` function, and then write the functions on which the `main` function depends. As our flowchart showed, the program must first ask the user to input values. But before we ask the user for those values, there must be variables in which to store the data. Code List CSII-1 shows the `main` function.

CODE LIST CSII-1

```cpp
// main function
int main()
{
  double principal, interest_rate;
  int first_year, first_month,
      total_months, month_count,
      current_year, current_month;
  oostring Wait;   // used in "Press Enter to Continue" input

  get_user_input(principal, interest_rate, first_year,
                 first_month, total_months);

  current_year = first_year;
  current_month = first_month;

  cout.setf(ios::fixed);      // prevent exponential notation
  for (month_count = 0; month_count < total_months; month_count++)
   {
    print_date(current_year, current_month);
    cout << "$" << setprecision(2) << principal << '\n';
    calculate_principal(principal, interest_rate);
    if (current_month < 12)
     {                    // If not yet December, increment month
      current_month++;
     }
    else                  // else stop output until Enter is pressed,
     {                    // set month back to January, and increment year
      cout << "\nPress Enter to Continue...\n";
      getline(cin, Wait);
      current_month = 1;
      current_year++;
     }
   }
  return 0;
}
```

After the variables are declared, the `main` function calls `get_user_input` to get the necessary values from the user. Once those values are returned to the `main` function, `current_year` and `current_month` are initialized to the initial values entered by the user.

Next, the fixed format option is set to ensure that the output does not appear in exponential notation. The fixed option also allows the setprecision to set the number of decimal places to the right of the decimal point. Now we are ready for the loop that prints the output.

We will use a for loop to print the table because we know the number of times we need to iterate. The for loop uses a loop counter variable named `month_count`.

The first statement in the loop calls a function named `print_date`, which prints the name of the month followed by the year. The principal is then printed on the same line of the screen. Next, the `calculate_principal` function takes the principal and interest rate and returns a new principal amount for the next month. The principal will grow with each iteration of the loop.

The remainder of the loop is an if structure used to increment the month and, when necessary, the year. Each time the year is incremented, the output pauses to allow the user time to read the output.

STEP-BY-STEP ▷ CSII.1

1. Enter the program code shown in Code List CSII-2 into a blank editor screen. You can replace Jonathan's name with your own.

2. Add the `main` function at the bottom of the source code file.

3. Save the source code file as **compound.cpp** and leave it open for the next Step-by-Step exercise.

CODE LIST CSII-2

```
// compound.cpp
// By Jonathan Kleid
// Calculates future value of an amount of money placed in an interest
// bearing account over time.

#include <iostream.h>
#include <iomanip.h>
#include "oostring.h"

// function prototypes
void get_user_input(double &principal, double &interest_rate,
                    int &first_year, int &first_month,
                    int &total_months);
void calculate_principal(double &principal, double interest_rate);
void print_date(int year, int month);
```

Now that we have analyzed the `main` function, let us look at the functions required to finish the program.

The `get_user_input` function (shown in Code List CSII-3) receives variables by reference, prompts the user for values for the variables, and returns the values to the main function. The function uses do while loops to repeat prompts until valid values are input.

```
// Function that gets the input values from the user.
void get_user_input(double &principal, double &interest_rate,
                    int &first_year, int &first_month,
                    int &total_months)

  cout << "Enter the starting principal: ";
  cin  >> principal;
  cin.ignore(80,'\n');
  cout << "Enter the current interest rate (Ex. 0.09 for 9%): ";
  cin  >> interest_rate;
  cin.ignore(80,'\n');
  do
   {
     cout << "Enter the first year: ";
     cin  >> first_year;
     cin.ignore(80,'\n');
     if ((first_year < 1900) || (first_year > 2050))
       {
        cout << "Invalid year.\n";
       }
   } while((first_year < 1900) || (first_year > 2050));

   do
    {
     cout << "Enter the first month (1 for Jan., 2 for Feb., etc...): ";
     cin  >> first_month;
     cin.ignore(80,'\n');
     if ((first_month < 1) || (first_month > 12))
       {
        cout << "Invalid month.\n";
       }
    } while((first_month < 1) || (first_month > 12));

   cout << "Enter the total number of months: ";
   cin  >> total_months;
   cin.ignore(80,'\n');
}
```

S TEP-BY-STEP ▷ CSII.2

1. Add the `get_user_input` function to the source code on your screen.

2. Leave the source code file open for the next Step-by-Step exercise.

The `print_date` function (shown in Code List CSII-4) is primarily a switch structure that prints the name of the month based on the month number that is passed to the function. The year and month are passed by value because there is no need to return the values to the `main` function. After the switch structure prints the month, a statement prints the year.

CODE LIST CSII-4

```
// Function that prints the month and year to the screen.
void print_date(int year, int month)
{
  switch(month)
   {
     case 1:
       cout << "Jan";
       break;
     case 2:
       cout << "Feb";
       break;
     case 3:
       cout << "Mar";
       break;
     case 4:
       cout << "Apr";
       break;
     case 5:
       cout << "May";
       break;
     case 6:
       cout << "Jun";
       break;
     case 7:
       cout << "Jul";
       break;
     case 8:
       cout << "Aug";
       break;
     case 9:
       cout << "Sep";
       break;
     case 10:
       cout << "Oct";
       break;
     case 11:
       cout << "Nov";
       break;
     case 12:
       cout << "Dec";
       break;
   }
  cout << " " << year << ": ";
}
```

The final function required for the program is a simple function (shown in Code List CSII-5) that calculates the new principal amount. The variable `principal` is passed by reference because the new principal amount must be passed back to the `main` function. The interest rate is passed by value because there is no need to pass it back to the `main` function.

CODE LIST CSII-5

```
// Function that adds the interest earned and calculates the
// new principal amount.

void calculate_principal(double &principal, double interest_rate)
{
    principal = principal + (principal * (interest_rate / 12));
}
```

S TEP-BY-STEP ▷ CSII.3

1. Enter the `print_date` and `calculate_principal` functions.

2. Save the source code file and leave it open for the next exercise.

Testing and Debugging

Once the code for a program has been entered, the program must be tested and debugged before it can be used and distributed as a reliable program.

S TEP-BY-STEP ▷ CSII.4

1. Issue the command to compile the program. If errors occur during the compilation, check your source code for syntax errors or other typographical errors.

2. When the program compiles and runs successfully, test it with the following input.

   Starting Principal: 1000.00
   Interest Rate: 0.08
   Year: 2001
   Month: 4 (April)
   Number of months: 12

3. Calculating by hand, we have determined that the input above should produce the output below. Compare the program's output to the values below to see whether the program is working correctly.

   Apr 2001: $1000.00
   May 2001: $1006.67
   Jun 2001: $1013.38
   Jul 2001: $1020.13
   Aug 2001: $1026.93
   Sep 2001: $1033.70
   Oct 2001: $1040.67

(continued on next page)

Nov 2001: $1047.61
Dec 2001: $1054.59
Jan 2002: $1061.63
Feb 2002: $1068.70
Mar 2002: $1075.83

4. When the program functions properly, save the source code and close.

Documenting and Maintaining

The final step is to write documentation and maintain the program. Some of the lines in the program already contain comments. The analysis in this case study is similar to the external documentation written for some programs.

The user documentation for a program such as this should explain how the program expects the input to be entered. For example, the user should be shown the proper format for entering each of the required inputs.

STEP-BY-STEP ⟹ CSII.5

1. Write user documentation for the program. Begin with a paragraph describing the purpose of the program.

2. Next, describe the necessary inputs and

explain the formats required for each.

3. If you entered the documentation in a text editor or word processor, print it.

Modifying the Program

As an additional exercise, modify the program to display the interest earned each month, in addition to the new principal. You may also want to change the program so that a yearly total of interest earned is printed.

ARRAYS, DATA FILES, AND OBJECT-ORIENTED PROGRAMMING

UNIT 6

Estimated Time for Unit: 3 hours

OBJECTIVES

When you complete this lesson, you will be able to:

■ Describe what arrays are and how they are used.

■ Declare a vector object.

■ Index elements in a vector.

■ Explain why arrays are needed.

■ Use loops to work with vectors.

■ Use other features of the vector object.

⏱ **Estimated Time: 1 hour**

VOCABULARY

array
elements
subscript
template class
vector

Understanding Arrays

An *array* is a list of variables or other data structures that are accessed using a single identifier. For example, suppose you need to store a list of five integers. You could declare five integer variables using a statement like the following one.

```
int a, b, c, d, e;
```

There is nothing to stop you from declaring five separate variables and managing the list of integers that way. However, writing code to manage the five variables as a list becomes difficult. In an array, an entire list is accessed using a single identifier. You then use a number to access a specific item in the array. In this lesson, you will use an object-oriented array called a *vector* to implement arrays.

Arrays are useful in a variety of situations. Suppose you need to store exam grades for an entire class of students.

 Note

Vector is a term from mathematics that describes a quantity identified by a magnitude and a direction. However, the term is also often used to describe an array.

Rather than have a separate variable for each student's grade, you could declare an array (or vector) that can hold the exam grades for all of the students in the class. Each student's grade would occupy a position in the list. So, for example, you could retrieve the third student's grade by taking the third grade from the array.

Declaring a Vector Object

Declaring a vector object is similar to declaring a string object. A string object, in fact, is basically an array of characters. You could think of a string object as a vector of characters that has some special methods included for dealing with text.

A vector object, however, is more generic. Whereas a string object is always an array of characters, a vector object can be an array of any data type. So when you declare a vector object, you must specify a data type. The following statement is an example of the simplest form of vector declaration.

```
vector <int> MyVector;
```

In this statement, `vector` is the name of the class and `MyVector` is the name of the particular vector object you are declaring. In between you place the data type in angle brackets. You must supply a data type when declaring; otherwise, a vector or the program will fail to compile.

Concept Builder

The vector class used in this lesson has standard features and behavior. All vector classes, however, are not the same. When you work with other vector classes, you may find differences in the way they are used and how they handle data.

Template Classes

The vector class is an example of a template class. A *template class* is designed to customize the data type at the time the program is compiled. When you write a program that declares an object from a template class, the data type you specify in the code is applied to the class when the program is compiled. The resulting object will include the data type specified when you declared the object.

Three Ways to Declare

Like a string object, a vector object can change its length as necessary. For this reason, it is not absolutely necessary that you determine in advance the length of the vector. However, if you know the required length of the vector, it is a good idea to specify the length when the object is declared. The vector class also includes a nice feature that allows you to initialize each item (called *elements*) with a value at the time the object is declared.

Let us look at the three ways to declare a vector object.

Hot Tip

If you declare an empty vector, you must later resize the vector or copy another vector into the empty vector. You will learn how to resize vectors and copy vectors later in this lesson. If you attempt to manually store data in an empty vector, you will get an error.

EMPTY VECTORS

A vector that does not have a specified length is called an *empty vector*. To declare an empty vector, just specify the data type and identifier, as shown in the next example.

```
vector <float> MyValues;
```

SPECIFYING THE NUMBER OF ELEMENTS

To declare a vector object of a specific length, specify the number of elements the vector should contain, as shown in the following example.

```
vector <float> MyValues(100); // a vector with 100 elements
```

INITIALIZING THE VECTOR

To declare a vector object of a specific length and initialize the elements at the same time, specify a value along with the number of elements, as shown in the next example.

```
vector <float> MyValues(100,0); // a vector with 100 elements
                                // initialized to 0
```

Compiling a Program Using the Vector Class

Compiling a program using the vector class is actually easier than using the string class. Because the vector class is a template class, the entire class is contained in the file vector.h. All you have to do to successfully compile and use the vector class is include the vector.h file and have that file available in the same directory as your program or in some other directory where the compiler will look for the file. The line required to include the vector.h file is shown next.

```
#include "vector.h"
```

The program shown in Code List 13-1 declares three vectors. The first one (Vector1) is an empty vector, Vector2 is a 10-element uninitialized vector, and Vector3 is a 10-element vector with each element initialized to zero.

CODE LIST 13-1

```
// vectorex.cpp

#include <iostream.h>
#include "vector.h"

int main()
{
  vector <int> Vector1;
  vector <int> Vector2(10);
  vector <int> Vector3(10,0);

  return 0;
}
```

STEP-BY-STEP ▷ 13.1

1. Enter the program in Code List 13-1 into a blank editor screen.

2. Save the source code as **vectorex.cpp**.

3. Copy the **vector.h** file from your data files to the folder where **vectorex.cpp** is saved or to your compiler's Include directory.

4. Compile and run the program. There will be no visible output from the program. Leave the program open and continue with the lesson.

Indexing Elements in a Vector

Once you have created a vector, it is easy to put data into the vector and pull data from it. To set an element of the vector, indicate the element to which you want to assign a value using square brackets. For example, the following code assigns the value 2.5 to the third element of the vector named MyValues. The value in the square brackets is called a *subscript*.

```
MyValues[2] = 2.5;
```

You may think that the preceding line of code has an error. Are you wondering why using a subscript of 2 causes the third element to be accessed? What you are seeing is a feature of C++ that beginning students often find confusing. In C++ vectors, the subscript refers to the position of an element from the beginning of the list. The vector assumes that the starting point for the list is the first element. The first element is zero spaces from the beginning. Therefore, the remaining elements are offset by one space. So, the third element is two spaces from the beginning.

When you want to retrieve a value stored in the vector, you use a statement like the following one. The same offset numbering system applies when you are retrieving data. So the following statement copies the value in the third element of the vector to the variable named `value`.

```
value = MyValues[2];
```

S TEP-BY-STEP ▷ 13.2

1. Add the following lines to **vectorex.cpp** below the declarations.

```
Vector2[0] = 1;
Vector2[1] = 2;

cout << Vector2[0] << endl;
cout << Vector2[1] << endl;
cout << Vector3[0] << endl;
```

2. Compile and run the program. Analyze the output to see that the values were stored in

the vectors. The zero value in `Vector3` is a result of the value specified when the vector was declared.

3. Add a line to the program to output the value in the third element of `Vector2`. Compile and run to see the value that appears in the element by default because the vector was not initialized when it was declared.

4. Save and close the program.

When Are Arrays Needed?

Why would you want to store an array of integers or floating-point numbers? Actually, you will find lots of uses for arrays of data. Let us look at some examples.

Suppose you want to write a program that stores the high temperature for every day of the month and then calculates an average. You could use a 31-element vector, similar to the next one, to store the high temperature for every day of any given month.

```
vector <int> daily_temp(31,0);
```

The elements of the preceding vector would be accessed using subscripts 0 to 30. Remember that the first element is accessed with the subscript 0 and the 31st element is accessed using the subscript 30.

Let us look at another example. Suppose you have written a computer game and you want to display the 10 highest scores between games. The following vector declaration could hold the scores. The statement declares a 10-element array of unsigned long integers.

```
vector <unsigned long> score(10);
```

 Note

When using a vector to store data such as the 10 highest scores of a game, the scores will be lost when the program ends. To keep scores for the next time the game is run, you would have to save the scores to disk and then reload them into a vector when the game restarts. In the next lesson, you will learn how to save data to files.

Using Loops to Work with Vectors

Let us consider the preceding vector above that stores the high temperatures for a series of days. It would be convenient to prompt the user for values for the vector using a for loop. Code List 13-2 shows a for loop that prompts the user for temperatures for the vector. The loop's index variable is used to index the vector, resulting in very efficient code.

CODE LIST 13-2

```
// The following loop gets the high temperatures from the user for as
// many days as the user specified in num_values.
for(index = 0; index <= (num_values - 1); index++)
{
  cout << "Enter the high temperature for day " << index + 1 << ": ";
  cin >> daily_temp[index];  // input value into array
}
```

Inside the loop are two statements. The first is an output statement that lets the user know what day's temperature is being entered. Notice that the code adds 1 to the index to account for the difference between the index required for the vector and the day number expected by the user. The second statement gets the temperature using a cin statement and places it in the vector by indexing the vector with the index variable.

A loop can also be used to efficiently output the values in a vector. Code List 13-3 shows the code required to output the values from the daily_temp vector.

CODE LIST 13-3

```
// Print the values in the array to the screen.
cout << "The array contains high temperatures for " << num_values
     << " days.\n";
cout << "The values are as follows.\n";
for(index = 0; index <= (num_values - 1); index++)
{
  cout << "Day " << index + 1 << ": " << daily_temp[index] << endl;
  total = total + daily_temp[index]; // update total for averaging
}
```

Notice that only one statement is required for outputting the values. However, even though the program is going to the trouble of looping through the entire list of values, we add one line of code to calculate a total of all the temperatures. This total will be used to calculate an average high temperature. Although you cannot see from these segments of code, the total variable was initialized to zero when it was declared.

Calculating the average temperature requires only one line of code, as shown in Code List 13-4. Because the total and num_values variables are integers, we use typecasting to allow a floating-point result to be achieved. The average_high variable has been declared as a double.

```
// Calculate average by typecasting total and num_values to doubles
// before dividing and assigning the result to average_high.
average_high = double(total) / double(num_values);
```

STEP-BY-STEP ▷ 13.3

1. Retrieve the source code file named **hightemp.cpp**. The program that appears includes the code you have just analyzed. If necessary, copy the **vector.h** file to the same folder that contains **hightemp.cpp**.

2. Study the code on your screen to see how the entire program works.

3. Compile and run the program.

4. Test the program by providing five temperatures as input.

5. Run the program again. When prompted for the number of days for which you have data, enter a value less than 1 or greater than 31. The program should prompt you to enter a valid value. Enter a valid value and complete the session with the program.

6. Close the program.

Other Vector Features

Earlier in the lesson you learned that the vector class and the string class are similar. Like a string object, a vector object can report its length. Because a vector is a more generic data structure than a string, you can also manually resize a vector. In addition, you can assign an entire vector to another vector object.

Obtaining the Length of a Vector

The length method is used to determine the length of a vector. There are a variety of reasons why you might need to know the length of a vector. For example, suppose you want to write a loop to print out all the values in a vector. By obtaining the length, you can determine how many times the loop must iterate. The following code shows how to determine the number of elements in a vector.

```
num_elements = MyVector.length();
```

Resizing a Vector

You can specify a new size for a vector using the resize method. The resize method can make a vector longer or shorter. If you lengthen a vector, the elements added to the vector will be uninitialized. If you shorten a vector, the data in the elements at the end of the vector will be lost. The following code will resize the MyVector vector to a new length of 50 elements.

```
MyVector.resize(50);
```

Assigning One Vector to Another

Assigning the contents of one vector to another is easy. A statement like the following one is all that is necessary.

```
MyVector1 = MyVector2;
```

The vector receiving the contents of the other is resized and all of its existing data is lost. Assigning a vector in this manner is a good way to make a copy of a vector before performing some process on the data.

STEP-BY-STEP ▷ 13.4

1. Retrieve the source code file named **vectorex.cpp** that you saved in Step-by-Step 13.2. Either open the project you were using in that exercise or create a new project that successfully compiles the vector class.

2. Add the lines of code from Code List 13-5 to the end of the program, before the `return` statement.

3. Compile and run the program again. Notice the length of the vector before and after the resize method is called.

4. Add the ines of code from Code List 13-6 to the end of the program, before the `return` statement.

5. Compile and run the program again. Notice that assigning the contents of `Vector2` to `Vector1` changed the length of `Vector1` to match the length of `Vector2`. `Vector1` is now an exact copy of `Vector2`.

6. Save and close the program.

CODE LIST 13-5

```
cout << "Vector3 is " << Vector3.length()
     << " elements in length.\n";
Vector3.resize(5);
cout << "Vector3 was resized to " << Vector3.length()
     << " elements in length.\n";
```

CODE LIST 13-6

```
cout << "Vector1 is " << Vector1.length()
     << " elements in length.\n";
Vector1 = Vector2;
cout << "Vector1 is now " << Vector1.length()
     << " elements in length.\n";
```

Summary

- An array is a list of variables or other data structures that is accessed using a single identifier.

- A vector object is an object-oriented array.

- The vector class is a template class, so you are allowed to declare a data type for the vector before the class is compiled.

- You can declare an empty vector, a vector of a particular size, or an initialized vector of a particular size.

- You must include the vector.h file in order for the vector class to compile.

- Individual elements in a vector are accessed using a number called a subscript.

- Loops provide a convenient way to process the data in vectors.

- Other vector features include obtaining the length of a vector, manually resizing a vector, and assigning the contents of one vector to another.

VOCABULARY REVIEW

Define the following terms:

array

elements

subscript

template class

vector

LESSON 13 REVIEW QUESTIONS

TRUE/FALSE

Circle the T if the statement is true. Circle the F if it is false.

T F   1.   An array is a list in which each element is accessed using a different identifier.

T F   2.   A vector is an object-oriented array.

T F   3.   The string class is more generic than the vector class.

T F   4.   When you declare a vector object, you must specify a data type.

T F   5.   There are three ways to declare a vector.

T F   6.   If you attempt to manually store data in an empty vector, the vector will resize to accommodate the data.

T F   7.   A vector of 10 elements is indexed using the subscripts 0 to 9.

T F   8.   Loops are often used to process data in vectors.

T F   9.   The sizeof method is used to obtain the length of a vector.

T F   10.   The vector object will not allow data to be lost if you resize it.

WRITTEN QUESTIONS

Write your answers to the following questions.

11. Why is an array more convenient to use than individual variables when storing a list?

12. From what field of study does the term *vector* come?

13. What makes a template class different from a standard class?

14. Why is the vector class written as a template class?

15. What information must be provided when declaring an empty vector?

16. What information must be provided when declaring a vector of a specified length with each element initialized to a specific value?

17. What subscript range is used to index the vector declared by the following statement?

```
vector <int> j(100);
```

18. When would knowing the length of a vector be necessary?

19. When a vector is manually enlarged, what value is contained in the new elements?

20. When assigning one vector's contents to another vector object, what happens to the length and existing contents of the vector receiving the contents of the other vector?

LESSON 13 PROJECTS

PROJECT 13A

Write the code required for the following.

1. Write a statement that declares an empty vector of type long named `LongVector`.

2. Write a statement that declares a vector named `n` of type float with 10 uninitialized elements.

3. Write a statement that declares a vector named z of type int with 100 elements initialized to zero.

4. Write a loop that will print the values in a 20-element vector named `quantity` to the screen.

5. Write a loop that will initialize the values in a 100-element vector of type double named x with the loop's index value. For example, the element at subscript 0 should have the value 0 and the element at subscript 11 should have the value 11.

PROJECT 13B

Modify **hightemp.cpp** so that it reports the coolest and warmest days in the vector.

PROJECT 13C

Write a program that declares a vector of 10 floating-point values. Have the program prompt the user for each of the 10 floating-point values and store them into the vector. The program should then report how many of the values entered are larger than the value in the first element of the vector. For example, if the values entered are 5.2, 6.1, 2.8, 8.9, 3.3, 2.0, 9.7, 1.4, 7.3, and 5.5, the program should report that five of the values in the vector are larger than the value in the first element. Save the source code as **floatvec.cpp**.

CRITICAL THINKING

Write a program that declares a 16-element vector of type double named x. The program should use a loop to initialize each element with the square root of the subscript. For example, the element at subscript 9 (the tenth element) should be initialized with the square root of 9, which is 3. The program should then include a second loop that prints the contents of the vector. The output should appear like the following example. Use three digits of accuracy to the right of the decimal point. Save the program as **sqroot.cpp**.

```
The square root of 0 is 0.000
The square root of 1 is 1.000
The square root of 2 is 1.414
The square root of 3 is 1.732
The square root of 4 is 2.000
The square root of 5 is 2.236
The square root of 6 is 2.449
The square root of 7 is 2.646
The square root of 8 is 2.828
The square root of 9 is 3.000
The square root of 10 is 3.162
The square root of 11 is 3.317
The square root of 12 is 3.464
The square root of 13 is 3.606
The square root of 14 is 3.742
The square root of 15 is 3.873
```

DATA FILES

File Concepts

Many useful programs collect all input from the keyboard and print all output to the screen. However, the ability to input data from a disk file and send output to a disk file opens the door to many more possibilities. A program that organizes names and addresses, for example, must store the data somewhere other than RAM. Otherwise, the data is lost when the program ends.

In this lesson, you will learn about sequential-access and random-access data files. You will learn how to open and close a sequential-access file, how to write data to a file, how to read data from a file, and how to add data to the end of an existing file. You will also learn how to detect the end of a file and how to use multiple files at the same time.

Data files are not difficult to understand. Storing data in a file simply involves taking data from your computer's RAM and copying it to a disk. Retrieving data from a file is just the opposite. Data stored on disk is copied into variables or other data structures in RAM.

Why Use Data Files?

Recall that your computer's memory (RAM) holds data only as long as the computer is on. Furthermore, data in RAM is lost as soon as your program ends. Disks and other forms of secondary storage hold data even after the computer is turned off. Therefore, any data that your program needs again should be stored on disk so that it can be reloaded into your program.

For example, suppose you have a program that prints mailing addresses on labels and envelopes. Unless a data file is used to store the addresses, the user has to enter the data from the keyboard every time the program runs.

Another reason to use data files is the amount of space available on a disk as compared to RAM. In the example of the program that prints addresses, a data file could store hundreds or even thousands of addresses—many times the number that could fit in RAM.

Sequential-Access versus Random-Access Files

There are two types of data files: sequential access and random access. The difference between the two is in how they access the data stored in them.

SEQUENTIAL-ACCESS DATA FILES

A *sequential-access file* works like an audiocassette tape. When you put a cassette tape in a stereo, you must fast forward or rewind to get to a specific song. You must move through the songs sequentially until you reach the one you want to hear. Data stored in a sequential-access data file is placed one after the other like songs on a cassette tape. To retrieve specific data from a sequential-access data file, you must start at the beginning of the file and search for the data or records you want while moving through the file.

Sequential-access files are the most widely used data files. Word processors save documents in sequential-access files. Spreadsheets, graphic files, and some databases are stored as sequential-access files.

A sequential-access file can contain data of mixed types and sizes. For example, a word processor file may begin with general information about the document, followed by the text of the document itself. There may even be codes that control formatting mixed in with the document's text. The programmers who developed the word processor program place data in the file using their own rules. When the program loads the document from disk, the same rules are followed in order to correctly interpret the data file.

Figure 14-1 represents a sequential-access file storing a list of names. Notice that the names vary in length. To find the fourth name in the list (Beau Chenoweth), the three names that precede it must be read first.

FIGURE 14-1

A sequential-access file requires that data be read from the beginning of the file each time it is accessed.

Shelley Neff	James MacCloskey	Kim Fan	Beau Chenoweth	Sarah Boyd	Britney Sooter

RANDOM-ACCESS DATA FILES

A *random-access file* works like an audio compact disc (CD). With the touch of a button, you can immediately access any song on the CD. You can play the songs on a CD in any order, regardless of the order they appear on the CD. A random-access data file allows to you to move directly to any data in the file.

Random-access files are most often used to store databases. A database with a large number of records is more efficiently managed with a random-access file because you can move quickly to any desired record in the database.

The secret to a random-access file is that data is written to the file in blocks (records) of equal size. In reality, the file appears on the disk as a sequential-access file. Because the file is made up of equally sized blocks, a program can predict how far to move forward from the beginning of the file in order to get to the desired data.

Figure 14-2 represents a random-access file. Regardless of the length of the name, the same amount of disk space is occupied by the data. While the random-access file allows almost instant access to any data in the file, the disadvantage is that random-access files often occupy more disk space than sequential-access files.

FIGURE 14-2

A random-access file allows any record in the file to be accessed directly.

Shelley Neff	James MacCloskey	Kim Fan	Beau Chenowe

In this book, you will write programs that use only sequential-access data files; however, the concept of a random-access file is important.

Opening and Closing Files

Using a sequential-access file requires that you complete a few simple (but important) steps. First, the file must be opened. Data can then be stored or retrieved from the file. Finally, the file must be closed.

A file is a container for data. Whether you think of a file as a drawer, a folder, or a box, the concept of opening and closing the file makes sense. Before you can put something in a file or take something out, the file must be opened. When you have finished accessing the file, it must be closed.

In a paper filing system, a folder or drawer left open may result in loss of important information. Closing a computer file may be even more important. A data file left open by a program can be destroyed if a power failure occurs or if a program crash occurs. A closed data file is almost always protected from such occurrences.

Declaring a File Stream

You have been using streams to get data from the keyboard and to the screen. Getting data to and from files also involves streams called *file streams*. The cin and cout streams are already set up for you. You must, however, declare the stream objects you will use to access files. When declaring a file stream, you select a stream type and a name for the stream.

How you declare a file stream varies depending on how you intend to use the file. If you will be storing data to the file (called *writing*), you declare a file stream of type ofstream as shown:

```
ofstream outfile;  // Declare a file stream for writing to file.
```

If you will be getting data from a file (called *reading*), you declare a file stream of type ifstream as shown:

```
ifstream infile;  // Declare a file stream for reading a file.
```

To help you remember the file stream types, understand that ofstream is short for "output file stream" and ifstream is short for "input file stream."

You can use any valid identifier for file streams. The preceding examples used the names outfile and infile because they describe the purpose of the stream. In some situations, you may want to use a name that describes the data in the file, such as customers_in or high_scores.

After you have declared a stream object, the next step is to open the file.

Note

The ofstream and ifstream classes are made available by including the header file named fstream.h.

Opening a File

When you *open* a file, a physical disk file is associated with the file stream you declared. You must provide the name of the file you want to open, and you must specify whether you want to put data in the file (write) or get data from the file (read). Consider the statements in Code List 14-1.

Note

If you need to work with more than one file at a time, you can declare more than one file stream and assign each file stream to a different file on the disk.

CODE LIST 14-1

```
ofstream high_scores;  // Declare a file stream for writing to file.
high_scores.open("SCORES.DAT", ios::out); // Create the output file.
```

The statements in Code List 14-1 declare a file stream named `high_scores` and open a file on disk with the filename scores.dat. After the filename, you must specify the way you want to access the file, called *stream operation modes*. There are several modes available, most of which you will learn about as you need them. For now, you need to know only two: `ios::out` and `ios::in`. Use `ios::out` when creating an output file and `ios::in` when opening a file for input. Your compiler may not require that you specify the stream operation mode when using these basic modes. It is a good idea, however, to specify the mode in all cases.

Note

Compilers differ slightly in the way they handle file operations. The way files are opened can vary among compilers as well. If you have trouble with the exercises in this lesson, consult your compiler's documentation.

If a file named scores.dat already exists in the same location, the existing file will be replaced with the new one. If no such file exists, one is created and made ready for data.

You must be careful when opening a file for output. You will not receive a warning if a file of the same name as that you are opening already exists. Sometimes you will want the existing file to be erased, but if not, it is up to you to use filenames that will not harm other data.

Let us look at another example. The statements in Code List 14-2 will open a file named mydata.dat for input using a file stream named `infile`.

CODE LIST 14-2

```
ifstream infile;  // Declare a file stream for reading a file.
infile.open("MYDATA.DAT", ios::in); // Open the file for input.
```

Because opening a file associates a file stream with an actual file on your computer, the filename you provide must be a legal filename for your operating system.

Closing a File

After a file has been opened, you can begin writing to it or reading from it (depending on the stream operation mode). When you complete your work with the file, you must *close* it. The following statement closes the file pointed to by the file stream named `infile`.

```
infile.close(); // Close the input file.
```

The statement format is the same whether you are closing an input or output file.

Writing Data to Files

Writing data to a sequential-access data file employs the insertion operator (<<) that you use when printing data to the screen. Instead of using the output operator to direct data to the standard output device (cout), you direct the data to the file stream. For example, the program listed in Code List 14-3 prompts the user for his or her name and age, opens a file for output, and writes the data to the output file.

CODE LIST 14-3

```
// filewrit.cpp

#include <iostream.h>
#include <fstream.h>  // necessary for file I/O
#include "oostring.h" // necessary for string object

int main()
{
 oostring user_name;
 int age;
 ofstream outfile; // Declare file stream named outfile.

 cout << "Enter your name: "; // Get name from user.
 getline(cin, user_name);
 cout << "Enter your age: ";  // Get age from user.
 cin >> age;

 outfile.open("NAME_AGE.DAT",ios::out);  // Open file for output.

 if (outfile)  // If no error occurs while opening file
  {           // write the data to the file.
   outfile << user_name << endl;  // Write the name to the file.
   outfile << age << endl;        // Write the age to the file.
   outfile.close(); // Close the output file.
  }
 else         // If error occurred, display message.
  {
   cout << "An error occurred while opening the file.\n";
  }
 return 0;
}
```

Notice the user is prompted to provide input in a manner similar to previous programs with which you have worked. Next, the statement `if (outfile)` appears. This code is the functional equivalent of `if (outfile != 0)`. Thus, if an error results in the attempt to open the file, the file stream (`outfile`) is assigned the value of 0.

A number of conditions can cause an error to occur as a file is opened. The disk could be protected so that new data cannot be written to it. If you are attempting to open a file on a floppy disk, there is always the possibility that the disk is in the wrong drive. Because a disk drive is a hardware device, there may also be mechanical problems. Whatever the case, you must check to be sure that the file was opened successfully before sending data to the file.

Hot Tip

By this time you are sending output to cout by habit. When outputting to a file, make sure you use the file stream name in place of cout.

STEP-BY-STEP 14.1

1. Enter the program shown in Code List 14-3. Save the source code as **filewrit.cpp**.

2. Compile and run the program. *Note:* You will need to add the **oostring.cpp** file to the project and have the **oostring.h** file in the same folder with **filewrit.cpp**.

3. Enter your name and age at the prompts. The program creates the **name_age.dat** file in the same folder.

4. When the program ends, open **name_age.dat** using your compiler's text editor. The data you entered is in readable form in the file.

5. Close your program and **name_age.dat**.

When writing to files using the technique of Step-by-Step 14.1, the output file receives data in text form in the same way output sent to cout appears on the screen. The output must be separated with spaces or end-of-line characters or the data will run together in the file. The reason you write data to a file is so that it can be read in again later. Therefore, you must separate data with spaces or end-of-line characters when you write it to a text file.

The program in Code List 14-4 uses a loop to ask the user for a series of numbers. Each number the user enters is stored in a file named floats.dat. When the user enters a zero, the program ends.

Note

In most compilers, the `#include <fstream.h>` directive makes the use of iostream.h unnecessary because fstream.h contains everything iostream.h has and more. In this lesson, we include both for compatibility.

```cpp
// loopwrit.cpp

#include <iostream.h>
#include <fstream.h>   // necessary for file I/O

int main()
{
 float x;            // variable for user input
 ofstream outfile;  // Declare file stream named outfile.

 outfile.open("FLOATS.DAT",ios::out);  // Open file for output.

 if (outfile)
  {
   cout << "Enter a series of floating-point numbers.\n"
        << "Enter a zero to end the series.\n";
   do   // Repeat the loop until user enters zero.
    {
     cin >> x;                 // Get number from user.
     outfile << x << endl;  // Write the number to the file.
    } while (x != 0.0);
  }
 else
  {
   cout << "Error opening file.\n";
  }
 outfile.close();  // Close the output file.
 return 0;
}
```

STEP-BY-STEP 14.2

1. Enter the program shown in Code List 14-4. Save the source code as **loopwrit.cpp**.

2. Compile and run the program. Enter at least five or six floating-point numbers and then be sure to end by entering a zero.

3. When the program ends, open **floats.dat** using your compiler's text editor. The numbers you entered are in readable form in the file.

4. Close **floats.dat** and **loopwrit.cpp**.

Reading Data from Files

The main reason data is written to a file is so that it can later be read and used again. In other cases, your program may read a data file created by another program.

As you learned earlier in this lesson, before you can read data from a file you must open the file for input using a file stream. The statements in Code List 14-5 are an example of declaring an input file stream and opening a file named mydata.dat for input.

CODE LIST 14-5

```
ifstream infile;  // Declare a file stream for reading a file.
infile.open("MYDATA.DAT", ios::in); // Open the file for input.
```

Once the file is open, you can read the data, using methods familiar to you. However, reading from a data file can be a little more complicated than getting input from the keyboard. In this lesson you will learn two methods of reading from data files. Other methods can be used, but these methods should give the desired results without too much complication.

First, you will learn a method that can be used when the file contains only numeric data. Then you will learn how to read data that includes strings or a combination of strings and data.

 Important

When you open a file using `ios::in`, the file must already exist. Some compilers will create an empty file and give unpredictable results. Other compilers may give an error message.

Reading Numeric Data

When reading strictly numeric data, you can use the extraction operator (>>) as if you were getting input from the keyboard. Instead of using cin as the input stream, use your file stream name. The program in Code List 14-6 reads the numbers you wrote to disk in Step-by-Step 14.2, prints the numbers to the screen and then calculates the sum and average of the numbers.

CODE LIST 14-6

```
// numread.cpp

#include <fstream.h>
#include <iostream.h>
#include <iomanip.h>

int main()
{
 float x, sum;
 int count;
```

(continued on next page)

```
ifstream infile; // Declare file stream named infile.

infile.open("FLOATS.DAT",ios::in);  // Open file for input.

sum = 0.0;
count = 0;

if (infile)  // If no error occurred while opening file
 {            // input the data from the file.
 cout.setf(ios::fixed);
 cout << "The numbers in the data file are as follows:\n"
     << setprecision(1);

 do  // Read numbers until 0.0 is encountered.
  {
    infile >> x;          // Get number from file.
    cout << x << endl;   // Print number to screen.
    sum = sum + x;        // Add number to sum.
    count++;              // Increment count of how many numbers read.
  } while(x != 0.0);

  // Output sum and average.
  cout << "The sum of the numbers is " << sum << endl;
  cout << "The average of the numbers (excluding zero) is "
      << sum / (count - 1) << endl;
 }
 else           // If error occurred, display message.
 {
 cout << "An error occurred while opening the file.\n";
 }
 infile.close();  // Close the output file.
 return 0;
}
```

STEP-BY-STEP ▷ 14.3

1. Retrieve the file **numread.cpp**. The program shown in Code List 14-6 appears.

2. Make sure the **floats.dat** file is in the same directory with **numread.cpp**.

3. Compile and run the program. The numbers you entered in Step-by-Step 14.2 should appear, along with the sum and the average of the values.

4. Close the source code file.

Reading String Data and Mixed String and Numeric Data

When reading string data, use the `get` function as you do to read strings from the keyboard. Like using `get` with the keyboard, using `get` to read from files requires that you flush the stream to remove the end-of-line character.

When a file includes both string data and numeric data (such as the name and age saved in Step-by-Step 14.1), you should read all the data as string data and convert the strings that contain numbers to numeric variables. This is done using a function called `atoi` or using another related function. The `atoi` function converts a number represented in a string to an actual integer value that can be stored in an integer variable.

The program completed in Step-by-Step 14.1 stores the variable name as a string and age as an integer. However, the program in Code List 14-7 illustrates how both values can be read as strings and the age can be converted to an integer prior to printing the values to the screen.

CODE LIST 14-7

```cpp
// strread.cpp

#include <fstream.h>
#include <iostream.h>
#include "oostring.h"

int main()
{
 oostring user_name;
 oostring user_age;
 int age;
 ifstream infile; // Declare file stream named infile.

 infile.open("NAME_AGE.DAT",ios::in);  // Open file for input.

 if (infile)  // If no error occurred while opening file
  {           // input the data from the file.
   getline(infile,user_name); // Read the name and
   getline(infile,user_age);  // the age from the file into strings.

   // Convert the age in the string to an integer.
   age = user_age.converttoint();

   cout << "The name read from the file is " << user_name << ".\n";
   cout << "The age read from the file is " << age << ".\n";
  }
 else  // If error occurred, display message.
  {
   cout << "An error occurred while opening the file.\n";
  }
 infile.close();  // Close the input file.
 return 0;
}
```

1. Retrieve **strread.cpp**. The program in Code List 14-7 appears on your screen.

2. If necessary, copy the **name_age.dat** file to the same folder that contains **strread.cpp**. You will need to add the **oostring.cpp** file to the project and have the **oostring.h** file in the same folder.

3. Before running the program, analyze the source code to see the purpose of each statement.

4. Compile and run the program. The name and age you saved in Step-by-Step 14.1 should appear in the output.

5. Close the source code file.

Sequential File Techniques

You now know how to write and read sequential-access data files. In this section, you will learn techniques that will help you work more efficiently with files. You will learn how to add data to the end of a file, detect the end of a file, use multiple data files at the same time, and prompt the user for the name of a data file.

Adding Data to the End of a File

One of the limitations of sequential-access files is that most changes require that you rewrite the file. For example, to insert data somewhere in a file, the entire file must be rewritten. You can, however, add data to the end of a file without rewriting the file. Adding data to the end of an existing file is called *appending*. To append data to an existing file, open the file using the `ios::app` stream operation mode, as shown in the following statement.

 Note

If the file you open for appending does not exist, the operating system creates one just as if you had opened it using `ios::out` mode.

```
outfile.open("MYDATA.DAT",ios::app);  // Open file for appending.
```

The program in Code List 14-8 opens the name_age.dat data file and allows you to add more names and ages to the file. The only difference between the program in Code List 14-8 and the program you ran in Step-by-Step 14.1 is the stream operation mode in the line that opens the file.

CODE LIST 14-8

```
// fileapp.cpp

#include <iostream.h>
#include <fstream.h>  // necessary for file I/O
#include "oostring.h" // necessary for string object

int main()
{
 oostring user_name;
 int age;
```

```
ofstream outfile; // Declare file stream named outfile

cout << "Enter your name: "; // Get name from user.
getline(cin, user_name);
cout << "Enter your age: ";  // Get age from user.
cin >> age;

outfile.open("NAME_AGE.DAT",ios::app);  // Open file for appending.

if (outfile)  // If no error occurs while opening file
 {             // write the data to the file.
  outfile << user_name << endl;   // Write the name to the file.
  outfile << age << endl;         // Write the age to the file.
  outfile.close();  // close the output file
 }
else          // If error occurred, display message.
 {
  cout << "An error occurred while opening the file.\n";
 }
return 0;
}
```

STEP-BY-STEP ▷ 14.5

1. Open the program **fileapp.cpp**. The program in Code List 14-8 appears, except that the statement that opens the file for output has not yet been changed to append data.

2. Run the program with the `ios::out` stream operation mode. *Note*: You will need to add the **oostring.cpp** file to the project and have the **oostring.h** file in the same folder with **fileapp.cpp**.

3. Enter your name and age as input.

4. Open the output file (**name_age.dat**) and note that the file's only contents are what you just entered. Close **name_age.dat**.

5. Run the program again. This time enter Ben Conrad for the name and 16 for the age.

6. Open **name_age.dat** again to see that your name and age have been replaced in the file. Close **name_age.dat**.

7. Change the statement that opens the file for output to match the statement in Code List 14-9.

8. Run the program again. This time enter your name and age again.

9. Open **name_age.dat** again to see that Ben Conrad's name and age have not been replaced by yours. Because the file was opened for appending, your name and age were added to the end of the file.

10. Close **name_age.dat**. Close the program.

CODE LIST 14-9

```
outfile.open("NAME_AGE.DAT",ios::app);  // Open file for appending.
```

225

Detecting the End of a File

Often the length of a file is unknown to the programmer. In Step-by-Step 14.3, the series of numbers you read into your program ended with a zero. Because you knew the data ended with a zero, you knew when to stop reading. In other cases, however, you may not have a value in the file that signals the end of the file. In those cases, there are other techniques for detecting the end of the file.

When reading strings from a file, the getline method returns a value of true as long as it finds valid data to read. If the end of the file is reached, the getline method will return a value of false. Therefore, a loop like the one in Code List 14-10 will read all the lines in a data file and stop reading when the end of the file is reached.

CODE LIST 14-10

```
while(getline(infile,instring))
  {
      cout << instring << endl;
  }
```

STEP-BY-STEP ▷ 14.6

1. Open the program **str_end.cpp**. The program includes a loop like the one in Code List 14-10.

2. If the file named **strings.dat** is not already in the same directory as **str_end.cpp**, copy it there now. You will also need to add the **oostring.cpp** file to the project and have the **oostring.h** file in the same folder with **str_end.cpp**.

3. Compile and run **str_end.cpp**. The contents of the **strings.dat** file are read from the file and printed to the screen.

4. Close the program.

When reading numeric values, you must detect whether the operation has failed, indicating that the end of the file has been reached. Code List 14-11 shows a loop that reads numbers into the variable x until the operation fails. Also notice that the line which prints the value to the screen is in an if structure that prevents the value of x from being printed if the input operation failed.

CODE LIST 14-11

```
do  // Read numbers until the end of file is encountered.
 {
   infile >> x;          // Get number from file.
    if(!infile.fail())  // If the end of file is not
    {                    // reached...
     cout << x << endl;  // Print number to screen.
    }
 } while(!infile.fail());
```

The `fail` function does not detect when the last line in the file is read. Instead, it detects when the program attempts to read past the end of the file. The results of reading past the end of the file vary. But in most cases, the last number in the file is read again. The if structure prevents the last value in the file from being printed twice.

The `fail` function returns the value of true if an attempt has been made to read past the end of the file. To use the `fail` function, use the name of the file stream, a period, and `fail()`, as shown in Code List 14-11.

Note

The `fail` function detects a variety of file errors, not just end of file. Some compilers support an `eof` function that can be used in place of `fail` to find the end of a file. The `eof` function, however, can have unpredictable results. The `fail` function is recommended because in the event of any error, attempting to read from the file should be discontinued.

STEP-BY-STEP ▷ 14.7

1. Open the program **num_end.cpp**. The program includes a loop like the one in Code List 14-11. The program is a modified version of **numread.cpp** that does not require the last number in the file to be zero. Instead, it detects the end of the file.

2. If the file named **nums.dat** is not already in the same directory as **num_end.cpp**, copy it there now.

3. Open **nums.dat** to see that it contains four floating-point numbers and that the list does not end in zero.

4. Compile and run **num_end.cpp**. The program operates like **numread.cpp**.

5. Close the program.

Using Multiple Files

As mentioned earlier, you can have more than one file open at a time. Just declare and use a separate file stream for each file. Why would you want more than one file open at a time? There are many reasons. Let us look at two of them.

Suppose you need to add some data to the middle of a file. Since you cannot insert data in a file, you must read the data from the original file and write it to a new file. At the position where the new data is to be inserted, you write the data to the new file and then continue writing the rest of the data from the original file.

Concept Builder

When using multiple files in a program, open files only as you need them and close them as soon as possible to avoid data loss in the event of power failure or program crash.

Another example of when more than one file may be necessary is when processing information in a file. Data may be read from one file, processed, and saved to another file.

Summary

■ Data files allow for the storage of data prior to a program's ending and the computer's being turned off. Data files also allow for more data storage than can fit in RAM.

■ A sequential-access file is like an audiocassette tape. Data must be written to and read from the file sequentially.

■ A random-access file is like a compact disc. Any record can be accessed directly.

■ The first step to using a file is declaring a file stream. Some file streams are for writing data and some are for reading data.

■ After a file stream has been declared, the next step is to open the file. Opening a file associates the file stream with a physical data file.

■ After data is written or read, the file must be closed.

■ The insertion operator (<<) is used to write to a data file.

■ When reading numeric data, use the extraction operator. When reading string data or when reading from a file with both string and numeric data, read the data into string objects.

■ Adding data to the end of an existing file is called appending.

■ The getline method detects the end of the file when reading strings from a file. The `fail` function detects the end of a file when reading numbers.

■ You can use more than one file at a time by declaring multiple file streams.

VOCABULARY REVIEW

Define the following terms:

appending	random-access file
close	sequential-access file
file streams	stream operation modes
open	

LESSON 14 REVIEW QUESTIONS

TRUE/FALSE

Circle the T if the statement is true. Circle the F if it is false.

T F 1. A computer's RAM can generally hold much more data than will fit in a data file.

T F 2. To retrieve data from a sequential-access data file, you must start reading at the beginning of the file.

T F 3. Any file stream can be used for both input and output.

T F 4. Opening a file associates a physical disk file with a file stream.

T F 5. The statement that closes a disk file must include the filename.

T F 6. When a file contains a mixture of numeric and string data, all the data should be read into string objects.

T F 7. The `ios::app` stream operation mode is used when adding data to the end of an existing file.

T F 8. The getline method returns a value of false if the end of the file is not yet reached.

T F 9. The `fail` function detects the end of a file and other file errors.

T F 10. Working with two files simultaneously requires two file streams.

WRITTEN QUESTIONS

Write your answers to the following questions.

11. What are the two types of data files?

12. What type of data file is the most widely used?

13. What is the danger of leaving a file open?

14. What happens if you open an existing file for output using `ios::out`?

15. What is a condition that could cause an error when opening a file?

16. How can you test to see whether an error occurred while opening a file?

17. Why are end-of-line characters included when data is written to a file?

18. What term describes adding data to the end of an existing file?

19. When does the `fail` function return a value of true?

20. What is an example of a situation where more than one file may need to be opened at once?

PROJECT 14A

SCANS

Write a program that asks the user's name, address, city, state, and ZIP code. The program should then save the data to a data file. Save the source code as **addrfile.cpp**. (*Note:* You will need to add the **oostring.cpp** file to the project and have the **oostring.h** file in the same folder.)

PROJECT 14B

SCANS

Modify the program written in Project 14A so that it appends a name and address to the data file every time the program is run, rather than rewriting the output file. Run the program several times to append several names and addresses to the output file.

PROJECT 14C

SCANS

Write a program that reads the data saved in Project 14B and prints the data to the screen. Save the source code as **nameprnt.cpp**.

CRITICAL THINKING

Modify **hightemp.cpp** so that it gets its temperatures from a data file, rather than from the keyboard. Create a text file with sample temperatures in order to test the program.

OBJECT-ORIENTED PROGRAMMING

OBJECTIVES

When you complete this lesson, you will be able to:

- Compare and contrast procedural programming and object-oriented programming.

- Use a simple class.

- Design and implement a simple class.

- Describe the concepts of reusability, containment, and inheritance.

⏱ **Estimated Time: 2 hours**

VOCABULARY

constructors
containment
has-a relationship
inheritance
information hiding
is-a relationship
member functions
members
object-oriented paradigm
object-oriented
  programming
paradigm
procedural paradigm
reusability
scope-resolution operator

Procedural Programming versus Object-Oriented Programming

As the field of computer science has grown over the years, several different methods have been developed for programming computers. The first programming was done by flipping switches on a control panel or feeding machine language instructions into a computer. Recall from Lesson 1 that the development of assembly language was followed by the development of high-level languages, which made programming easier.

One of the more recent developments in programming is known as *object-oriented programming* (OOP), which in some ways continues the trend toward higher-level programming languages. OOP, however, does more than that: it changes the way a programmer uses data and functions.

The different methods used for writing programs are known as paradigms. A *paradigm* is a model or a set of rules that defines a way of programming. Two primary paradigms are used to program computers today: the procedural paradigm and the object-oriented paradigm.

You learned some concepts of OOP and some of its important terms in Lesson 6. This lesson will review some of those concepts and extend them with additional insight and information. You will also have the opportunity to build your own class in this lesson.

Procedural Paradigm

The procedural paradigm is the paradigm you have used in this book up to this point. The *procedural paradigm* focuses on the idea that all algorithms in a program are performed with functions and data that a programmer can see, understand, and change. In a program written procedurally, the focus is on the functions that will process the data. The programmer then devises ways to pass the required data to and from the functions, which do the processing. To successfully write procedural programs, the programmer must understand how all data is stored and how the algorithms of the program work.

When you learned about strings, you learned that strings are stored in character arrays. Working with character arrays requires you to know the technical details of the character array and the functions that manipulate the array. To avoid this technical detail, we chose to use a string class, which is an object-oriented character array.

Procedural programming has served programmers well for many years and will continue to do so for some time. But computer scientists are always searching for a better way to develop software. By taking a look at the world around them, they discovered that the world consists of objects that perform work and interact with each other. When applied to programming computers, the result is a different paradigm: object-oriented programming.

Concept Builder

There are many programming paradigms in computer science. Some of the paradigms are procedural, functional, object-oriented, and logic. Most common languages such as C, FORTRAN, and standard PASCAL are procedural. C++, Smalltalk, and Java are well-known object-oriented languages. The functional paradigm includes languages such as LISP and Scheme. Finally, Prolog is a language in the logic paradigm.

Object-Oriented Paradigm

The *object-oriented paradigm* centers on the idea that all programs can be made up of separate entities called *objects*. A program built from these objects is called an *object-oriented program*. Each of the objects used to build the program has a specific responsibility or purpose. In a string object, for example, the string itself and all the operations that can be performed with the string are part of the object. The string object can initialize itself, store a string provided to it, and perform other functions such as reporting the length of the string the object holds. In other words, instead of an object's being directly manipulated by other parts of the program, an object manipulates itself. Building programs using the object-oriented paradigm is called object-oriented programming or OOP.

Communication among objects is similar to communication among people. You cannot look inside someone's head to see what he or she knows. You must ask questions and allow the person to provide a response. In OOP, data is transferred through messages that are exchanged among objects. The data in an object is not intended to be accessed directly by code that is outside of the object. You have already used messages while working with the string and vector classes. Rather than going into the object and finding out the length, you used a length method to "ask" the object its length. In effect, you sent a message and received a response.

Concept Builder

Messages can do more than simply initialize an object or return a length of a string or vector. A message can perform a high-level task such as sort information in the object. A string object can even include a method to check the spelling of the text in the string.

Communication among objects takes the form of messages because objects hide all of their data and internal operations. As you learned in Lesson 6, this "hiding" of data and code is known as encapsulation. By using encapsulation, objects can protect and guarantee the integrity of their data. In procedural programming, poorly written functions can often change important data, causing problems throughout the program. The threat of a poorly written function changing data is reduced when using the object-oriented paradigm.

There is more to object-oriented programming than the concepts and features mentioned in these lessons. The first step, however, is to visualize how a program can be implemented using objects, learn what is in an object, and understand how objects communicate with other parts of the program. Object-oriented programming in C++ does not take the place of what you have already learned. Instead, it extends the features of the language and gives you a new way to organize programs. The structures and data types you have been using are also used in object-oriented programs. In fact, what you have learned in previous lessons will provide the foundation you need to be successful as an object-oriented programmer.

Using a Simple Circle Class

In previous lessons, you have used a string class, a vector class, and stream classes. Internally, those classes are fairly complicated. In this lesson, you will use a class that defines a circle and allows you to include circle objects in your programs. This circle object is very simple. It allows you to declare a circle and define its radius. The object then reports the area of the circle. Through this simple example, you will see how encapsulation and messages make it possible for you to use the object without knowing how the data is stored in the object or how the algorithms are implemented. Later in the lesson, we will look at how the circle class is written.

Classes

Recall that the definition for an object is known as a class. Our circle class will be named simply *circle*. The class *circle* tells the compiler how to create each object of type circle. You declare a circle object the same way you declared other objects. The following statement declares a circle named `my_circle`.

```
circle my_circle;
```

When the compiler encounters this declaration, it refers to the circle definition to find out how much memory to reserve for a circle object. The object is then created in memory and given the name `my_circle`. In the same way that many different variables of the same data type can be created, many different objects of the type circle can be created. Each different object of the type circle is independent of the other circle objects in the program. If you were to declare two circle objects, you would have two independent objects, which could be used to represent two distinct circles.

Note

When multiple objects are declared from the same class, the code required to perform the operations (methods) is not duplicated in memory for each object. The data for each object is stored separately in memory, but all objects defined by the same class share the same code.

STEP-BY-STEP 15.1

1. Load the program **oop.cpp**. The program in Code List 15-1 appears.

2. If necessary, copy the **circle.h** file to the folder that contains **oop.cpp**.

3. Look at the program and see how the objects are declared and how messages are passed between the objects. Notice that there is no way of knowing how the circle objects store the radius or how they calculate area.

4. Run the program.

5. Leave the source code file open while you analyze the program in the paragraphs that follow.

Concept Builder

Another way to look at the relationship between a class and an object is to consider examples in the real world. If the definition of a human being were a class, then you and I are instances of that class. We are not the same person, but we both have the characteristics of the human class.

```
// oop.cpp
// This object-oriented program shows the use of simple
// objects which represent circles.

#include "circle.h"        // contains the circle class
#include <iostream.h>

int main()
{
 circle Circle_One;        // declare objects
 circle Circle_Two;        // of type circle
 double User_Radius;
 double Area;

 cout << "\nWhat is the radius of the first circle? ";
 cin  >> User_Radius;

 // send a message to Circle_One telling it to set its
 // radius to User_Radius
 Circle_One.SetRadius(User_Radius);

 cout << "\nWhat is the radius of the second circle? ";
 cin  >> User_Radius;

 // send a message to Circle_Two telling it to set its
 // radius to User_Radius
 Circle_Two.SetRadius(User_Radius);

 // send a message to Circle_One asking for its area
 Area = Circle_One.Area();

 cout.setf(ios::fixed);
 cout << "\nThe area of the first circle is " << Area << ".\n";

 // send a message to Circle_Two asking for its area
 Area = Circle_Two.Area();

 cout << "\nThe area of the second circle is " << Area << ".\n";

 return 0;
}
```

Writing a Program to Use the Circle Class

Let us analyze the source code you ran in the previous exercise. After the beginning comments, there are two compiler directives, shown again in Code List 15-2.

```
#include "circle.h"        // contains the circle class
#include <iostream.h>
```

The first compiler directive includes the header file circle.h. The circle.h header file contains the definition for the circle class. Without the class definition, the compiler would not know how to create a circle object, nor would it know what properties a circle object has. The next compiler directive includes the iostream.h header file so that the program can get input from the user and output data to the screen.

In the main function, the program declares two copies of the circle class, Circle_One and Circle_Two (see Code List 15-3). A variable to hold a radius and an area of a circle is also declared. The variables User_Radius and Area are used in your program and are not part of either object.

```
int main()
{
  circle Circle_One;       // declare objects
  circle Circle_Two;       // of type circle
  double User_Radius;
  double Area;
```

The program then prompts the user for the radius of the first circle. After the program receives the user's response, it sends a message to Circle_One requesting that it set its radius to User_Radius, as shown in Code List 15-4.

```
cout << "\nWhat is the radius of the first circle? ";
cin  >> User_Radius;

// send a message to Circle_One telling it to set its
// radius to User_Radius
Circle_One.SetRadius(User_Radius);
```

After the radius of Circle_One has been set to User_Radius, the program prompts the user for the radius of the second circle and sets the radius of Circle_Two using the same method that was used to set the radius of Circle_One.

Finally, the program sends a message to each of the circle objects and requests its area. The area of Circle_One is assigned to Area and then output to the screen. Then the area of the second circle is also retrieved and output to the screen (see Code List 15-5).

```
// send a message to Circle_One asking for its area
Area = Circle_One.Area();

cout.setf(ios::fixed);
cout << "\nThe area of the first circle is " << Area << ".\n";

// send a message to Circle_Two asking for its area
Area = Circle_Two.Area();

cout << "\nThe area of the second circle is " << Area << ".\n";
cout.unsetf(ios::fixed);

return 0;
}
```

There are many different ways the radius could be stored in the object as well as different ways the area could be calculated. Is the size of the circle stored in the form of the radius or the diameter? How is the area calculated? You do not know the answers to these questions. To use the object, however, you do not need this information.

Designing and Implementing the Circle Class

You now have lots of experience using classes that have been created for you. At some point, however, you will need to design a class or modify an existing class. Implementing a class is not difficult, but it does involve some new syntax that you may have not seen before.

Designing a Class

Designing a class requires you to think in an object-oriented way. For example, consider a typical telephone answering machine. It encapsulates the functions of an answering machine as well as the data (your incoming and outgoing messages). The buttons on the answering machine are the equivalent of messages. Pushing the Play button sends a message to the answering machine to play the stored messages. It is not hard to understand that an answering machine is an object which contains all the storage and functions it needs within itself.

To design a class, you must think of computer programs in the same way you think of an answering machine or other objects around you. If you were to design the circle class you used in the previous section, you should first take into account what needs to be stored and what functions are necessary. In other words, you define the purpose of the object. The purpose will determine how an object is coded, what data it will hold, and how its operations will be implemented.

In the case of the circle, all that is required to define a circle is a radius. You then decide what functions the object needs to perform. For example, you may want the circle to report its area and circumference. The circle also needs to be able to set its radius.

A class should be designed with enough functions and data to perform its responsibilities—no more and no less. You have never seen an answering machine that can function as a stapler. Likewise, a class should not perform an unrelated task. You also do not need to store more data than is necessary. For example, since the radius is all that is necessary to define a circle, you should not store both a radius and a diameter.

Object-oriented design (often abbreviated OOD) involves much more than the guidelines outlined here. For this lesson, the goal is just to get a taste of object-oriented design.

Implementing a Class

The best way to learn how to implement a class is to study the code of an implemented class. Code List 15-6 is the header file circle.h that was used in Step-by-Step 15.1. You have used header files before. However, you may not have ever opened one to see what is inside. A header file is a source code file that typically includes code or declarations of code that you intend to include in more than one program. Classes are normally defined in header files so that they may be reused.

Note

Header files normally contain declarations of variables, functions, and classes, but not the implementation of the functions and classes. This is the case with almost all header files that come with a C++ compiler. However, in some situations, the functions and classes may also be implemented in the same header file.

CODE LIST 15-6

```
// circle.h

#ifndef _CIRCLE_H
#define _CIRCLE_H

const double PI=3.14159;

class circle
{
 public:
        // constructors
        circle();              // default constructor
        circle(const circle &); // copy constructor

        // member functions
        void    SetRadius(double);
        double Area();

 private:
        // data
        double radius;
};

// default constructor
circle::circle()
{
   radius = 0.0;
}
```

(continued on next page)

```
// copy constructor
circle::circle(const circle & Object)
{
  radius = Object.radius;
}

// method to set the radius of the circle
void circle::SetRadius(double IncomingRadius)
{
  radius = IncomingRadius;
}

// method to find the area of the circle
double circle::Area()
{
 return(PI*radius*radius);
}

#endif
```

Before continuing, familiarize yourself with the code in Code List 15-6. The implementation of the circle class will be broken down and examined in the paragraphs that follow.

COMPILER DIRECTIVES

At the beginning of the file are the compiler directives `#ifndef` and `#define`. These are used to prevent the class from being defined twice, which can create problems. The `#define` directive instructs the compiler to define a symbol and to remember that the symbol exists. The `#ifndef` directive checks the compiler's symbol table for a specified entry.

In this case, these compiler directives are used together to make sure that the circle class has not already been defined. The `#ifndef` directive checks for the existence of a symbol named _CIRCLE_H. If the entry is not found, the `#define` directive defines the symbol and the source code that follows defines the circle class. If the _CIRCLE_H symbol is already defined, it means that this header file has been compiled already and the definition of the circle class is skipped.

At the end of Code List 15-6 is the compiler directive `#endif`, which ends the original `#ifndef` directive. The `#ifndef` compiler directive works with the `#endif` directive to form an if structure similar to those you have worked with in previous lessons. The `#ifndef` directive instructs the compiler to compile everything between the `#ifndef` and the `#endif` if the symbol is not defined.

CLASS DEFINITION

A class definition is made up of several different parts (see Code List 15-7). The definition begins with the keyword `class`, followed by the class name and an opening brace. The definition ends with a closing brace and a semicolon. Functions and variables that are prototyped and declared in a class definition are called ***members***.

Note

If the semicolon after a class definition is omitted, the compiler will report several errors. Therefore, if multiple errors are encountered when compiling a class, check for the presence of the semicolon at the end of the class definition.

```
class circle
{
 public:
        // constructors
        circle();                  // default constructor
        circle(const circle &);    // copy constructor

        // member functions
        void   SetRadius(double);
        double Area();

 private:
        // data
        double radius;
};
```

After the opening brace is the keyword `public` followed by a colon. The `public` keyword tells the compiler to let the programmer using the class have access to all the variables and functions between the `public` and `private` keywords. Any variables and functions after the `private` keyword cannot be accessed from outside the object. The `private` keyword allows a circle object to protect its data. This data protection is known as *information hiding*, which is an important benefit provided by encapsulation. By using information hiding, objects can protect the integrity of their data.

The constructor prototypes follow the `public` keyword (see Code List 15-8). *Constructors* tell the compiler how to create the object in memory and what the initial values of its data will be. Constructors are given the same name as the class.

```
// constructors
circle();                  // default constructor
circle(const circle &);    // copy constructor
```

The circle class has two constructors. The first constructor is known as the default constructor. The default constructor is used when the object is declared. The second constructor is known as the copy constructor. A copy constructor receives a reference to another object as an argument and is used when objects are passed to functions by value.

At this stage, constructors can be confusing. All you need to understand right now is that constructors allow you to declare objects. Classes often have multiple constructors to allow you to declare objects in different ways. For example, recall how the vector class allowed you to declare an empty vector, a vector of a specific length, or a vector of a specific length initialized to a value. Each of those different ways to declare a vector requires a separate constructor within the class.

After the constructors are the member function prototypes (see Code List 15-9). *Member functions* allow programmers using an object to send information to it and receive information from it. Member functions are the messages used for communication in object-oriented programming.

```
// member functions
void    SetRadius(double);
double Area();
```

The circle object needs two member functions: one to set the radius and one to retrieve the area. Member function prototypes are written just like normal function prototypes with a `return` type, a name, and an argument list. Recall that it is not necessary for a prototype to include the names of the parameters, just the type. The implementation of the member functions follows the definition of the class.

The `private` keyword comes after the member function prototypes. The only data required for the circle object is the radius, so it is declared as a float with the identifier `radius`, as shown in Code List 15-10.

```
private:
        // data
        double radius;
};
```

Because `radius` is after the `private` keyword, a programmer using a circle object cannot access the radius directly, so member functions must be used. After the `radius` variable, the definition of the circle class is closed with the closing brace and a semicolon.

IMPLEMENTING MEMBER FUNCTIONS

To implement a member function, you must use a special syntax. The function is implemented like a normal C++ function except that the class name and the *scope-resolution operator* (::) precede the function name. Constructors are slightly different from other member functions because they do not have any `return` type—not even void.

Constructor implementation in the circle class is very simple (see Code List 15-11). The default constructor sets the radius equal to zero. The copy constructor sets the radius equal to the passed object's radius.

```
// default constructor
circle::circle()
{
  radius = 0.0;
}

// copy constructor
circle::circle(const circle & Object)
{
  radius = Object.radius;
}
```

The implementation of the other member functions is also simple. Code List 15-12 shows how the `SetRadius` function sets the radius equal to the value it is passed, and the `Area` function calculates and returns the area of the circle.

CODE LIST 15-12

```
// method to set the radius of the circle
void circle::SetRadius(double IncomingRadius)
{
  radius = IncomingRadius;
}

// method to find the area of the circle
double circle::Area()
{
 return(PI*radius*radius);
}
```

STEP-BY-STEP ▷ 15.2

1. Open the **circle.h** header file.

2. Modify the class definition to include a member function that returns the radius of the circle. The class definition should be modified to include the prototype for the `GetRadius` function shown in Code List 15-13.

3. Add the function below to the end of the circle.h file, before the #endif line.

   ```
   double circle::GetRadius()
   {
     return(radius);
   }
   ```

4. Save **circle.h** and open **oop.cpp**.

5. Add the statement from Code List 15-14 below the line that reports the area of the first circle.

6. Add the statement from Code List 15-15 below the line that reports the area of the second circle.

7. Compile and run the modified program.

8. Close the program.

CODE LIST 15-13

```
class circle
{
 public:
        // constructors
        circle();                // default constructor
        circle(const circle &); // copy constructor

        // member functions
```

(continued on next page)

```
        void    SetRadius(double);
        double  Area();
        double  GetRadius();

    private:
        // data
        double radius;
};
```

```
cout << "The radius of the first circle is "
     << Circle_One.GetRadius() << ".\n";
```

```
cout << "The radius of the second circle is "
     << Circle_Two.GetRadius() << ".\n";
```

Reusability, Containment, and Inheritance

You have seen some of the advantages of using object-oriented programming. Three more advantages of the paradigm are reusability, containment, and inheritance.

Reusability

Among the greatest advantages that object-oriented programming offers is *reusability*. After an object is designed and coded into a class, that class can be reused in any program. This means that productivity may be increased because less code has to be written. In addition, because less code is written, fewer errors can occur. Although procedural code can be reused, object-oriented code is often easier to use, especially when using more advanced techniques of data handling. For example, you have used the string and vector classes in a number of programs.

Containment

One of the features of objects that make them so reusable is that objects can contain other objects and use them to implement another object. For example, suppose you want to create a class that defines a car. If you already have a wheel object that defines the properties of a wheel, your car object can use the wheel class to declare four wheel objects. This type of relationship among objects is called *containment* because the car object contains four wheel objects. The relationship is also referred to as a *has-a relationship* because a car has a wheel (four wheels, in this case).

You have used a vector class to implement arrays. There is another commonly used class called a matrix class. A matrix class allows you to implement a two-dimensional array of rows and columns. In most cases, a matrix class contains a vector of vectors. Therefore, a matrix class demonstrates reusability and containment. You will use a matrix class in Case Study III.

Inheritance

Inheritance is the ability of one object to inherit the properties of another object. For example, you might have a building class that defines the properties of a building. The building class could define attributes such as the dimensions of the building, the number of floors, and the types of materials used to construct the building. Suppose you have debugged and perfected your building class, but what you need is a house object. A house has all the attributes of a building as well as additional attributes, such as number of bedrooms, number of bathrooms, and size of garage.

Rather than write a new class from scratch or modify the building class, you can create a house class that inherits the properties of the building and then extends those properties with properties that describe the house. The house object and the building object have what is called an *is-a relationship*, meaning the house is a building.

When one class inherits the properties of another, the class from which the properties are inherited is known as the parent class. The class that inherits the properties of another is the child class or derived class. In the example above, the building class is the parent class and the house class is the child class. The building class can also be described as a base class upon which other classes are built.

An object created from the derived class can call a parent class's member functions as if they were members of the derived class. Users of the class do not need to know what members are implemented in each class. In fact, the users of the class do not need to know that the class is derived, as long as they know what members are available to them.

Inheritance can be multilevel. For example, a class called garden_home could inherit properties of the house class that inherits properties of the building class (see Figure 15-1). Multilevel inheritance is one of the features that makes the work done in an object-oriented program more reusable.

FIGURE 15-1
Inheritance can continue for multiple levels.

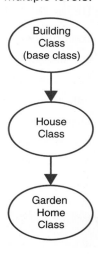

Summary

- A paradigm is a model or set of rules that define a way of programming.

- In the procedural paradigm, the functions and algorithms are the focus, with data viewed as something for the functions to manipulate.

- The object-oriented paradigm dictates that data should be placed inside of objects and that these objects should communicate with each other in the form of messages.

- Object-oriented programming (OOP) is the process of developing programs using the object-oriented paradigm.

- Constructors tell the compiler how to create an object in memory and what the initial value of its data will be.

- Member functions provide a way for a programmer to pass data to and get data from an object.

- Reusability is a major benefit of object-oriented programming.

- Containment is the term used to describe an object that contains one or more other objects as members.

- Inheritance is the term used to describe an object that inherits properties from another object.

- The class from which an object inherits properties is called a parent class or base class. The class that inherits the properties is called a child class or derived class.

- Inheritance can be multilevel.

VOCABULARY REVIEW

Define the following terms:

constructors	members
containment	object-oriented paradigm
has-a relationship	object-oriented programming
inheritance	paradigm
information hiding	procedural paradigm
is-a relationship	reusability
member functions	scope-resolution operator

LESSON 15 REVIEW QUESTIONS

TRUE/FALSE

Circle the T if the statement is true. Circle the F if it is false.

T F 1. A paradigm is a model or set of rules that define a way of programming.

T F 2. The procedural paradigm involves sending messages.

T F 3. Object-oriented programming reduces the problems caused by poorly written functions changing data that should not be changed.

T F 4. The circle class calculates the area of the circle.

T F 5. Functions and variables that are prototyped and declared in a class definition are called objects.

T F 6. Classes often have more than one constructor.

T F 7. Constructors have a void `return` type.

T   F   8. Classes can be easily reused in multiple programs.

T   F   9. Containment creates an is-a relationship among objects.

T   F   10. Inheritance can be multilevel.

WRITTEN QUESTIONS

Write your answers to the following questions.

11. What are the two primary programming paradigms discussed in this lesson?

12. What paradigm centers on the idea that all programs can be made up of separate entities called objects?

13. The circle class allows you to declare a circle. What data is provided by the programmer using the circle class?

14. What code is necessary to declare two circle objects: `CircleA` and `CircleB`?

15. Why are classes normally defined in a header file separate from your main program?

16. What is the purpose of a constructor?

17. What is an example of a class that you have reused in the lessons of this book?

18. What is a parent class?

19. When you write a program that includes string objects, are you using containment or inheritance?

20. Is a program that extends the properties of a class using containment or inheritance?

PROJECT 15A

Write a program similar to **oop.cpp** that declares two circle objects. The program should set the radius of the first circle to 1.5 and then obtain the area of the first circle from the object. The program should then set the radius of the second circle to the area of the first circle. As output, the program should provide the area of both circles. Save the program as **oop2.cpp**.

PROJECT 15B

Add a method to the circle class that returns the circumference of the circle. Modify **oop.cpp** to report the circumference of the circle.

PROJECT 15C

SCANS

Write a program named **bucktest.cpp** that declares a bucket object based on the class definition in bucket.h, which is provided for you. Open bucket.h to see the methods in the class. The program should perform the following operations:

1. Declare an object of type bucket.

2. Use the `SetGallonSize()` method to set the bucket size to 5.0 gallons.

3. Use the `FillBucket()` method to fill the bucket with 3.2 gallons of water.

4. Use the `GetWeight()` method to output the weight of the 3.2 gallons of water.

CRITICAL THINKING

SCANS

Using the circle class definition as a model, create a file named **square.h** and implement a class that models a square and includes an `Area` method. Also write a program to test the square class. Name the test program **sqrtest.cpp**.

REVIEW QUESTIONS

MATCHING

Write the letter of the description from Column 2 that best matches the term or phrase in Column 1.

Column 1	Column 2
_____ 1. appending	**A.** A model or set of rules for a way to program
_____ 2. array	**B.** Functions that allow communication with an object
_____ 3. constructors	**C.** Functions and variables prototyped and declared in a class definition
_____ 4. containment	
_____ 5. file streams	**D.** A list of data structures accessed with a single identifier
_____ 6. inheritance	**E.** Results in a has-a relationship
_____ 7. member functions	**F.** Results in an is-a relationship
_____ 8. members	**G.** Functions that create an object in memory
_____ 9. paradigm	**H.** Objects that provide a connection to a data file
_____ 10. template class	**I.** Adding data to the end of a file
	J. A class designed to have the data type customized when compiled

WRITTEN QUESTIONS

Write your answers to the following questions.

1. What are the three ways to declare a vector?

2. What subscripts are used to index a three-element vector?

3. What happens to the data in a vector if you manually shorten the vector?

4. In a sequential-access file, where must you begin reading?

5. When a file contains a mixture of numeric and string data, into what type of object should the data be read?

6. What stream operation mode is used when adding data to the end of an existing file?

7. What programming paradigm involves classes and objects?

8. Why do classes often have more than one constructor?

9. In object-oriented programming, why is reusability important?

10. Give an example of when you have used containment in this course.

APPLICATIONS

APPLICATION 6-1

1. Write the code statement necessary to make the vector class available to your program.

2. Write the code necessary to declare a 50-element vector of type int, initialized to 1, named IntVect.

3. Write the code necessary to determine the number of elements in IntVect and store that value in a variable named NumElements.

4. Write the code necessary to declare a file stream named outstream to be used for writing to a file.

5. Write the code necessary to close the file attached to the outstream file stream.

APPLICATION 6-2

Write a program named **postage.cpp** that declares two vectors of six elements each of type double. One vector should be named weight and one should be named rate. The program should use a loop to prompt the user for a weight in ounces and a postage rate for that weight and store the values in parallel elements of the vectors. After the six weights and rates have been gathered and stored in the vectors, a loop should print a table of the weights and rates to the screen. You can use any data you wish to test the program. A suggested data set appears below.

Weight	Rate
1.0	0.33
2.0	0.55
3.0	0.77
4.0	0.99
5.0	1.21
6.0	1.43

APPLICATION 6-3

Modify the **rodeo.cpp** program that you saved in Application 5-3 to save each transaction to a data file. The program should open a file stream to a data file and write the information as the order is taken, in a format similar to the sample below.

```
Sandwich 1.25
Chips 0.50
Large Drink 1.00
Sub Total 2.75
Total 2.92
```

APPLICATION 6-4

Use the class you implemented in the Critical Thinking activity in Lesson 15 (**square.h** and **sqrtest.cpp**) as a starting point to create a rectangle class that models a rectangle and includes an `Area` method. The class should also include methods to set and retrieve the length and width properties of the object. Name the class file **rect.h** and the test program **recttest.cpp**.

 INTERNET ACTIVITY

1. Open your Web browser.

2. Use a Web search engine such as www.yahoo.com to locate information about object-oriented programming (OOP). Also search for OOA (object-oriented analysis) and OOD (object-oriented design).

3. After you see what your search finds, go to **http://www.programcpp.com/basics**.

4. One the home page, click the link called **Internet Activities from the book** and then go to the **Unit 6** link. On that page, you will find links to sites that provide information on object-oriented programming and design.

5. Write a paragraph or more describing something you learned while researching object-oriented programming and design on the Web.

MILEAGE LOOK-UP TABLE

⏱ Estimated Time: 1 hour

SCANS

Overview

The look-up table is a widely used data structure that can be implemented using a two-dimensional array or matrix. An example of how a look-up table can be used is to determine the amount of deduction from an employee's paycheck. The amount of gross pay and the number of dependents the employee claims are used to look up a deduction amount in a table. Even microprocessors sometimes use look-up tables to help them perform some operations more quickly.

In this case study, you will analyze a program that uses a matrix as a look-up table of mileage between major cities. The program will ask for two cities as input and provide output of the number of miles between the cities.

The Matrix Class

In Lesson 15 you learned that a matrix is a two-dimensional array that can be implemented using a vector of vectors. In this case study, you will use a matrix class that has been created for you. The matrix class is contained in the file matrix.h and requires vector.h because the matrix class uses containment to create a vector of vectors.

The matrix class is similar to the vector class. The major difference is that a matrix is made up of rows and columns like a spreadsheet, rather than just a list. Let us look at some examples that use the matrix class.

Declaring a Matrix Object

Because the matrix class is a template class, you must specify a data type when declaring the matrix object.

```
matrix <float> MyFloatMatrix;  // instantiate a matrix with size 0 x 0
```

You can declare a matrix and specify the size in rows and columns. The following example declares a matrix with three rows and two columns. The first value is always the number of rows and the second value is always the number of columns.

```
matrix <char> CharMatrix(3,2);
```

You can instantiate a matrix and specify the size and a value with which to initialize each element. In the following example, `MyMatrix` is initialized with four rows and three columns, each holding the value 0.

```
matrix <int> CharMatrix(4,3,0);
```

Obtaining the Size of a Matrix

You can determine the number of rows in the matrix using the `numrows` function.

```
rows = MyMatrix.numrows();
```

You can determine the number of columns in the matrix using the `numcols` function.

```
columns = MyMatrix.numcols();
```

Resizing a Matrix

You can specify a new size for the matrix using the `resize` function. Keep in mind that resizing the matrix can result in lost data. The following example resizes the matrix to have five rows and seven columns.

```
MyMatrix.resize(5,7);
```

Indexing Elements in a Matrix

You can set the elements of the matrix individually. The following example sets the element in the first row of the second column to 3.

```
MyMatrix[1][2] = 3;
```

You can retrieve the elements of the matrix individually. The following example retrieves the value of the element in the third row of the second column.

```
value = MyMatrix[3][2];
```

Assigning One Matrix to Another

You can assign the contents of one matrix to another. The matrix receiving the contents of the other is resized.

```
MyMatrix1 = MyMatrix2;
```

Building the Look-Up Table

The look-up table is the heart of this case study's program. The program will store each possible output value in a matrix. Instead of calculating the distance between two cities, the program will look up the distance in a table (the matrix). Figure CSIII-1 shows the look-up table required for our program.

To keep the problem manageable, 10 cities have been selected for the look-up table. To find the mileage between two of the cities, locate the row of your originating city and the column of your destination. The intersection of that row and column gives the road mileage between the cities.

This look-up table will be implemented in the program as a matrix.

	Atlanta	Boston	Chicago	Cincinnati	Dallas	Denver	Detroit	Los Angeles	New York	Seattle
Atlanta	0	1037	674	440	795	1398	699	2182	841	2618
Boston	1037	0	963	840	1748	1949	695	2979	206	2976
Chicago	674	963	0	287	917	996	266	2054	802	2013
Cincinnati	440	840	287	0	920	1164	259	2179	647	2300
Dallas	795	1748	917	920	0	781	1143	1387	1552	2078
Denver	1398	1949	996	1164	781	0	1253	1059	1771	1307
Detroit	699	695	266	259	1143	1253	0	2311	637	2279
Los Angeles	2182	2979	2054	2179	1387	1059	2311	0	2786	1131
New York	841	206	802	647	1552	1771	637	2786	0	2815
Seattle	2618	2976	2013	2300	2078	1307	2279	1131	2815	0

Implementing the Look-Up Table

In our program, the look-up table must be implemented as a matrix. We will declare the matrix and then initialize it later in the program with values from a data file. The following statement declares the matrix and initializes the 10-by-10 matrix to 0.

```
matrix <int> cities(10,10,0);
```

The Completed Program

Code List CSIII-1 is a listing of the entire completed program. Let us compile and run the program, then analyze it piece by piece.

```
// mileage.cpp

#include <iostream.h>    // necessary for input/output
#include <fstream.h>     // necessary for file input/output
#include "matrix.h"      // necessary for matrix class

// function prototypes
void get_cities(int &originating_city, int &destination_city);
```

```
// main function
int main()
{
 // integer matrix declared for the look-up table
 matrix <int> cities(10,10,0);

 int originating_city;  // holds the choice of the starting point
 int destination_city;  // holds the choice of the ending point
 int row_counter;       // used to count rows in loops
 int column_counter;    // used to count columns in loops
 char answer;           // used for ending or not ending the loop
 ifstream input_file;   // holds file pointer for input file


 input_file.open("mileage.dat",ios::in); //open file for input
 for(row_counter = 0 ; row_counter < 10 ; row_counter++)
 { // iterate through input file to get data for each row
   for(column_counter = 0 ; column_counter < 10 ; column_counter++)
   { // iterate through input file to get data for each column
     input_file >> cities[row_counter][column_counter];
   }
 }
 input_file.close();   // close the input file

 do
  { // iterate until user chooses not to continue

    // call get_cities function to get input from the user
    get_cities(originating_city, destination_city);

    originating_city--; // decrement the number of the originating and
    destination_city--; // destination cities for use in the array

    // index array using the decremented city numbers and print mileage
    cout << "\nMileage = " << cities[originating_city][destination_city]
         << endl;

    // ask user if he/she wants to repeat look-up
    cout << "\nContinue? [Y]es [N]o: ";
    cin >> answer;
    // loop as long as user answers y or Y
  } while ((answer == 'y') || (answer == 'Y')); // end of do loop
  return 0;
} // end main function

// function that gets the input from the user
void get_cities(int &originating_city, int &destination_city)
{
  cout << "\nOriginating City    Destination City\n";
  cout << "--------        --------\n";
```

(continued on next page)

```
cout << " 1 Atlanta            1 Atlanta\n";
cout << " 2 Boston             2 Boston\n";    // table of starting
cout << " 3 Chicago            3 Chicago\n";   // and ending points
cout << " 4 Cincinnati         4 Cincinnati\n";
cout << " 5 Dallas             5 Dallas\n";
cout << " 6 Denver             6 Denver\n";
cout << " 7 Detroit            7 Detroit\n";
cout << " 8 Los Angeles        8 Los Angeles\n";
cout << " 9 New York           9 New York\n";
cout << "10 Seattle           10 Seattle\n";

cout << "\nOriginating City [1-10]: ";
cin >> originating_city;

cout << "\nDestination City [1-10]: ";
cin >> destination_city;
} // end of get_cities function
```

S TEP-BY-STEP ▷ CSIII.1

1. Open **mileage.cpp**. The program in Code List CSIII-1 appears on your screen.

2. Compile and run the program. In order for the program to compile and run, **matrix.h**, **vector.h**, and **mileage.dat** must be present in the same folder. Run the program with several combinations of cities.

3. Enter the same city number for both the originating and the destination city. The mileage should be reported as 0.

4. Exit the program and leave the source code file open.

The program begins with a comment that identifies the program, followed by the compiler directives necessary for console input and output, file input and output, and the matrix class definition. The program consists of only two functions (`main` and `get_cities`), so only the `get_cities` function requires a prototype.

Next, the `main` function begins. As usual, the `main` function begins with variable declarations, as shown again in Code List CSIII-2. In addition to the matrix discussed earlier, two variables that hold the numbers of the originating and destination cities are declared. Two other variables are declared that are used as counters in the for loops that load the values from the data file into the matrix. Another variable is declared that is used to store the user's response to a question of whether to continue. Finally, a file pointer is declared so that a data file can be used.

```
// integer matrix declared for the look-up table
matrix <int> cities(10,10,0);

int originating_city;  // holds the choice of the starting point
int destination_city;  // holds the choice of the ending point
int row_counter;       // used to count rows in loops
int column_counter;    // used to count columns in loops
char answer;           // used for ending or not ending the loop
ifstream input_file;   // holds file pointer for input file
```

Following the variable declaration, the program opens the data file mileage.dat, which contains the data needed to initialize the matrix (see Code List CSIII-3). Two nested for loops initialize the matrix. The first loop iterates through all the rows in the matrix, while the second loop is responsible for initializing each column in the current row with a value from the data file. When each position in the matrix has been initialized, the data file is closed.

```
input_file.open("mileage.dat",ios::in); //open file for input
 for(row_counter = 0 ; row_counter < 10 ; row_counter++)
 { // iterate through input file to get data for each row
   for(column_counter = 0 ; column_counter < 10 ; column_counter++)
   { // iterate through input file to get data for each column
     input_file >> cities[row_counter][column_counter];
   }
 }
input_file.close();  // close the input file
```

After the matrix is initialized, the main function enters the loop shown in Code List CSIII-4. The loop calls the get_cities function to get the originating and destination cities from the user. The variables originating_city and destination_city are passed by reference to allow the user's input to be passed back to the main function.

```
do
 { // iterate until user chooses not to continue

   // call get_cities function to get input from the user
   get_cities(originating_city, destination_city);

   originating_city--; // decrement the number of the originating and
```

(continued on next page)

```
destination_city--; // destination cities for use in the array

// index array using the decremented city numbers and print mileage
cout << "\nMileage = " << cities[originating_city][destination_city]
    << endl;

// ask user if he/she wants to repeat look-up
cout << "\nContinue? [Y]es [N]o: ";
cin >> answer;
  // loop as long as user answers y or Y
} while ((answer == 'y') || (answer == 'Y')); // end of do loop
```

The values returned for the cities are in the range of 1 to 10. Recall, however, that array and matrix subscripts in C++ begin with zero. Therefore, the look-up table is indexed using the values 0 to 9. To adjust for the difference, the statements shown again in Code List CSIII-5 subtract 1 from the values in the variables to prepare them to index the matrix.

CODE LIST CSIII-5

```
originating_city--;  // Decrement the number of the originating and
destination_city--;  // destination cities for use in the array
```

Now that the city numbers have been adjusted to properly index the matrix, a single statement (shown in Code List CSIII-6) is used to look up the value and output the result.

CODE LIST CSIII-6

```
// index array using the decremented city numbers and print mileage
cout << "\nMileage = " << cities[originating_city][destination_city]
    << endl;
```

Finally, the `main` function asks the user if he or she wants to repeat the look-up process. The control expression of the do while loop tests the user's response to determine whether the loop should repeat or exit.

The `get_cities` function, shown in Code List CSIII-7, is very straightforward. First, a table of cities is displayed to give the user the options. Next, the user is asked for the originating city and, finally, the destination city. The ampersands (&) in the function declaration cause the parameters to be passed by reference, so the values entered by the user can be returned to the `main` function.

```
// function that gets the input from the user
void get_cities(int &originating_city, int &destination_city)
{
  cout << "\nOriginating City       Destination City\n";
  cout << "---------------        ---------------\n";
  cout << " 1 Atlanta             1 Atlanta\n";
  cout << " 2 Boston              2 Boston\n";      // table of starting
  cout << " 3 Chicago             3 Chicago\n";     // and ending points
  cout << " 4 Cincinnati          4 Cincinnati\n";
  cout << " 5 Dallas              5 Dallas\n";
  cout << " 6 Denver              6 Denver\n";
  cout << " 7 Detroit             7 Detroit\n";
  cout << " 8 Los Angeles         8 Los Angeles\n";
  cout << " 9 New York            9 New York\n";
  cout << "10 Seattle            10 Seattle\n";

  cout << "\nOriginating City [1-10]: ";
  cin >> originating_city;

  cout << "\nDestination City [1-10]: ";
  cin >> destination_city;
} // end of get_cities function
```

Modifying the Program

As an additional exercise, modify the program to include Memphis, Tennessee. Table CSIII-1 shows the road mileage between Memphis and the other 10 cities.

TABLE CSIII-1

Atlanta	371	Denver	1040
Boston	1296	Detroit	713
Chicago	530	Los Angeles	1817
Cincinnati	468	New York	1100
Dallas	452	Seattle	2290

Finally, modify the program to check the validity of the values entered by the user. *Hint*: Use a do while loop to continually call the `get_cities` function until valid input is received.

APPENDIX A

ASCII Table

ASCII Character	Decimal	Hexadecimal	Binary
NUL	0	00	000 0000
SOH	1	01	000 0001
STX	2	02	000 0010
ETX	3	03	000 0011
EOT	4	04	000 0100
ENQ	5	05	000 0101
ACK	6	06	000 0110
BEL	7	07	000 0111
BS	8	08	000 1000
HT	9	09	000 1001
LF	10	0A	000 1010
VT	11	0B	000 1011
FF	12	0C	000 1100
CR	13	0D	000 1101
SO	14	0E	000 1110
SI	15	0F	000 1111
DLE	16	10	001 0000
DC1	17	11	001 0001
DC2	18	12	001 0010
DC3	19	13	001 0011
DC4	20	14	001 0100
NAK	21	15	001 0101
SYN	22	16	001 0110
ETB	23	17	001 0111
CAN	24	18	001 1000
EM	25	19	001 1001
SUB	26	1A	001 1010

ASCII Character	Decimal	Hexadecimal	Binary
ESC	27	1B	001 1011
FS	28	1C	001 1100
GS	29	1D	001 1101
RS	30	1E	001 1110
US	31	1F	001 1111
space	32	20	010 0000
!	33	21	010 0001
"	34	22	010 0010
#	35	23	010 0011
$	36	24	010 0100
%	37	25	010 0101
&	38	26	010 0110
'	39	27	010 0111
(	40	28	010 1000
)	41	29	010 1001
*	42	2A	010 1010
+	43	2B	010 1011
,	44	2C	010 1100
-	45	2D	010 1101
.	46	2E	010 1110
/	47	2F	010 1111
0	48	30	011 0000
1	49	31	011 0001
2	50	32	011 0010
3	51	33	011 0011
4	52	34	011 0100
5	53	35	011 0101
6	54	36	011 0110
7	55	37	011 0111
8	56	38	011 1000
9	57	39	011 1001
:	58	3A	011 1010
;	59	3B	011 1011
<	60	3C	011 1100

(continued on next page)

ASCII Character	Decimal	Hexadecimal	Binary
=	61	3D	011 1101
>	62	3E	011 1110
?	63	3F	011 1111
@	64	40	100 0000
A	65	41	100 0001
B	66	42	100 0010
C	67	43	100 0011
D	68	44	100 0100
E	69	45	100 0101
F	70	46	100 0110
G	71	47	100 0111
H	72	48	100 1000
I	73	49	100 1001
J	74	4A	100 1010
K	75	4B	100 1011
L	76	4C	100 1100
M	77	4D	100 1101
N	78	4E	100 1110
O	79	4F	100 1111
P	80	50	101 0000
Q	81	51	101 0001
R	82	52	101 0010
S	83	53	101 0011
T	84	54	101 0100
U	85	55	101 0101
V	86	56	101 0110
W	87	57	101 0111
X	88	58	101 1000
Y	89	59	101 1001
Z	90	5A	101 1010
[	91	5B	101 1011
\	92	5C	101 1100
]	93	5D	101 1101
^	94	5E	101 1110
_	95	5F	101 1111

ASCII Character	Decimal	Hexadecimal	Binary
`	96	60	110 0000
a	97	61	110 0001
b	98	62	110 0010
c	99	63	110 0011
d	100	64	110 0100
e	101	65	110 0101
f	102	66	110 0110
g	103	67	110 0111
h	104	68	110 1000
i	105	69	110 1001
j	106	6A	110 1010
k	107	6B	110 1011
l	108	6C	110 1100
m	109	6D	110 1101
n	110	6E	110 1110
o	111	6F	110 1111
p	112	70	111 0000
q	113	71	111 0001
r	114	72	111 0010
s	115	73	111 0011
t	116	74	111 0100
u	117	75	111 0101
v	118	76	111 0110
w	119	77	111 0111
x	120	78	111 1000
y	121	79	111 1001
z	122	7A	111 1010
{	123	7B	111 1011
|	124	7C	111 1100
}	125	7D	111 1101
~	126	7E	111 1110
DEL	127	7F	111 1111

APPENDIX B

THE BINARY NUMBER SYSTEM

Overview

Data is a computer representation of something that exists in the real world. For example, data can be values such as money, measurements, quantities, or a high score. Data can also be alphabetic, such as names and addresses, or a business letter.

In a computer, all data is represented by numbers, and the numbers are represented electronically in the computer. To understand how electrical signals become numbers, let's begin by looking at a simple electric circuit that everyone is familiar with: a switch controlling a light bulb.

From Circuits to Numbers

When you think of an electric circuit, you probably think of it being either on or off; for example, a lightbulb is turned on and off by a switch. The lightbulb can exist in two conditions: on or off. In technical terms, the lightbulb has two states.

Imagine you had two lightbulbs on two switches. With two lightbulbs there are four possible states, as shown in Figure B-1. You could assign a number to each of the states and represent the numbers 0 through 3.

FIGURE B-1
There are four light combinations
possible with two lightbulbs.

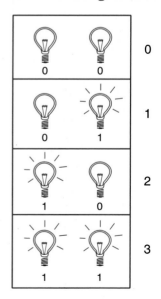

There are eight light combinations possible with three lightbulbs.

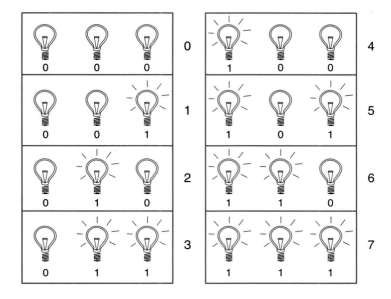

You cannot do much using only the numbers 0 through 3, but if more circuits are added, the number of states increases. For example, Figure B-2 shows how three circuits can represent the numbers 0 through 7 because there are eight possible states.

If you are the mathematical type, you may have noticed that the number of states is determined by the formula 2^n, where *n* is the number of circuits (see Table B-1).

TABLE B-1

Number of Circuits	Number of States	Numbers That Can Be Represented
1	$2^1 = 2$	0,1
2	$2^2 = 4$	0...3
3	$2^3 = 8$	0...7
4	$2^4 = 16$	0...15
5	$2^5 = 32$	0...31
6	$2^6 = 64$	0...63
7	$2^7 = 128$	0...127
8	$2^8 = 256$	0...255

Now instead of lights, think about circuits in the computer. A single circuit in a computer is like a single light; it can be on or off. A special number system, called the binary number system, is used to represent numbers with groups of these circuits. In the binary number system each binary digit, called a bit for short, is either a 0 or a 1. As shown in Figure B-3, circuits that are off are defined as 0, and circuits that are on are defined as 1. Binary digits (bits) are combined into groups of 8 bits called bytes.

FIGURE B-3

In the computer, signals that are off are defined as 0 and signals that are on are defined as 1.

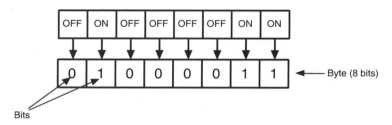

Bits

If a byte is made up of 8 bits, then there are 256 possible combinations of those 8 bits representing the numbers 0 through 255 (see Table B-1). Even though 255 is not a small number, it is definitely not the largest number you will ever use, so to represent larger numbers, computers group bytes together.

Binary versus Decimal

The binary number system may seem strange to you because you count using the decimal number system, which uses the digits 0 through 9. Counting in the decimal number system comes very naturally to you because you probably learned it at a very young age. But someone invented the decimal number system just like someone invented the binary number system. The decimal number system is based on 10s because you have 10 fingers on your hands. The binary number system is based on twos because of the circuits in a computer. Both systems, however, can be used to represent the same values.

In the decimal number system, each digit of a number represents a power of 10. That is why the decimal number system is also called the base 10 number system. Consider the number 3208, for example. When you read that number, you automatically understand it to mean three thousands, two hundreds, no tens, and eight ones. Represented mathematically, you could say $(3 \times 1000) + (2 \times 100) + (0 \times 10) + (8 \times 1) = 3208$, as shown in Figure B-4.

FIGURE B-4

Each digit of the decimal number 3208 represents a power of 10.

$$3 \times 1000 = 3000$$
$$2 \times 100 = 200$$
$$0 \times 10 = 0$$
$$8 \times 1 = 8$$
$$3208$$

3 2 0 8

In the binary number system, each digit represents a power of 2, as you saw in Table B-1. Working with powers of 2 is not as natural to you as working with powers of 10. But with a little practice you will see that base 2 numbers are not so mysterious. Consider the binary number 1101. Even though the number is four digits long, its value is nowhere near a thousand. The powers of 2 are 1, 2, 4, 8, 16, 32, and so on. So for this number, its decimal equivalent is $(1 \times 8) + (1 \times 4) + (0 \times 2) + (1 \times 1) = 13$, as shown in Figure B-5. So the binary number 1101 is equivalent to 13 in the decimal number system.

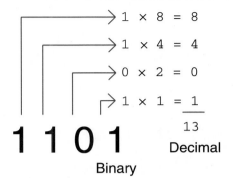

FIGURE B-5
Each digit of the binary number 1101 represents a power of 2, so conversion to the decimal system is easy.

Decimal Points and Binary Points

You have used decimal points for a long time. Did you know there is a binary point? A decimal point divides the ones place and the tenths place, or 10^0 from 10^{-1}. There is an equivalent in the binary number system called the binary point. It divides the 2^0 place from the 2^{-1} place.

With a binary point, it is possible to have binary numbers such as 100.1, which in decimal is 4.5. Can you convert the binary number 10.01 to decimal? If you got 2.25 as the answer, you are correct. Try converting the binary number 11.001001 to decimal.

REVIEW QUESTIONS

1. Define data.

2. How many bits are in a byte?

3. How many combinations of bits are possible with 3 bits?

4. How many combinations of bits are possible with 4 bits?

5. How many combinations of bits are possible with 5 bits?

6. How many combinations of bits are possible with 6 bits?

7. Convert the binary number 1010 to decimal.

8. Convert the binary number 10001 to decimal.

9. Convert the binary number 101111 to decimal.

10. Convert the binary number 11111111 to decimal.

APPENDIX C

THE PROGRAMMING PROCESS

Overview

Programmers are always tempted to immediately begin writing code to solve a problem. There is a better way. Sure, if you are writing a program to print your name on the screen a million times you might get by with just sitting down and keying in a program. But most programs are more complicated, and a more structured and disciplined approach to programming is necessary.

Although different programmers use different approaches, most good programmers follow five basic steps when developing programs:

1. Define the problem.

2. Develop an algorithm.

3. Code the program.

4. Test and debug the program.

5. Document and maintain the program.

Defining the Problem

Defining the problem to be solved requires an understanding of what the program is to accomplish.

For example, a program that calculates interest on a loan is fairly easy to define. Start by identifying the inputs and outputs. As input, the program needs the loan amount, the interest rate, and the number of months that the money is to be borrowed. A specific known formula can be applied to the data, and the amount of interest is the output.

Many programs are more difficult to define. Suppose you are defining a game program that involves characters in a maze. In your definition, the abilities of each character must be defined. In addition, the maze and how the characters interact with the maze and each other must also be defined. The list goes on and on.

Imagine how much there is to define before writing a program to handle airline reservations for a worldwide airline or the software that controls the launch of the space shuttle. Before any part of the program is written, the programmer must know exactly what the goal is.

Defining the problem does not take into consideration how the program will do the job, just what the job is. Exactly how a program accomplishes its work is addressed in the second step of the process.

Developing an Algorithm

The second step in the programming process is to develop an algorithm. An algorithm is a set of sequential instructions that are followed to solve a problem. Algorithms have been commonly used for years. A recipe for baking a cake, instructions for assembling a bicycle, and directions to a shopping mall are all examples of algorithms. The directions to a mall, shown in Figure C-1, are a set of steps that you execute sequentially.

Some algorithms involve decisions that change the course of action or cause parts of the algorithm to be repeated. Consider the algorithm for parking the car once you reach the mall. A more complicated algorithm is best illustrated with symbols in a flowchart as shown in Figure C-2.

FIGURE C-1

This algorithm leads you to a shopping mall.

> *Drive south on University Avenue to 50th Street.*
> *Turn right (west) on 50th.*
> *Drive west on 50th to Slide Road.*
> *Turn left (south) on Slide Road.*
> *Drive south on Slide Road until you see the mall entrance on the right.*

FIGURE C-2
Some steps in an algorithm may be repeated many times.

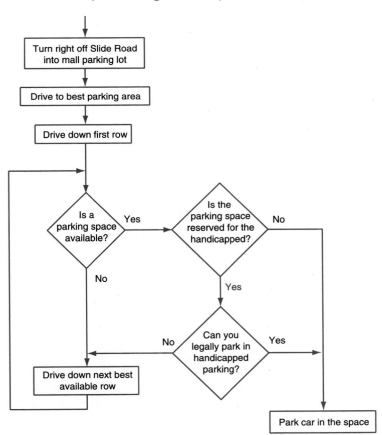

Programming a computer requires that you create an algorithm. The instructions the program gives the computer must tell the computer exactly what steps to do and in what order to do them. The computer executes each instruction sequentially, except when an instruction causes the flow of logic to jump to another part of the program.

When first developing an algorithm, you should avoid the temptation of initially writing in a programming language. A better method is to use pseudocode. Pseudocode expresses an algorithm in everyday English, rather than in a programming language. Pseudocode makes it possible for you to describe the instructions to be executed by the program. The precise choice of words and punctuation, however, is less important. Code List C-1 is an example of pseudocode for a mathematical program that prompts the user for an integer (a whole number without any decimal places) and squares it.

CODE LIST C-1

```
declare j and k as integers
prompt user for j
l = j * k
print l
```

Depending on the complexity of your program, developing algorithms can be a quick process or the most time-consuming part of developing your program.

Coding the Program

An algorithm's pseudocode is next translated into program code. This book teaches you the commands and structures you need to translate algorithms into actual programs.

Errors can be made during coding that can prevent the program from successfully compiling and linking. So part of the coding step involves resolving errors that prevent the program from running.

A common error is called a syntax error. A syntax error occurs when you key a command or some other part of the program incorrectly. Computers must be told exactly what to do. If someone leaves you a note that reads "Lock the back dore before you leave," you will be able to figure out what the instruction is. When the computer recognizes a syntax error, the programmer is notified immediately. Everything has to be just right or the computer will not accept it.

There are other errors that the computer may detect when compiling. Most of them are easily resolved. When all of those errors are resolved, the program will compile, link, and be ready to run. Even if a program runs, it may still fail to do its job correctly. That is where the next step of the programming process comes in.

Testing and Debugging

Testing and debugging is an important step that is too often ignored. Programs typically fail to operate 100% correctly the first time they are compiled or interpreted. Logic errors and other hidden problems called bugs must be located. Software must be tested and "debugged" to make sure the output is correct and reliable.

 Did You Know?

Back when computers used vacuum tubes, the heat and light generated by the tubes sometimes attracted bugs such as moths. The bugs sometimes caused short circuits, resulting in the need to "debug" the computer.

One way to test a program is to provide input for which the results are known. For example, a program that converts meters to feet can be easily tested by giving the program input values for which you know the output. Carefully select a wide variety of inputs. Use values that are larger or smaller than those which are typical. Use zero and negative numbers as inputs when allowable.

You should also test every part of a program. Make sure you provide input that tests every line of your code. Test each part of the program repeatedly to make sure that consistent results are obtained.

A type of error that can cause your program to stop running (or crash) is called a run-time error; it occurs when a program gives the computer an instruction that it is incapable of executing. A run-time error may lead to a program "crash." For example, if your program tries to divide a number by 0, a run-time error will occur on most systems. A run-time error could also occur if the system runs out of memory while your program is running.

You will experience lots of bugs and errors as a programmer. They are a part of every programmer's day. Even the best programmers spend lots of time testing and debugging. Throughout this book you will be warned of possible pitfalls and bugs so that you can avoid as many as possible. But the best way to learn how to avoid bugs is to experience them.

Documenting and Maintaining the Program

This step applies mostly to programs used in the real world. But since you may someday write such programs, you should be aware of this step as well. Programmers must document their work so that they and other programmers can make changes or updates later. Documentation may also have to be written for the program's users.

You should document your programs while you are programming and avoid saving the task for last. The time to write documentation for a program is while you are programming. By the time you finish the programming, you may have already forgotten some of what you did.

You may also be less likely to write proper documentation once a program is complete. You may think your time is better spent on another project, but you will be pleased to have the documentation when it is needed.

Documentation in the Program

Documentation that is included in the program itself is very important. Virtually all programming languages allow comments to be included in the source code. The comments are ignored by the interpreter or the compiler; therefore, the programmer can include notes and explanations that will make the program easier for people to read.

Documentation outside of the Program

Many times a program is complex enough that documents should be written that explain how the programming problem was solved. This documentation might be diagrams, flowcharts, or descriptions.

Documentation for the User

You have probably already been exposed to user documentation. Programs that are to be used by more than a few people usually include user documentation that explains the functions of the software.

Program Maintenance

Maintenance is an important part of the programming process. Most programs are written to help with a task. As the task changes, the program must also change. Users are likely to request additions and changes be made to the program. Maintaining a program is an important part of the process because it keeps the programmer's work up to date and in use.

During the maintenance phase of the programming process, bugs may be found that were not uncovered during the testing and debugging phase. It is also possible that better ways to accomplish a task in the program may be discovered. It is important to understand that the steps of the programming process may be repeated in order to refine or repair an existing program.

REVIEW QUESTIONS

1. List the five basic steps in the programming process.

2. Give an example of an algorithm used in everyday life.

3. Define the term bug as it relates to programming.

4. What is the purpose of documentation inside a program?

5. Write an algorithm that gives directions from one location to another. Choose a starting point (your home, for example) and give detailed, step-by-step directions that will lead anyone who might be reading the algorithm to the correct destination.

6. Draw a flowchart that describes the steps you follow when you get up in the morning and get ready for your day. Include as many details as you want, including things such as hitting the snooze button on your alarm clock, brushing your teeth, and eating breakfast.

APPENDIX D

ORDER OF OPERATIONS

Lesson 4 discussed the order of operations for the math operators. The chart below is a more complete table of the order of operators of all types. The operators shown in each group (divided by a line) have the same precedence level. The group with the highest precedence appears at the top of the table. Under the *Associativity* heading, you can see whether the operators are evaluated from right to left or left to right. If the operator you are looking for does not appear in the table below, check your compiler's documentation for a complete list. *Note*: Some of the operators in this table were not covered in this book. They are included for completeness.

TABLE D-1

Group	Symbol	Description	Associativity
Scope resolution	::	scope-resolution operator	left to right
Structure operators	->	structure pointer operator	left to right
	.	dot operator	
Unary operators	!	logical negation	right to left
	+	unary plus	
	-	unary minus	
	&	address of	
	*	dereferencing	
	++	increment operator	
	--	decrement operator	
	(typecast)	typecasting	
	sizeof	sizeof operator	
	new	memory allocation	
	delete	memory deallocation	
Multiplicative operators	*	multiplication	left to right
	/	divide	
	%	modulus	

(continued on next page)

Group	Symbol	Description	Associativity
Additive operators	+	addition	left to right
	-	minus	
Relational operators	<	less than	left to right
	<=	less than or equal to	
	>	greater than	
	>=	greater than or equal to	
Equality	==	equal to	left to right
	!=	not equal to	
Logical AND	&&	logical AND	left to right
Logical OR	||	logical OR	left to right
Assignment	=	assignment operator	right to left
	*=	compound assign product	
	/=	compound assign quotient	
	%=	compound assign remainder	
	+=	compound assign sum	
	-=	compound assign difference	

APPENDIX E

THE BOOL DATA TYPE

The bool data type (discussed in Lesson 3) was not originally in the C++ language. Before the bool data type, programmers used integers for all true and false values. As you learned, false is represented by 0 and true is represented by 1.

Some older C++ compilers do not support the bool data type. If your compiler is among those compilers, there is an easy fix. On the Electronic Instructor CD for this book is a file named bool.h. The contents of the file are shown below. If your compiler does not automatically support the bool data type, simply include bool.h in your program and an equivalent data type will be defined for you.

```
#ifndef _BOOL_H
#define _BOOL_H

typedef int bool;
const int FALSE = 0;
const int TRUE = 1;

#endif
```

The string class requires the bool data type. The oostring.h file includes the following statement.

```
//#include "bool.h"
```

By default, the #include "bool.h" statement is commented out of the string class. However, if your compiler does not support the bool data type, simply remove the slashes and the bool.h file will be included.

APPENDIX F

USING A DEBUGGER WHEN PROGRAMMING

What Is a Debugger?

A debugger is a program that helps programmers find errors in their programs. In many cases, a debugger is integrated into the compiler's programming environment to make it easy to use.

Debuggers offer many features that allow a programmer to see what is going on inside a running program. In this appendix, we'll concentrate on three of the most useful features: stepping through instructions, setting breakpoints, and watching variables.

Stepping Through Instructions

One of the most useful features of a debugger, especially for beginning programmers, is the ability to step through the lines of a program individually and see the effect each line has on the operation of the program. With this feature, the programmer can see the actual source code and control when the program executes the next line of code.

Stepping through instructions lets a programmer see things that otherwise would be difficult to verify, such as verifying that code within if structures is getting executed or watching the flow of logic through loops and function calls.

Setting Breakpoints

Another useful feature of a debugger is the ability to set a breakpoint. Setting a breakpoint is like putting a stop sign somewhere in your program. For example, if you are having trouble debugging a certain function, you can set a breakpoint that stops the program from executing at the point where the function is called. Once the program is stopped by the breakpoint, you can step through the instructions within that function to get a closer look at the problem area.

Watching Variables

Watching variables is particularly useful. While stepping through a program, you can select variables for which you would like to display their value as the program runs. The displayed values are updated each time you step through an instruction. As a result, you can see the value of a variable at any point in the program's execution.

APPENDIX G

C++ COMPILERS

Choosing, installing, and learning to use a C++ compiler may be the most difficult part of this course. This appendix will provide you with some guidance that will hopefully make the process easier.

Because the C++ compilers come from a variety of software companies, there is no one way to install and use a C++ compiler. To make the process easier, the Web site that accompanies this book includes information specific to the major compilers. For the most up-to-date information, including quick references for common compilers, see the address below.

http://www.programcpp.com/basics/compilers

General C++ Compiler Notes

■ Because C++ was written to be a portable language, the programs in this book can be run on DOS, Windows, Unix, or Macintosh compilers with a few exceptions. Minor inconsistencies may appear, especially in the way input and output is handled.

■ Working with data files often exposes minor variations in the way C++ compilers handle input and output. Test data file input and output with your compiler before allowing students to begin that lesson.

■ Use the most recent version of the compiler software your computer can run. Some older C++ compilers do not support the latest features of the language. For example, some older compilers do not support template classes, making it impossible to use the vector and matrix classes.

■ Verify whether your compiler includes the bool data type. See Appendix E for more information about the bool data type.

■ Most C++ compilers have a feature to group source code files into a project or workspace. When you begin to use classes, you will have to know how to create a project and add the required files to the project.

■ Learning to use your compiler's debugger can be a powerful teaching tool. See Appendix F for more information about how to use a debugger.

■ C++ has only basic screen formatting capabilities. Most compilers do not even include a clear screen command. The Web site previously mentioned will have some pointers for you. As a general rule, however, you should not expect to be able to create intricately formatted output using standard C++ features.

■ With some compilers, especially when running under Microsoft Windows, you may experience a situation in which the output of your program appears in a window and disappears almost immediately. If your compiler does not have a built-in feature to pause the output, you can include an additional input statement at the end of your program to cause execution to pause. Examples are available on the Web site mentioned.

275

- Sending output to a printer also varies among compilers and among operating systems. Examples are available on the Web site given earlier.

- The Web site of the company that developed the compiler you are using is a good resource. Links to the major compiler developers are available at the Web address mentioned earlier.

GLOSSARY

A

++ operator A C++ operator that increments an integer.

-- operator A C++ operator that decrements an integer.

Algorithm A set of sequential instructions that are followed to solve a problem.

American Standard Code for Information Interchange (ASCII) A code most computers use to assign a number to each character. The numbers are used to represent the character internally.

Appending The process of adding data to the end of an existing file.

Argument Data passed to a function.

Arithmetic operators Operators that perform math operations such as addition, subtraction, multiplication, and division.

Array A group of variables of the same data type that appear together in the computer's memory.

Assembly language A programming language that uses letters and numbers to represent machine-language instructions.

Assignment operator An operator (=) that changes the value of the variable to the left of the operator.

Automatic variables *See* Local variable.

B

Boolean variable A variable that can have only two possible variables: true or false.

Bottom-up design A program design method that involves beginning at the bottom of the VTOC (Visual Table of Contents) and working up.

Braces Special characters used to mark the beginning and ending of blocks of code.

C

Case sensitive A characteristic of the C++ language that provides for the interpretation of uppercase and lowercase letters differently.

Characters The letters and symbols available for use by a computer.

Close The final step of using a data file.

Comments Remarks in a program that are ignored by the compiler.

Compiler A program that translates a high-level language into machine language, then saves the machine language so that the instructions do not have to be translated each time the program is run.

Compiler directive Commands for the compiler, which are needed to effectively compile your program.

Concatenation Adding one string onto the end of another string.

Console I/O Using the screen and keyboard for input and output (I/O is an abbreviation of input/output).

Constant Stores data that remains the same throughout a program's execution.

Constructors Tell the compiler how to create an object in memory and what the initial values of its data will be.

277

Containment The term used to describe a has-a relationship among classes.

Control expression An expression that provides for a decision to be made in an if statement or to end a loop.

D

Data type A specification that defines the type of data that can be stored in a variable or constant.

Declaring Indicating to the compiler what type of variable you want and its name or identifier.

Decrementing Subtracting 1 from a variable.

Dot operator The operator used to access the members of a structure.

do while loop An iteration structure that repeats a statement or group of statements as long as a control expression is true at the end of the loop.

E

"E" notation Exponential notation.

Elements Variables in an array.

End-of-line character *See* New line character.

Executable file The output of a linker that can be executed without the need for an interpreter.

Exponential notation A method of representing very large and very small numbers (also called scientific notation).

Expression A math statement made up of terms, operators, and functions.

External variables *See* Global variable.

Extraction operator The operator that outputs data to a stream.

F

Field width The width of a formatting field when using the I/O manipulators.

File streams Objects that provide a data path to a file.

Floating-point number A number that includes a decimal point.

Flowchart A diagram made up of symbols used to illustrate an algorithm.

for loop An iteration structure that repeats one or more statements a specified number of times.

Function A block of code that carries out a specific task.

Fuzzy logic A logic system that allows for true, false, and variations in between.

G

Global variable A variable declared before the main function and accessible by any function.

Graphical user interface (GUI) A system for interacting with the computer user through pictures or icons.

H

Has-a relationship The relationship between classes where one class contains another class.

Header file A file that serves as a link between your program code and standard C++ code that is needed to make your program run.

High-level language A programming language in which instructions do not necessarily correspond with the instruction set of the microprocessor.

I

Identifier Names given to variables and constants.

if structure A programming structure that executes code if certain conditions are met.

if/else structure A programming structure that executes one block of code if certain conditions are met and another block of code if the same conditions are not met.

Incrementing Adding 1 to a variable.

Infinite loop An iteration structure in which iterations continue indefinitely.

Information hiding Data protection that is an important benefit of encapsulation.

Inheritance The ability of one object to inherit the properties of another object.

Initialize To assign a value to a variable.

Input stream A stream used to receive input.

Insertion operator The operator that gets data from a stream and puts it into a variable.

Instance The data for one object that has been created in memory and has the behaviors defined by the class.

Integer A whole number.

Interpreter A program that translates the source code of a high-level language into machine language.

I/O manipulators A set of format options available in C++ that may be placed directly in the output statement.

Is-a relationship The relationship in which one object inherits characteristics from another class.

Iteration A single loop or pass through a group of statements.

Iteration structures Programming structures that repeat a group of statements one or more times (loops).

K

Keyword Words that cannot be used as identifiers because they are part of the C++ language.

L

Library functions Functions that come with your compiler.

Linker A program that links object files created by a compiler into an executable program.

Literals Hard-coded values.

Local variable A variable declared within a function that is accessible only within the function.

Logical operators Operators that allow *and*, *or*, and *not* to be implemented as part of logical expressions.

loop A programming structure that repeats a group of statements one or more times.

Lowercase The noncapital (small letters) of the alphabet.

Low-level language A programming language in which each instruction corresponds to one or only a few microprocessor instructions.

M

Machine language The programming language (made up of ones and zeros) that a microprocessor understands.

main function The function by which every C++ program begins.

Member functions Allow programmers using an object to send information to an object and receive information from an object.

Members The functions and variables in a class definition.

Menu A set of options presented to the user of a program.

Message In object-oriented programming, the method used to transfer data.

Method Code inside an object that is necessary to perform the operations on the object.

Modulus operator The operator that provides integer division.

N

New line character The end-of-line character.

O

Object code The machine-language code produced by a compiler.

Object file The file produced by a compiler that contains machine-language code.

Object-oriented paradigm A way of programming in which data and operations are seen as existing together in objects that are similar to objects in the real world.

Object-oriented programming Building programs using the object-oriented paradigm.

One-way selection structure A selection structure in which the decision is whether to go "one way" or just bypass the code in the if structure.

Open The operation that associates a physical disk file with a file pointer so that data in the file may be accessed.

Operating system The program in charge of the fundamental system operations.

Order of operations The rules related to the order in which operations (such as math operations) are performed.

Overflow The condition where an integer becomes too large for its data type.

P

Paradigm A model or set of rules that defines a way of programming.

Parameter The variable that receives the value or any other identifier in the parentheses of the function declaration.

Pass To send an argument to a function.

Passing by reference A method of passing variables in which any changes you make to the variables are passed back to the calling function.

Passing by value A method of passing variables in which a copy of the value in the variable is given to the function for it to use.

Procedural paradigm A way of programming that focuses on the idea that all algorithms in a program are performed with functions and data that a programmer can see, understand, and change.

Programming language A language that provides a way to program computers using instructions that can be understood by computers and people.

Promotion The condition in which the data type of one variable is temporarily converted to match the data type of another variable so that a math operation can be performed using the mixed data type.

Prototype A statement that defines the function for the compiler.

Q

Quotient Quantity that results when one number is divided by another.

R

Random-access file A data file that allows you to move directly to any data in the file.

Relational operators Operators used to make comparisons.

Remainder Quantity remaining when a number does not divide evenly into another.

Reusability Using an object again after it has been coded and tested.

S

Scope The availability of a variable to functions.

Scope-resolution operator The operator that separates the class name and the function name in a member function.

Selection structures Structures that allow for logical decisions in C++ programs.

Sequence structures Execute statements one after another without changing the flow of a program.

Sequential-access file A file with which you must start at the beginning and search each record to find the one you want.

Short-circuit evaluation A feature of C++ that allows the program to stop evaluating an expression as soon as the outcome of the expression is known.

Source code A program in the form of a high-level language.

Special character A character that extends the normal alphanumeric characters.

Standard input device The default input device, usually the keyboard.

Standard output device The default output device, usually the screen.

Statement Line of C++ code; statements end with a semicolon.

Stream Data flowing from one place to another.

Stream operation modes A mode that specifies the way you want to access the file.

String A group of characters put together to make one or more words.

String class An object-oriented class that allows strings to be included in programs.

String object An object for storing and processing strings.

Subscript An index value that accesses an element of an array.

Switch structure A selection structure capable of handling multiple options.

T

Template class A class that can be used with any data type.

Top-down design A program design method in which the general organization and flow of the program are decided before the details are coded.

Truncate To drop the digits to the right of the decimal point, without rounding the value.

Truth tables Diagrams that show the result of logical operations.

Two-way selection structure A selection structure in which one block of code is executed if the control expression is true and another block is executed if the control expression is false.

Typecast operator An operator that forces the data type of a variable to change.

Typecasting Changing the data type of a variable using a typecast operator.

U

Underflow When a value becomes too small for a variable to hold accurately.

Uppercase The capital letters of the alphabet.

V

Variable Holds data that can change while the program is running.

Vector A one-dimensional array of any data type.

W

while loop An iteration structure that repeats a statement or group of statements as long as a control expression is true.

INDEX

O

Object(s)
  communication among, 232
  introduction, 77
  matrix, 250-251
  messages, 81
  vector, 205-206
  See also String objects

Object code, 9

Object file, 9

Object-oriented design (OOD), 237

Object-oriented languages, 232

Object-oriented programming (OOP)
  reusability, 242
  vs. procedural programming, 231-232

Opening files, 217

Operating systems, 3-4

Operations
  compilers and, 217
  order of, 55-56, 271-272
    logical, 124-125
    in switch structure, 139
  string, 80-83

Operator(s)
  ++ and --, 53-54
  << and >>, 89-90
  arithmetic, 48-51
  assignment, 46-48
    vs. relational operator, 121
  compound, 82
  dot, 81
  extraction and insertion, 89
  logical, 122-125
  modulus, 50
  in output statements, 51-52
  relational, 120-121
  typecast, 62

Or (||), 122

Order of operations, 55-56, 271-272
  logical, 124-125
  in switch structure, 139

Output statements
  special characters, 91
  using operators in, 51-52

Overflow, 64

P

Paradigm, 231

Parameters, 143
  vs. argument, 178

Parentheses ()
  to change order of operations, 55
  and order of logical operations, 124-125
  and semicolon, with while loop, 148

Pascal, as high-level language, 8

Passing by reference, 177, 179-180

Passing by value, 177-179

Passing data, 177

Points, decimal and binary, 265

Primitives, 30

Printing, hard copy, clearing screen and, 102

Problem, defining, 266

Procedural languages, 232

Procedural paradigm, 231-232

Program
  analyzing, case study, 111-114
  autonomous functions, 166
  building with functions, 164-169
  coding, 268
  compiling, 9

debugger, 274
  and testing, 268-269
  decision making in, 118-120
  documentation and maintenance, 202, 269-270
  flow, functions and, 169
  maintenance, 269-270
  modifying, 257
    case study, 115
    organization, 166
  testing and debugging, 268-269
  writing, to use circle class, 234-236
  See also C++, Standalone program

Programming
  binary number system, 5-6
  procedural, vs. OOP, 231-232
  using debugger when, 274
  See also Object-oriented programming (OOP)

Programming process, 195, 266-270

Promotion, 60-62

Prompts, descriptive, 101

Prototypes, 168-169, 182
  constructor, 239
  and semicolons, 170

Q

Quotation marks (""), 80

Quotient, 50

R

Random-access data files, 215-216

Random-access memory (RAM), and data files, 214-215

Read-only memory (ROM), 2

Top-down design, 166
    for compound interest, 197-198

True and false, representing, in
    C++, 120

Truncation, 62

Truth tables, 122

Typecast operators, 62

Typecasting, 60, 62-64

U

Underflow, 64-65

Unsetf, 93-95

Uppercase
    and case sensitivity, 19
    for constants, 40

User, documentation for, 269

V

Value
    passing by, 177-179
    returning, using Return
        statement, 180-182

Value range, of data types, 31-32
    floating-point, 38

Variables
    Boolean, 39, 74
    declaring, 254-255
        and naming, 33-35
            multiple, in statement, 35
    initializing, 33-34
        with literal, 77
    promoting, 61
    scope, 171-173
    typecasting, 62-63
    understanding, 30
    watching, with debugger, 274
    See also Data types

Vector(s), 204
    assigning one to another, 210
    empty, 205
    features, 209-210
    indexing elements, 206-207
    initializing, 205
    obtaining length, 209
    resizing, 205, 209
    using loops with, 208-209

Vector class, compiling program
    using, 206

Vector objects, declaring, 205-206

Visual Basic, as high-level
    language, 8

Visual Table of Contents (VTOC),
    165-166, 183, 196

Void function, 167

W

While loops, 147-151
    do while, 147, 149-151
    standard, 147-149
    vs. for loops, 149

Writing, data, to files, 216, 218-
    220

Z

Zero, dividing by, 52-53